Online Investing
on the
Australian
Sharemarket

4th EDITION

Roger Kinsky

Wrightbooks
A Wiley Brand

First published in 2013 by Wrightbooks
an imprint of John Wiley & Sons Australia, Ltd
42 McDougall St, Milton Qld 4064

Office also in Melbourne

Typeset in 11.5/13.4 pt ITC Berkeley Oldstyle Std

© Roger Kinsky 2013
The moral rights of the author have been asserted

National Library of Australia Cataloguing-in-Publication data:

Author:	Kinsky, Roger, author.
Title:	Online investing on the Australian sharemarket / Roger Kinsky.
Edition:	4th Edition.
ISBN:	9781118606568 (pbk.)
	9781118606605 (ebook)
Notes:	Includes index.
Subjects:	Electronic trading of securities—Australia.
	Stocks—Australia—Computer network resources.
	Investments—Australia—Computer network resources.
Dewey Number:	332.632202854678

Microsoft Excel screenshots reprinted with permission from Microsoft Corporation.

Cover design by Jeff Faust
Cover image: iStockphoto.com / Bojovic Predrag
Internal design by Peter Reardon, pipelinedesign.com.au

Printed in Australia by Ligare Book Printer

10 9 8 7 6 5 4 3 2 1

Disclaimer

Contents

Acknowledgements

I would like to thank all the companies that allowed me to reproduce charts and web pages included as examples in this book. I would also like to thank Trish Power, co-founder of SuperGuide.com.au, for reviewing the section on SMSFs in chapter 5 and for her helpful suggestions.

Introduction

Online share investing is an increasingly popular method of wealth management for Australian investors. The reasons for this include the following:

⇨ A growing number of Australians want more control over the financial decisions affecting their savings, whether they're invested in a share portfolio or a superannuation fund.

⇨ This trend is driven by scepticism about the need to pay management fees to others when the cost involved can't be justified by the performance.

⇨ The online method is the cheapest and most convenient way of trading shares and accessing the information and resources needed to make good share investing decisions.

The first edition of this book was written because there were very few online investing books published in Australia. Most were of overseas origin and weren't really relevant to Australia's unique investing environment. The book was well received and was followed by a second and third edition that were updated to keep pace with the constantly changing world of online trading and investing. The third edition was written six years ago and since then many changes have occurred, so this fourth edition was written to bring the book up to date with modern developments.

In today's busy world, I believe readers want to access the information they require quickly and easily without having to wade through reams of complex analysis or explanation. This idea was foremost in my mind at all times when writing this edition, so

I've taken the opportunity to simplify the book and make it even more user-friendly. As is the case with my other share investing books—*Teach Yourself About Shares, Shares Made Simple* and *Charting Made Simple*—in this edition of *Online Investing on the Australian Sharemarket* I've included case studies, examples and succinct tips where appropriate. These tips derive from my many years of experience as an online share trader and investor, and I trust they will help you to be successful and avoid the traps that might catch the unwary.

In this edition I've included consideration of mobile and smart phone applications as these are becoming an increasingly popular way of accessing the internet for share trading and information purposes. It also contains a new section on self managed superannuation, as this is a growth area with Australian investors, giving them more control over the financial decisions affecting their retirement nest eggs. At the same time they may be able to achieve a substantial saving in the annual fees charged by fund managers, and this saving can compound over the years to provide a substantial increase in their retirement benefit.

In chapter 1, I explain basic concepts and terminology associated with share trading and investing and the many advantages of doing so online, but also some potential pitfalls and how you can avoid them. In chapter 2, I outline the information and facilities available on the internet relevant to share investing so you'll be in a better position to decide the online data and facilities you want to access. In chapter 3, I discuss the different types of websites and provide details of some relevant sites with a short synopsis of each so you can decide whether the site is of interest to you. In chapter 4, I provide information about the costs and resources available with online brokers operating in Australia to help you make an informed decision about the broker that best fulfils your requirements. In chapter 5, I explain how you can set up with your broker of choice so you can trade online. In this chapter I also discuss self managed superannuation and how you can set up and manage your own fund online if it's a share investing method that suits your needs.

After reading these chapters you'll be in a position to trade shares online. Before doing so, it's most important to develop a trading and monitoring plan. In chapter 6, I discuss how to go about this and the factors you need to consider in your plan. In chapter 7, I outline the nuts and bolts of online share trading and the different types of orders you can place. I also consider the various mistakes you could make and how to best avoid them.

In chapter 8, I describe fundamental analysis as it's a most important research tool, especially for longer term share investing. In chapter 9 I outline the basics of charting and the technical analysis tools you can use, and show you how to analyse charts and draw conclusions. In chapter 10, I look at another method of share investing known as a top-down approach that's based on the analysis of indices. I outline the makeup of the indices and, most importantly, how you can use indices to your advantage. Finally, in chapter 11, I describe the risks associated with online share trading and investing and suggest strategies for managing those risks. After all, strategic risk management is the key to continuing success as a share trader or investor.

If you're completely new to online trading and investing, I've no doubt that after reading this book you'll be able to trade and invest successfully right from the start, even if you're a complete novice. If you already have some experience, I trust this book will provide additional information, strategies and tips to help you to become even more successful.

I've tried to make the book as up to date and error free as possible and the editorial staff have done a fine job of assisting me in this endeavour. However, perfection is very difficult to achieve in the real world, so if you spot any apparent discrepancies, if you have suggestions for improving the book, or if you'd simply like to provide feedback, please email me: rkinsky@bigpond.com

I'd be happy to hear from you and I will reply promptly to your email.

Finally, I wish you success as an online share trader or investor, and I trust that this book will prove valuable in helping you to achieve this goal.

Roger Kinsky
Woollamia, NSW
August 2013

Disclaimers

The Global Industry Classification Standard (GICS®) was developed by and is the exclusive property and a trademark of Standard & Poor's and MSCI. Neither MSCI, Standard & Poor's nor any other party involved in making or compiling any GICS classifications makes any express or implied warranties or representations with respect to such standard or classification (or the results to be obtained by the use thereof), and all such parties hereby expressly disclaim all warranties of originality, accuracy, completeness, merchantability or fitness for a particular purpose with respect to any of such standard or classification. Without limiting any of the foregoing, in no event shall MSCI, Standard & Poor's, any of their affiliates or any third party involved in making or compiling any GICS classifications have any liability for any direct, indirect, special, punitive, consequential or any other damages (including lost profits) even if notified of the possibility of such damages.

To the extent permitted by law, the Commonwealth Securities Limited and its related entities do not accept liability to any person for loss or damage arising from the use of this content. Please consult your own legal advice before using any content of this email. This content is not directed to, or intended for distribution to or use by, any person or entity who is a citizen or resident of or located in any locality, state, country or other jurisdiction where such distribution, publication, availability or use would be contrary to law or regulation or which would subject the Commonwealth Bank Group to any registration or licensing requirement within such jurisdiction. This information has been prepared without taking account of the objectives, needs, financial and taxation situation or needs of any particular individual. For this reason, any individual should, before acting on the information in this email, consider the appropriateness of the information, having regard to the individual's objectives, needs, financial and taxation situation and if necessary, seek appropriate independent financial and taxation advice. CommSec, is a wholly owned, but non-guaranteed, subsidiary of the Commonwealth Bank of Australia ABN 48 123 123 124 AFSL 234945 and both are incorporated in Australia with limited liability. CommSec is a participant of the ASX Group. Please consider the Product Disclosure Statement and CommSec's Financial Services Guide which can be downloaded from www. commsec.com.au or requested by calling 13 15 19 before making any decisions about products available from CommSec. If you have a complaint, CommSec's dispute resolution process can be accessed on 13 15 19. Fees and charges apply, and rates are subject to change. Terms and Conditions are available upon request.

Author's disclaimer

In this book I have included many tips and strategies that derive from my many years of experience as an online share trader and investor. I trust they will help you to be successful and avoid the traps that could catch the unwary. However, the sharemarket can move in unpredictable ways at times, so these shouldn't be construed as advice, but rather as suggestions that may or may not be appropriate for you depending on your particular share investing and trading circumstances.

chapter 1

Using the internet for share investing

In this chapter I'll explain some basic concepts and terminology associated with online share investing. I'll also outline why it's a good option to trade shares online, some potential pitfalls and how to avoid them. I'll start from the beginning, so if you have some knowledge and experience with shares and investing you may be able to quickly skim through this chapter.

Impact of the internet

It's no exaggeration to say that the internet has revolutionised human communication and the way business dealings are conducted. While it's always dangerous to make predictions about the future, I believe the technology is still in the formative stage and that further development and applications will continue for many years to come. It's easy to foresee a future in an Australian cashless society with all monetary transactions conducted in real time using a card linked electronically to a bank account. There's been a huge growth in online shopping, and this may continue to the point where retail stores selling consumer goods will be replaced by skeleton shops holding only one demonstration item with all orders being fulfilled using the internet.

Using the internet for share investing

Use of the internet for share investing is another example of the way the internet has revolutionised business dealings. Most securities exchanges throughout the world are now internet based, with a demise of the physical trading floor as all transactions are now internet-based using computers.

According to the Australian Bureau of Statistics, in June 2012 more than 9 million Australian households were connected to the internet, and with business connections the total came to over 12 million. This number doesn't include those accessing the internet using mobile phones and similar devices. In one year (to June 2012) connections to the internet increased by over 10%. As yet, there appears no end in sight to the mushrooming use of the internet, and share investing is no exception. In May 2011 about 7.1 million people, or 43% of the adult Australian population, owned shares either directly (via shares or other listed investments) or indirectly (via unlisted managed funds). The level of direct participation in the Australian sharemarket was 39%, or 6.59 million people, and this ranks Australia among the leading share-owning nations in the world on a per capita basis.

In Australia it's estimated there are approximately 1.5 million online investors. Many have become investors through privatisations and demutualisations and others have set up their own online self managed superannuation accounts using shares as the investment entity. With the growing use of the internet more and more investors are choosing to trade online rather than in the older, traditional way by telephone contact with an offline stockbroker. Of the Australian direct shareholding investors who traded in last two years, 65% used an online broker, with the majority being directly online and a small percentage using the telephone with an online broker.

As reported in *Sydney Morning Herald* weekend business 6–7 October 2012, there are an estimated 615 000 active online investors in Australia with almost 50 000 of these being classified as frequent traders (trading at least four times a month).

Control

The feedback I receive from readers of my books as well as statistical data convinces me that there's a growing trend for Australians to want to have direct control over their shares or other financial investments. To put it bluntly, many are becoming disillusioned with entrusting their investments to fund managers and investment advisers who charge an appreciable fee for service but whose advice doesn't result in investments that meet expectations. Even if the manager or adviser is able to achieve results that are better than or as good as a market index, the fees can soak up the additional benefit, so the investor ends up no better off (and often worse off).

It's not my purpose to denigrate fund managers and investment advisers who, no doubt, provide a worthwhile service for many investors. I'm just making the point that a growing number of investors want to take direct control of their own financial destinies and the internet is the ideal vehicle for doing so. There has been a substantial growth in self managed super funds (SMSFs), and this trend seems set to continue into the foreseeable future, clearly showing the trend toward self-managed investing.

Along with wanting to take control of their financial investments, the trend toward using the internet for share investing has been stimulated by the increasing competition among internet investment service providers. They have been trying to increase their market share using a two-pronged approach, namely:

⇨   reducing fees and charges

⇨   increasing the accessibility and depth of information and services provided.

It's now possible to trade online for a cost of only 0.1% of the trade value, with a minimum charge of less than $10. This makes online investing viable even for small investors and provides the opportunity for worthwhile trading profits with only relatively small market moves.

Tip

Increasing competition and use of the internet is good news for the online investor and you can expect continuing benefits in the future if you choose the online option.

Accessing the internet

Of the more than 9 million Australians connected to the internet, the vast majority are connected through broadband, with less than half a million still using dialup. Accessing the internet for share investing has traditionally been on desktop or laptop computers but in recent times there's been a mushrooming use of mobile devices for this purpose. There's a bewildering variety of these, and new versions are continually being developed and released. With mobile smart phones, there's the iPhone, Android and Windows phones, and there are several tablets including the iPad and Blackberry. These allow convenient access to the internet from any location where a strong enough signal can be obtained. There are a number of apps (applications) especially tailored for them which provide fast and convenient access to a website and more are continually coming on stream. Apart from the portability aspect, I suspect that a major reason why these devices are becoming increasingly popular for share investing is that so many Australians already own and use them for communication and social networking so there's no need to purchase and carry additional hardware. However, for share investing purposes I prefer to use a computer because the larger screen size allows easier reading of detailed information and better visual interpretation of charted data. For portable access you can use a laptop in various sizes—the smaller ones being particularly portable as they're not much larger than a book.

In order to access the internet you need an internet service provider (ISP) and pay a monthly charge. You may need to sign a contract that could tie you to the provider for one or more years. Computers require some type of internet connection device (such as a wireless dongle) that you attach to your computer, generally using a USB port, and that will be provided by the ISP. If you're using a smart phone or tablet device, access to the internet can be included in the contract with your phone service provider. You can also connect to the internet using a Wi-Fi network, and using Bluetooth you can use the wireless network to connect to other devices such as Bluetooth keyboards.

You'll usually have a choice of fee structures depending on the amount of monthly internet download capacity you require. If you exceed your limit the extra downloads can be costly so my suggestion is that it's better to choose a more expensive plan with sufficient download capacity for all your needs, rather than trying to skimp and save with the cheapest plan.

Tip

It's surprising how your download megabytes can mount up, so it's a good idea to give yourself plenty of scope when you enter into a contractual agreement with an ISP.

Other access considerations

Because of the ever-present risk of hacking or virus transmission you need to ensure you use a good protection program that automatically updates. Free computer-protection programs are available but I feel it's false economy not to use a really good program as these are obtainable for less than $50 per year. If you're using mains power it's also a good idea to use a surge protection device as a sudden power surge can zap your computer if you're not protected. It's also a good idea to turn your computer off at the mains power switch after you've shut down.

Share investing information is often in Adobe PDF format so you need to have the Adobe Acrobat reader program downloaded. You can download it for free and you need to download the updates as they become available.

You may often wish to obtain a hard copy of information you receive on the internet so a fast, good-quality printer is an important accessory. I use a high-speed laser printer for most of my printing but it's only black and white, so I also have a slower, ink jet colour printer for printouts where colour is important.

Tip

Much share investing data such as charts are detailed and are much easier to interpret on a large screen, so the larger the screen on your internet connection device, the better.

Investing

Investing implies the following two conditions:

⇨ You have some available money (also known as capital) over and above what you require for day-to-day living expenses. This money may have been derived from a number of sources: perhaps you've saved it from surplus after you've deducted expenses from your income; you might have inherited some money; received a tax refund; or had a financial windfall. In some cases, you have derived your investing funds by obtaining an investment loan. With shares this type of loan is known as a margin loan.

⇨ You put this money into a financial venture with the aim of obtaining a profitable return. That's to say, you want to put the money to good use and grow your wealth. This is known as 'putting your money to work' as opposed to 'your money taking a holiday'.

Investment instrument

Investment instrument is a general term that applies to any asset or commodity that's used for the purpose of investing. In this book I'll concentrate on shares but they are one type of investment instrument and there are many others, including: bonds, managed funds, hybrids, derivatives (such as CFDs, forex, options, warrants), fixed-interest securities such as debentures and so on.

Tip

If you're not an experienced investor I suggest you avoid trading the more sophisticated types of investment instrument and stick to plain-vanilla type shares.

Capital

Capital is a business term that means wealth. It can be money or cash that's directly available (such as cash in the bank) or the monetary value of any assets owned by a business. So the only difference between cash and capital is that capital isn't necessarily in the form of directly available cash.

Tip

While a business may have a certain amount of capital (as shown by the books of account), a great deal of this may be tied up in assets or stock that don't necessarily have the same cash value if the business tries to sell them.

Stocks, shares and portfolio

One way a company (or corporation) raises capital for start up or growth is by 'going public'; that is, by becoming a public company. The capital is obtained by issuing a number of shares at a certain price and the capital so obtained is known as equity capital.

Shares are units of ownership in a company, so when you invest in shares you effectively become a part-owner in that company and this gives you a say in the company's management. That is, you have voting rights and can vote at company meetings open to shareholders. Shares are also known as equities because shareholders have an ownership position, or equity, in the company and a claim to a share of the company's assets and profits.

The total number of shares issued by a company is known as 'stock' but the word 'stock' is often used to describe the company itself. For example, you can own a number of different stocks (such as Telstra, ANZ Bank and so on) and you can own a different number of shares in each. Your total personal total holding of all shares you own is your 'portfolio'.

Initial public offering (float)

When a company first offers shares that can be taken up by the general public this is known as an initial public offering (IPO) or float. The float is usually underwritten, which means that a broking firm or financial institution undertakes to purchase any shares left over if the offering is under-subscribed. Shares in an IPO can be purchased by an investor by application only using a document known as a prospectus that contains all information of relevance to potential investors.

Some floats have proved successful long-term investments. I wish I'd bought Commonwealth Bank shares when they floated in September of 1991 at $5.40. Now worth over $60 this is a capital gain of over 1000%, and as well as this capital gain, there's been consistently good dividends paid to shareholders. However, this is an exceptional example and most floats are risky for the simple reason that there's no track record of the business as a public company.

Tip

I suggest you don't invest in an IPO unless you have some very reliable information that leads you to the belief that the investment is likely to be profitable.

Securities exchange (stock exchange)

In order for the shares in a public company to be traded by the public at large (rather than by private treaty), they need to be listed with a securities exchange and the company issuing the shares is then known as a listed company. Before it can operate in Australia, the securities exchange must have a licence granted by the Australian Securities and Investments Commission (ASIC). Most Australian companies are listed with Australian exchanges but a few are listed with overseas exchanges, if their business is more relevant to an overseas country. Some shares are listed on both Australian and overseas exchanges and these can be traded directly by investors overseas at times when our exchange is closed.

In order to be listed, the company has to pay fees and comply with listing rules that can be quite stringent and are designed to protect investors. After listing, the company must comply with ongoing rules and may be investigated for possible breaches or behaviour that appears suspect—such as a sudden change in the share price or volume of shares traded without any obvious reason. Listing rules also stipulate that any new information of relevance to shareholders must be submitted to the exchange and be available to the public before being divulged to anyone or released to the press. This rule is designed to eliminate 'insider trading'; that is, where a select number of investors in the know can profit from information that's not available to the general public.

In Australia, the following securities exchanges operate:

⇨ Australian Securities Exchange (ASX), which incorporates the Australian Stock Exchange and the Sydney Futures Exchange. It provides listing and trading in securities and derivatives including shares, futures, options and warrants. It also provides clearing and settlement of trades through the CHESS system. (I'll outline the CHESS system shortly.)

⇨ National Stock Exchange (NSX), which specifically caters for the listing of small to medium enterprises.

⇨ Chi-X stock exchange, a global exchange that operates in Australia and at the time of writing provides trading in the top 200 Australian shares.

⇨ Asia Pacific Stock Exchange (APX), which caters especially for the Asia–Pacific region and offers Chinese market participants an alternative listing venue to the Shanghai and Shenzhen stock exchanges in China.

⇨ Indigenous Stock Exchange (ISX), which caters especially for Indigenous organisations.

Of these exchanges, the ASX is by far the largest and most widely used in Australia with over 90% of market share and more than 2000 listed entities, so it's the one I'll be concentrating on in this book.

Delisting and suspension

A listed company can become delisted; that is, it will no longer be listed with the securities exchange and the shares can't be traded using the exchange trading facility. A common cause of delisting is that the company restructures or is taken over and then becomes a new entity. Other causes of delisting are bankruptcy or any major breaches of legal requirements or exchange rules, or for non-payment of fees. Delisting is usually permanent in nature.

Voluntary suspension of the shares may also be imposed by the exchange at the request of the directors, usually because some major change is in the offing and the directors want to prevent speculative trading based on rumour rather than fact. Suspension is generally only a temporary event, generally for only a day or two, but it can be longer. When there's a suspension of share trading it's known as a trading halt because the shares can't be traded using the exchange trading facility during the time of suspension.

Tip

Voluntary suspension of share trading can be good or bad news for investors depending on the nature of the change being considered by the directors, but enforced delisting is bad news as any shares owned by investors become virtually worthless. Remember that the value of anything really depends on what a willing buyer will pay for it, so if it can't be sold, it's essentially valueless.

Market capitalisation

Market capitalisation (often abbreviated to market cap) is the share price multiplied by the number of shares on issue. It's a measure of the size of a company as reflected by the total number of investor dollars. The largest Australian companies have market caps in hundreds (or thousands) of millions of dollars, whereas the smallest ones may be only a hundred or so million dollars.

Value of a share

The value of a share can be influenced by many factors, such as the size of the company, its present or future profitability and so on, but in fact, the market determines the value of a share. The value of a share is commonly thought to be the last sale price, based on the assumption that this is the price at which the shares will trade in the immediate future. However, this isn't a constant price—it can change continually with each trade.

Tip

There's no precise way of determining the actual value of a share holding—the best you can do is get a reasonable estimate based on the last share price of the shares, but should you want to convert the shares to cash your cash in hand can be considerably different. There used to be a value called the 'par value' that was supposed to reflect some intrinsic value of a share but this is obsolete in Australia and is no longer quoted or used.

Types of shares

There are many different types of shares, including the following:

⇨ Ordinary shares (also known as fully paid ordinary shares or FPOs)—these are the most common shares owned and traded.

⇨ Contributing shares—these shares are not fully paid and the company may call on shareholders to contribute additional funds until a future time when the shares become fully paid.

⇨ Preference shares—these shares are given some preferential treatment over ordinary shares, such as first right to a dividend or company assets in the event of liquidation.

⇨ Convertible shares or hybrids—these shares are usually shares that have a fixed dividend rate based on some predetermined criteria. They usually can be converted to ordinary shares at some later point in time.

⇨ Company-issued options—these give the holder the right (but not the obligation) to obtain shares in the company at some future point in time.

⇨ Rights—these are similar to company-issued options except the time period is usually much shorter and the rights are issued only to current shareholders.

⇨ Bonus shares—these are additional shares issued free of charge to current shareholders. In the past companies often issued these as a reward to shareholders but bonus issues are now very rare.

⇨ Trust units — some companies (typically property conglomerates) are structured as trusts and issue units rather than shares. However, if the units are listed and tradeable, the distinction isn't important from an investor's viewpoint other than that there's a different taxation rate applicable to trust payouts to shareholders compared to share dividends.

Tip

When you consider the dividend yield make sure you also check the level of franking. Many property trusts (and other trusts) have high yields but the catch is that the dividend is almost always unfranked and therefore far less valuable than the same dividend fully franked (franking will be discussed shortly).

Classifying shares

Conventionally, shares are classified into various types, as follows:

⇨ Blue chip — these are the shares issued by the large, well-known market leader type organisations, including the major banks and large, established companies such as Telstra, Woolworths, Wesfarmers and so on. They have a large market share and a good track record of stable, long-term profits and usually also dividend payments. The shares are expensive but are considered to be the safest, so they're also known as 'defensives' because they're less prone to large price falls should the market turn down. They're a favourite of 'mum and dad investors'; that is, average Australians with no special share investing or trading expertise who want a relatively safe haven for their money.

⇨ Green chip — these are shares in smaller organisations that have a stable track record but are a little more risky than blue chips and less expensive. This could include regional banks, medium-sized established retailers, industrials and others.

⇨ Fallen angel—a blue or green chip share that's fallen on hard times with a big reduction in profitability and consequently a big drop in the share price.

⇨ Speculative—these are shares in smaller companies that don't have a proven track record of profitability. They generally don't pay a good dividend (and often no dividend at all) and they're considered to be risky as they often trade on 'blue sky potential'; that is, possible future profitability (that may or may not actually eventuate).

⇨ Penny dreadful—as the name suggests, these are shares that trade at a low price (sometimes only a few cents) and are very speculative. They present the possibility of huge profits if they experience a favourable turn in fortunes but also the possibility of total wipeout (that is, bankruptcy).

Tip

If you're a newcomer to online trading, I suggest you avoid speculative and penny dreadful shares. While they offer the prospect of large profits, you can also lose heaps in price downturns. The share price can even fall so much that the shares become virtually worthless, in which case you'll lose all the money you've invested in them.

Volatility

Volatility is a measure of the extent and rapidity of percentage price fluctuations, and can refer to the market as a whole or to any particular shares or investment instrument. I use the term 'percentage' because a $1.00 price change in a $10.00 share is 10% and if this happened in one day it would indicate high volatility. However, a $1.00 price change in a $50 share is 2% and indicative of a much lower volatility. Volatility is also known as 'choppiness', a descriptive term because it's very similar to a body of water that can be relatively calm or choppy depending on the surface wave action.

Tip

As I'll explain in later chapters, volatility and price risk are closely related so the more volatile shares are also the most risky. Needless to say, blue and green chip shares are usually the least volatile and speculative and penny dreadful shares the most volatile.

Trading and parcel

Trading is the act of buying or selling. When you trade shares, you buy or sell a 'parcel'; that is, a certain number of shares with a certain value. For example, you may place an order to buy (or sell) a parcel of 1000 shares that may be trading for $3.50, so having a parcel value of $3500.

Tip

It's important to realise that shares can't be bought without a seller (or sellers), nor sold without a buyer (or buyers), and in all cases both buyers and sellers must agree on the price and quantity.

Board of directors

It's obviously impossible for shareholders in a public company to make consensus decisions on every issue that arises, so these decisions are made by a group elected by the shareholders known as the board of directors (or board). They're often retired company directors or politicians or persons of note. The board periodically hold board meetings (usually once a month) and make decisions on behalf of the shareholders.

Annual report

The company is required to publish an annual report showing financial and other information of importance to shareholders. This is usually a document of a hundred or so pages and shareholders can opt to have it mailed to them or else made available electronically.

Tip

Most average shareholders won't have the time or expertise to wade through the annual report in detail so it's more convenient to look at summary reports or shareholder briefing reports that summarise the details of most interest to shareholders.

Annual general meeting (AGM)

As well as monthly board meetings, the company is required to hold an annual general meeting (AGM) of all shareholders so they can have a say and vote on important issues. In practice, the majority of shareholders don't attend AGMs so decisions are usually based on the preferences of a small number of large shareholders.

Tip

If you have the time to attend an AGM and the location is reasonably convenient to you, it's well worth doing so, at least once.

Profiting from shares

Profit from shares can come from two sources: dividends and capital gains.

Dividends are payments to the shareholders, usually from after-tax profits. Dividends may be franked, unfranked or partly franked depending on the amount of Australian tax paid by the company on its profits. From an investor's viewpoint, fully franked dividends are best because you obtain a full tax credit from the Australian Taxation Office (ATO) for the profit tax paid by the company. These are known as imputation credits (or franking credits), and even if you don't pay income tax you can receive them as a cash payment. So your effective (after tax) investment return from a fully franked dividend is higher than if the same dividend is unfranked or partly franked. In fact, a fully franked dividend gives an effective return (after tax) that's 42.9% higher than the unfranked dividend.

Dividends are usually paid every six months—those paid in the first half of the company's financial year are known as interim dividends and those paid in the second half of the year are known as final dividends. Typically the final dividend is greater than the interim dividend. In many cases, shareholders have the option of taking dividends in shares rather than cash—often at a discount price. This is known as a dividend reinvestment plan (DRP) and is an excellent method of building up your shareholding over the longer term while avoiding the temptation to spend a cash dividend.

Tip

If you're investing for the long term, seek shares that pay good fully franked dividends. If a DRP is available and you can manage without the cash payout, I suggest you join the DRP as it's a great way of building up your share wealth over the longer term.

Capital gains are profits made when shares are sold at a higher price than the purchase price, or more exactly, when the net revenue from the sale exceeds the total cost of purchase. If you're holding shares that have risen in price, your profit is known as 'paper profit' and it's not taxable until you actually sell. When you sell shares showing a paper profit this is known as 'taking profits' or 'crystallising profits'. You then make a realised capital gain, which is money in the bank for you that must be declared as income in the financial year of the sale.

Tip

You really need to have a good understanding of tax considerations applying to shares as these can influence your trading decisions. My book Teach Yourself About Shares *has a comprehensive treatment of both capital gains tax and dividend tax.*

Return on capital

As an investor (or trader) it's important to focus on return on capital (also known as profit on the capital invested) rather than the dollar amount of profit. For example, a profit of $1.00 per share on a $10.00 share is a 10% return (which is rather good) but if the share price is $50.00 the return reduces to a paltry 2%.

Tip

Always focus on return on capital rather than the dollar value of capital gains or dividends.

Dividend yield

The dividend yield is the total dividend (interim + final) divided by the current share price and expressed as a percentage. It is effectively the return on capital from dividends.

Tip

When considering dividends, focus on the dividend yield rather than the dollar value as the yield, as dividend yield is the return on capital.

Grossed-up yield

Because you get a taxation benefit from a dividend that's franked, the effective (after tax) yield is higher for a franked share than for an unfranked share. This is known as the grossed-up yield and you can calculate it by multiplying the yield by a grossing-up factor. For fully franked shares, the grossing-up factor is 1.429 (at the present company tax rate of 30%). For grossing-up factors for partly franked dividends please consult my book *Teach Yourself About Shares*.

Tip

Always take into account the benefits of franking when comparing dividend yields. For example a 5% fully franked yield is better for you than a 7% unfranked yield.

Ex-dividend date

There's a cut-off date for the payment of the next dividend to shareholders and it's known as the ex-dividend date. If you hold (or buy shares) prior to this date you'll get the next dividend but if you buy them on this date (or later) you'll miss out on the current dividend. Usually on the ex-dividend date the share price will fall by the value of the dividend and franking credits, so if you buy on the ex-dividend date or later you'll buy at a better price but miss the current dividend and franking credits (if any) associated with it.

If you sell shares on the ex-dividend date (or later) you'll still get the current dividend because you owned them prior to the ex-dividend date. If you're in the DRP it's important to be aware of this implication because after you sell the shares you'll be allocated the dividend in shares, and if you've sold all your shares you'll be left holding a small parcel of nuisance shares.

Tip

Before you buy or sell shares, always check the ex-dividend date and be aware of its implications.

Obtaining or disposing of shares

The most common way you can obtain or dispose of shares is by trading them; that is, by buying or selling them on the sharemarket. However, there are other ways your shareholding can change:

⇨ you can receive shares in lieu of a dividend payment

⇨ you can receive shares as a beneficiary of an estate

⇨ you can receive shares because of a demutualisation; that is, a change from a cooperative structure to a company structure

⇨ shares can be transferred as an off-market transfer—that is an ownership change that doesn't involve the market; for example, from one family member to another or from private ownership to a self managed super fund (SMSF).

Investor vs trader

While it seems obvious that a person who invests is an 'investor' and a person who trades is a 'trader', with shares there's a more subtle distinction. In most cases before you become a share investor you need to trade because you can't invest in shares unless you own them and you generally become a share owner by purchasing the shares. While an investor needs to trade, the frequency of the trades is the key factor in the distinction between an investor and a trader. Investors trade relatively infrequently and holds their shares over the longer term, whereas traders trade frequently and hold their shares for a shorter term. For example, many traders are 'day traders' because they don't hold their shares for more than one day; that is, they buy and sell the same shares on the same day.

As I've said the main difference between an investor and a trader is the frequency of their trades. Because a trader trades frequently, there's little opportunity to profit from dividends so a trader usually aims for capital gains profit only. For investors, dividends can be an important source of profit.

I've summarised the difference in table 1.1.

Table 1.1: investor and trader compared

	Trading frequency	Holding term	Source of profit
Investor	Trades infrequently	Long term	Dividends, imputation credits and capital gains
Trader	Trades frequently	Short term	Primarily capital gains

Tip

If you're considering giving up your day job and becoming a full-time share trader, think again. Studies show that very few people can derive a good income from full-time share trading and most who attempt it end up with burnt fingers. The most reliable way of deriving income from shares is from longer term share investing.

Brokers

You must be licensed in order to trade instruments listed with an exchange. Because you don't hold this licence, you need to use a licensed agent to execute the trade on your behalf. Licensed share trading agents are known as stockbrokers, sharebrokers, or simply 'brokers'. Brokers may operate online (using the internet) or offline (by mail, phone or fax). In order for a broker to execute trades on your behalf you need to first enter into a contract with them where you agree to the terms and conditions set out in their PDS (product disclosure statement). I'll explain how to do this in later chapters.

Brokerage

A broker trading shares on your behalf charges a fee and this fee is known as brokerage. Brokerage is usually a proportion of the dollar value of the trade, with a certain minimum fee for low-value trades. In addition to brokerage, some brokers who provide a more comprehensive service to customers charge ongoing fees that apply whether or not you trade. I'll discuss some of these fees and charges in later chapters.

Tip

Fees and charges for services performed are subject to GST. However, the GST charge is usually included in the quoted fee structure and isn't an additional charge (as is the case with most purchases of goods or services in Australia).

Share codes

If you want to trade offline, you'll most likely give your broker verbal instructions such as 'buy (or sell) 1000 shares for me in XYZ Company at $x'. When using the internet you need to convert verbal conversations into a dialogue a computer understands. You do this by using a code that's unique to the financial instrument you're interested in. For ordinary shares, this code is a three-letter one; for example the code for the Commonwealth Bank is CBA, for Woolworths it is WOW. For more sophisticated financial instruments the code can be up to six characters and include numbers as well as letters. I'll explain how to access codes online in later chapters.

Tip

If you're a longer term investor, after a while you'll probably remember the codes of the shares in your portfolio. Nevertheless, it's a good idea to have them written down in a conveniently accessible place, especially when you're contemplating a trade.

Indices

An index is a single statistic that amalgamates the price of a number of shares. Of itself, the index has no real meaning but changes in the index provide an indication of market changes. Australia has now adopted global index classifications and codes relevant to each index, which I discuss in greater detail in chapter 10. Like shares, index codes are three-letter ones.

There are two types of indices, namely sector indices and market indices.

Sector index

To make life somewhat easier for investors, the Australian sharemarket is broken down into sectors; that is, the types of business companies are chiefly involved in—for example: finance, materials, energy and so on.

Market index

The market itself is broken down into groups of shares that aren't necessarily in the same sector but have some other feature in common. For example, the most common market index in Australia is the All Ordinaries index (code XAO), comprising the 500 largest companies by market capitalisation.

Tip

The All Ords is the most commonly referred to index in television and financial news in the press as it gives a good indication of the entire Australian sharemarket.

World sharemarkets

Even if you're not really interested in investing overseas, world markets usually impact on the Australian market. In particular, the US market is of great importance to Australian investors as the Australian market often follows the lead of Wall Street. For example, if key US indices such as the Dow Jones and Nasdaq are up at the close of US markets and prior to the opening of our market, our market will often move up during the first hour or so of trading. Similarly, if US markets are down at close, our market will often move down during the initial trading phase.

Tip

Whether or not our market follows the trend set by overseas markets depends upon the mood of the investors, but very often US markets set the initial tone of our market.

Share registries

A share registry is a list of all shareholders in a company with all relevant details such as their contact information, number of shares held, when the shares were obtained or disposed of, dividends and other payments, and so on. Few listed companies maintain their own share registries but prefer to contract the work out to a specialist provider such as Computershare or Link Market Services. The important point is that if you have a query about your shareholding or dividend payments you need to contact the share registry and not the company itself. Registries are accessible on the internet and you can log in and check your details using a log in code and password.

Tip

You'll know who maintains the share registry of shares you own as it will be shown on shareholder information you receive when you purchase the shares. This information will also be shown each time you receive a dividend statement.

Shareholder information

When you become a shareholder, you can elect how you'll receive your shareholder information such as dividend statements, annual reports, notice of meetings, reports to shareholders and suchlike. You have three choices, namely:

⇨ receive all information by post

⇨ receive all information by email

⇨ receive some information by post and some by email.

The choice is a personal one and depends on your situation. Written information provides a permanent record that can be filed but of course you can print out any information you receive by email so the only benefit of using the post is that it saves you the trouble of printing. This is of importance with information such as annual reports which are often 100 or so coloured pages.

Provided you back up any important documents on an external thumb drive or hard drive, having a hard copy isn't critical because even if your computer crashes the data won't be lost. For shares held in my SMSF I opt to obtain shareholder information by email because at the end of each year I need to transmit this by email to my SMSF provider so it needs to be in electronic form.

Tip

If you elect to receive your shareholder information electronically it will save the company money, and as a shareholder this will eventually be of benefit to you. Also it's better for the environment. Make sure you back up any important electronic information on an external storage device so that in the event of a computer crash the data is retrievable.

Data providers

Compiling shareholder information and presenting it in the required manner requires specialist skills and software. Most securities exchanges and brokers don't compile their own data but use a specialist provider to do this work for them. For example, the ASX uses Standard & Poor's to compile market indices such as the All Ordinaries index and CommSec uses Morningstar to provide the share investing data given on their website.

As there are a number of data providers who may be using different algorithms and data sources, there can be differences in the information that's presented.

Tip

If you spot any errors or anomalies in data provided by a service provider or between different service providers it's worth investigating further. Your query will most likely be referred back to the data provider who should be able to provide an answer.

Online and offline brokers

When you invest online you use the facilities available on the internet to trade and to obtain all the information you require. When you invest offline you deal with a person such as a broker, financial agent or adviser. Before the advent of online trading, all brokers operated offline, meaning that you needed to contact them by phone, fax or mail when you wanted to trade. The broker would place the order with the exchange on your behalf and usually would also give you advice about the trade if you asked for their opinion.

Nowadays, the distinction between online and offline brokers is becoming rather less clear cut because you can contact an offline broker by sending an email or text message or contact them using their website. Some brokers offer a hybrid service that fuses traditional, full-service broking with the increased convenience and reduced cost associated with an online broking platform.

Tip

I suggest you don't start trading online until you've read right through this book.

Why invest online?

The decision whether to trade and invest online or offline isn't a simple one because the waters are muddied as online and offline brokers vary considerably in the charges and facilities they provide. For example, some offline brokers provide a full range of investment services such as advising you of the shares you should hold or trade, trading on your behalf, and keeping track of your portfolio and finances. Others provide a trade-only service where they simply place the trades on your behalf without providing any advice or suggestions.

Online brokers are rather more uniform in the range of services provided (which I'll discuss in greater detail in later chapters) but their fees and charges can vary considerably, and there are also some differences in the information you can access and in the way that it's presented. Nevertheless, it's possible to come to some general conclusions regarding the advantages and disadvantages of online investing.

Advantages

⇨ You're in complete control and make all your own decisions.

⇨ Online trading costs less. Typically you can trade shares to the value of $10 000 online for $20 (or even as little as $10), and that's only 0.2% or less. A telephone trade (even without advice) usually costs about $50 (or more).

⇨ The reduced brokerage makes trading relatively small parcel values online a feasible option. This allows investors with small amounts of capital to profitably trade online.

⇨ There's a huge amount of relevant information you can access free of charge on the internet. Much of this information is not conveniently available in any other way.

⇨ Trading data and financial information are usually up to date and are often in available real time. On the other hand, information such as recent sale prices or a price chart published in a book or magazine will be up to date only at the time of writing and can be weeks or months old. Online information sometimes applies to the previous day's trading or there may be a delay of 20 minutes or so. But certainly, you won't be looking at information that's weeks or months old.

⇨ You can look at data in chart or table form which is much easier to analyse than verbal information provided over the phone.

⇨ You can access information and research on a 24/7 basis—you're not restricted to office hours.

⇨ Online connections are usually very fast, efficient and don't rely on telephone calls and the availability of the party you're calling at the time you're doing so.

⇨ Information provided on the internet by an online service provider tends to be more factual and contain less personal bias. There's evidence that in the past, offline investment advisers didn't always give impartial advice and would sometimes favour investments they had a particular financial interest in.

⇨ Provided you have internet access you can invest online and obtain the information you need regardless of your location in Australia and you don't need to make a long-distance or mobile phone call.

⇨ You can invest online using portable computers, smart phones, iPads and similar devices.

⇨ Because all online instructions and contracts are in written form there's less chance of verbal communication errors.

⇨ You can easily experiment and test your systems and plans using the internet. Provided you don't actually trade shares you can't get into any trouble or expense by doing so. Back-testing your system or method is easy online and this is an excellent way of developing a trading system.

Disadvantages

⇨ You can't talk to a knowledgeable person. When you invest online you're using a dispassionate computer that won't have a conversation with you. This isn't necessarily as big a disadvantage as you might think because of the huge growth in social networking with sites such as Facebook, Twitter and YouTube, as well as many online chat rooms and forums that allow you to ask questions and seek ideas from other online users.

⇨ There's a risk that a hacker could access your personal online information. Also, there's a risk of virus or other infection so you need a good virus protection program.

⇨ You may occasionally be bumped off (lose internet connection) but this is relatively rare nowadays and usually happens only if you're using wireless and you're in an area where the reception isn't strong.

⇨ You need a degree of computer literacy and financial competence in order to take full advantage of the information and facilities available online. However, you don't need a great deal of knowledge to start with and, even if you're a rank beginner, after you've read this book you should be well on your way.

⇨ You need to be vigilant to avoid errors that otherwise might be detected by an offline broker who's familiar with your situation.

Evolutionary approach

If you haven't invested online but are considering doing so, a good option is an evolutionary rather than a revolutionary approach. That's to say you can 'test the water' by setting up an online account and trading a few relatively small parcels of shares. As your experience and confidence grow you can expand your operations until you eventually invest solely using the internet if you're satisfied that it's the best way to go.

Tip

Consider an evolutionary approach to online investing. You don't need to plunge in with an 'all or nothing' approach right from the start.

Forecasts and tips

In my experience, most of the information obtained on the internet is accurate and can be relied on except when it's a forecast or tip. Always regard forecasts and tips as speculative, even when the forecast is the consensus of a number of 'expert' financial advisers. In particular, be aware of information or ideas expressed in internet forums and chat rooms as it's personal opinion and therefore contains a certain amount of bias.

Tip
Don't act on a forecast or tip without careful consideration and conducting your own research.

Information overload

The internet contains a massive amount of information that's constantly growing in volume. There are about 2000 shares and other entities listed with the ASX with large amounts of data about each that you can access on the internet. In addition, the facilities available to online investors are constantly growing as websites become more sophisticated. For example, there are at least 60 different technical analysis indicators you access and use on internet sites. Furthermore, in many cases you'll get conflicting indications from different indicators, and as a result, whether you're a novice or an experienced investor, you can easily fall into the trap of 'paralysis by analysis' where you get confused and bogged down by too much information. On the other hand, you might decide to simplify your approach and concentrate on only a selected number of statistics or indicators, and as a result omit consideration of some vital ones.

In other words, there's an optimum balance between insufficient information and information overload, as illustrated in figure 1.1.

Figure 1.1: optimum information

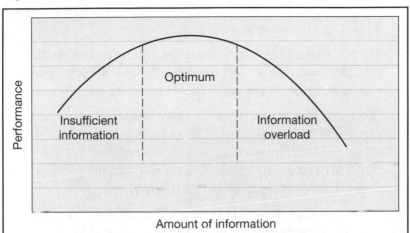

The trick is to try to get yourself into the optimum zone where you have sufficient information to make good investment decisions but not so much that you get bogged down. In this book I'll try to guide you in this direction and focus on the essentials that you need and omit the peripheral distractions. This will get you started in the right direction, and as you become more experienced you can refine your information systems as necessary to suit your needs.

Tip

Generally speaking, information simplification is better than overload. It's a mistake to believe that 'more is necessarily better'. Some very successful trading systems have been developed that focus on only a handful of key statistics and indicators.

Key points

⇨ The internet has revolutionised share trading and the way information about shares is obtained. An increasing number of investors are obtaining information and trading shares using the internet.

⇨ It's easy and convenient to trade shares using the internet and I urge you to seriously consider this option as there are many advantages to doing so.

⇨ There's been increasing competition among online service providers and this is good news for the online investor as you can expect continuing benefits by going online.

⇨ You can access the internet for share investing purposes with many devices, including mobile phones (of several different types), tablets, laptops and desktop computers. For the purpose of analysing charts and statistics available online, the larger the screen the better.

⇨ When you trade online you're in full control and dealing with a computer and not a person, so you need to check carefully to ensure that all details are correct before you place an online order.

⇨ There are many different types of shares but if you're not an experienced investor it's generally best to stick to plain-vanilla ordinary shares.

⇨ You profit from shares in two main ways: from capital gains and dividends. You make capital gains when you sell shares for a higher price than you purchased them and you obtain dividend income when shares you hold pay dividends to shareholders.

⇨ Recognise the value of franking (or imputation) credits as these considerably boost the value of dividends.

⇨ You'll generally maximise share investing profitability if you invest in shares that pay a good, well-franked dividend and at the same time offer the prospect of capital gains.

⇨ Information obtained over the internet is generally up to date and accurate. However, you shouldn't rely on any information about the future whether that consists of personal opinions presented in forums and chat rooms or forecasts made by one or more financial analysts.

⇨ There's so much information and so many facilities available on the internet that you can get bogged down with information overload. You need to strike an optimum balance and remember that it's generally better to err on the side of simplicity rather than complexity.

⇨ You can adopt an evolutionary rather than revolutionary approach by setting up an online account and trading a few shares in relatively small parcel sizes. As you become more experienced and confident you can expand your usage before finally transferring completely to the online method.

⇨ There are a few pitfalls for the unwary online investor but they can be avoided. After reading this book in its entirely you should be well on your way to avoiding the traps and becoming a successful online investor.

chapter 2

Online share investing resources

You can't use the facilities and resources available on the internet for share investing if you don't know what they are. Therefore the first step in becoming a successful online investor is to research what online resources are available to you so you can tap into and use the ones appropriate to your needs.

In this chapter I'll outline the information and facilities available on the internet relevant to share investing so you'll be in a better position to decide the information you'll want to access and the facilities you'll wish to use. This chapter is a summary of the resources available and provides only an outline of each. Most are examined in greater detail later on in the book.

Resources available online

Available online resources are summarised in table 2.1. Clearly it's not an exhaustive list but it certainly outlines the most important resources and facilities available online.

Tip

In most cases I don't quote the specific websites where you can access these resources; instead sites are listed in chapter 3.

Table 2.1: resources available online

General information	Charting facility
Listed stocks and their codes	Research tools
Delisted stocks	Watch list
Name changes and amalgamations	Portfolio
Initial public offerings (IPOs)	Trading history
Sectors and indices	Alerts
Market news	Forums and chat rooms
Company announcements	Recommendations
Director trades	Online broker comparisons
Shareholder briefings (presentations)	Shareholder benefits
Company profile	Managed funds
Financial data	Self managed superannuation
Forecasts	Margin loans
Online trading facility	Contracts for difference (CFDs)
Trading depth	Paper trading and investment games
Trading volume	Online book and software purchases
Course of trades	

I'll now provide a brief description of each of the resources outlined in this table.

General information

There are many websites that provide general information about shares, share investing and share trading. Worldwide websites often contain useful information and facilities, but it's generally best to access Australian sites as these are more focused on our market and the facilities available to Australian investors.

Often websites have a 'Help' button or similar facility that provides additional information on request. In addition, some sites have explanatory drop-down menus attached to specific terms on the site. In some cases there's an alphabetical glossary or descriptions of terms, which can be very useful when you want to check on the meaning of a particular term, statistic or technical indicator.

Most websites have a 'Contact us' form that allows you to post any queries and have them answered by email.

Listed stocks and their codes

As I mentioned in chapter 1, when a tradeable instrument is listed with a securities exchange it's assigned an alphabetic code, which for ordinary shares is a three-letter one. You need to use the codes when you trade or look up information about shares or other investment instruments and I suggest you keep a master list of the ones you own (or are interested in) for easy reference.

You can obtain a master list (in alphabetical order) of all tradeable instruments listed with an exchange with the relevant code from their website. Many other sites (including online trading sites) enable you to obtain the code if you enter the name of the company or investment instrument you're interested in.

Delisted stocks

As I mentioned in chapter 1, the shares in a company can be delisted by an exchange for a number of reasons. If you try to trade shares or access information about shares you're interested in and you can't do so, delisting is the most likely reason.

You can obtain a list of delisted stocks on the exchange's site (and also on other sites) with an explanation for the delisting.

Name changes and amalgamations

Apart from delisting, another reason you may not be able to trade or obtain information about shares you're interested in is because there's been a name change, amalgamation or takeover. You can use the internet to find out if this has been the case. For example, details of name changes and amalgamations of ASX listed stocks over the last five years are listed on the ASX site.

Initial public offerings (IPOs)

If you're interested in IPOs you can use the web to find out about upcoming IPOs and the key dates and you'll usually be able to download the relevant prospectus. However, if you wish to subscribe, you'll still need to manually complete the application form and post it in with your payment.

Sectors and indices

Many websites allow you to determine the sector group a company is included in. Also, you can find out which shares are included in each of the market indices. You're also able to track trends in sectors or market indices, both for Australian and overseas markets, and access charts of sector and index movements. These charts are similar to price charts for shares.

Market news

This facility enables you to obtain the latest market news for both Australian and overseas markets. Generally, you're given a broad overview of markets, including general market trends as well as trends in the major indices and commodities and any significant changes in investor sentiment. Some websites also give brief details of companies in the news because of some major change or pending change.

Many websites (and most online trading sites) allow you to track trends in overseas markets prior to the opening of the Australian market. Some sites can also email you a daily or weekly market bulletin if you request it.

Company announcements

According to securities exchange listing rules, listed companies are required to provide details of any major changes to the exchange before releasing the information by any other means to any other person or the public at large. The information is submitted to the exchange in the form of an announcement that's published on the website of the exchange and available to anyone with access to the site. In Australia the ASX site is the major exchange, so it's the logical place to search for announcements. However, many other sites (including online trading sites) tap into the ASX site and list the announcement headings and provide links to the exchange site so you can access the announcement in detail if you wish

Announcements are made every day, and if you try to read them all you'll be overwhelmed. It's important to restrict your search to shares in which you have an interest and to specific timeframes. Many websites allow you to search all today's announcements, or announcements for specific shares over the past week, month, six months or year. Some websites will email you headline announcements if you register and request this service. This facility allows you to quickly scan a list to see if there are any that interest you. Links are provided so you can read the announcements in full if you wish to.

The ASX site differentiates announcements that are considered to be price sensitive and these are noted with an exclamation mark (or other symbol on other sites).

The types of announcements commonly made include:

⇨ the lodging of financial reports (such as interim or final reports)

⇨ shareholder presentations

⇨ dividend announcements and DRP price allocations

⇨ substantial changes in share ownership (including directors' interests)

⇨ restructuring plans (such as acquisitions or the sale of divisions or subsidiaries)

⇨ substantial changes in company activities

⇨ substantial sales or acquisitions of new assets

⇨ significant litigation cases that have commenced or concluded

⇨ significant changes in resources, such as when an oil well produces, or fails to produce, substantial reserves

⇨ changes in governance

⇨ issues of new shares (such as a rights issue)

⇨ earnings estimates or preliminary financial results

⇨ responses to ASX inquiries (for example, those resulting from sudden unexplained jumps or drops in share prices)

⇨ suspension of share trading

⇨ appointments of receivers (for companies declared bankrupt).

Tip

If you notice a sudden and dramatic share price movement, it is a good idea to check the announcements facility to see whether the company has released any information that could explain the price change.

Director trades

In Australia, directors of listed companies can legally trade shares in their own companies. Knowledge of director trades is regarded as useful information for share investors and traders, for the obvious reason that a director of a company should be well aware of the current financial situation and likely future performance of the business. Consequently substantial value share trading by a director or directors could be a significant pointer to the future.

Tip

There are websites where you can search for recent director trades and this is a facility that's well worth investigating. When a director purchases shares of significant value in her own company, this can be indicative of a vote of confidence and that the share may be worth purchasing. On the other hand, selling shares of significant value could be a sign of less confidence about the future.

Shareholder briefings (presentations)

At the AGM, the chairperson of the board and the CEO usually make a presentation to shareholders. This is a simplified summary of the activities of the company and sales and profits trends, as well as future outlook. It's often presented in slide form as a PowerPoint presentation. Most shareholders don't attend AGMs so a fairly recent innovation has been to make these presentations accessible on the internet. This is a great way for shareholders (or prospective shareholders) to get an understanding of the company and its activities without having to wade through a hundred or so pages of detailed information and statistics contained in the annual report.

Company profile

The company profile provides information about the principal activities and aspirations of listed companies. You can research basic details, such as the location of the company's head office, what its main products are and where they are sold, how long the company has been in operation, who the directors are, what acquisitions or mergers it has been involved in, and so on.

You can also find out how many shares are on issue, who the major shareholders are and the name and contact details of its share registry. If a company pays dividends you can find out the ex-dividend date. You will also be able to ascertain the date of the next annual general meeting (AGM) when it's scheduled.

Financial data

This facility enables you to access a company's financial records and research important current and past financial data, such as profit and earnings per share, dividend per share, assets, liabilities, loan capital, equity capital and gearing. This type of information is also known as fundamental statistics.

Some data providers have a facility called 'Earnings surprises' which allows you to compare the last few earnings results with those that were expected by the market. A history of significant earnings surprises is an indication of more volatile (and therefore risky) shares.

Tip

In chapter 8 I provide more details about company profiles and important financial statistics.

Forecasts

Data given in the company's financial record is historical. However, the sharemarket is forward looking and investors are more focused on future prospects than past results. Many websites publish forecast earnings and growth figures compiled by financial analysts based on available information and trends.

Tip

You should always consider the future when considering any share trade or investment, but regard forecasts as a guide rather than a reliable indication of future performance.

Online trading facility

This facility allows you to trade online using a computer (or other device) connected to the internet. As well as Australian shares, some online trading sites enable you to trade other instruments such as:

⇨ managed funds

⇨ international shares

⇨ bonds and other fixed-interest securities

⇨ currencies, or foreign exchange rates (forex)

⇨ derivatives, such as warrants, exchange-traded options (ETOs) and futures

⇨ contracts for difference (CFDs).

Tip

As I mentioned in chapter 1, the more sophisticated trading instruments can offer the prospect of increased capital gains but they also carry a greater risk so are best avoided by all but very experienced or specialist traders.

Trading depth

Trading depth refers to the number and quantity of buy or sell orders for a stock at each price. In some cases, there may be a large number of orders in the system, so on online trading sites it's common to show only 10 or so buy and sell orders with prices closest to the last trade price. Because of the dynamic nature of share trading, the trading depth can change rapidly with time as orders are fulfilled and as prospective buyers or sellers enter or leave the market.

Trading volume

Volume is the quantity of shares in a stock that have been traded. This can be up to a point in time during a day or the total at the end of a day. It's important to be aware that for each buy transaction there must be an equal and opposite sell transaction so the volume of shares traded is the number bought or the number sold (not the sum of the two).

Course of trades

This facility allows you to access sales history at any point in time during the day; that's to say, the price and the number of shares traded in each parcel. When there are many trades, this is indicative of liquidity. (This is also sometimes called 'course of sales'.)

Tip
I discuss the interpretation and use of trading depth, volume and course of trades in detail in chapter 7. It's easier to interpret course of trades data by accessing it in chart form.

Charting facility

Information such as share price movements, volume of trades and so on is easiest to interpret when presented as a chart. Many online sites have a charting facility that provides many types of charts relevant to share investing and often the charts can be customised in various ways by the user. Many websites also provide indicators that provide tools for chart analysis.

Tip
The analysis of share charts is known as 'technical analysis' and I discuss how to do technical analysis in chapter 9.

Research tools

Because there's a large number of listed shares, it's obviously very time consuming to trawl through all of them when you're searching for shares that are suitable for your investing needs. The research tools facility allows you to use a computer to do the searching for you and come up with a short list of shares that satisfy your requirements. For example, you can obtain a list of shares whose price relative to earnings (P/E) or dividend yield is within a certain range stipulated by you.

Tip

A research tools facility is provided on many sites (including online trading sites) and is a big time saver for you.

Watch list

Many online sites allow you to set up a watch list where you can more easily keep track of price movements or announcements with a selected number of shares. These can be those you've invested in or are interested in. Once you've set up the watch list, all you need to do is access the list through the website and you'll be able to tell at a glance how the price has moved that day (compared to the day before) for each of the shares in your list.

Tip

Some websites allow you to set up a list of shares and have an email sent to you when one of them makes an announcement. This is a great way of keeping in touch with developments in shares you're interested in.

Portfolio

Your portfolio is the list of all the stocks you own and the number of shares in each. Online trading sites usually set up a portfolio automatically for you when you buy shares through the site or have shares allocated to you in lieu of dividends (a DRP). When you purchase additional shares these are added to your portfolio, and if they are shares in the same stock they will automatically be added to your holding. When you sell shares through the site, these are automatically deleted from your portfolio.

Your online portfolio is updated periodically so it shows the last sale price of each of your shares, the value of each parcel and the total value of your portfolio. It may also show the profit or loss on each parcel and the total profit and loss of your portfolio. This is trickier if you've bought shares in the same stock at different times and at different costs or where you've had shares allocated to you in lieu of dividends.

As well as your online trading site, there are other public access sites that allow you to set up your portfolio with shares you own or hypothetical ones, in which case the portfolio you set up will be the same as a watch list.

Tip

I discuss setting up and managing your online portfolio in detail in chapter 6.

Trading history

Most online trading sites allow you to access your trading history and so keep track of all your transactions with your online broker. The site will also show the cash balance in your trading account.

While you should keep your own records of your share trades, it is useful to be able to access this information through your online trading site (particularly at tax time).

Tip

Cash transfer for the settlement of share trades occurs three business days after the day the trade occurred (known as T+3), so the cash balance in your trading account and the shares in your online portfolio won't reflect any share trades you've made in the last three business days — in other words it will be three days out of date.

Alerts

It's possible to arrange automatic email or mobile phone alerts (via text messages) for shares you nominate. You may have to pay for this service but some sites provide it free of charge. You can be alerted for different criteria such as:

⇨ *Price alert:* when the share price reaches a threshold value which can be a low value (such as a stop-loss level) or a high value (such as a profit-stop level). You can preset or alter these values at any time.

⇨ *Announcement alert:* when there's been an announcement by the company.

⇨ *Volume alert:* when the number of shares traded that day reaches a threshold value set by you.

⇨ *Status alert:* when the status of the shares changes; for example, the shares go ex-dividend or options expire or the company is delisted or taken over.

Tip

Before you arrange for any alerts check to see if there's a fee involved, and if so what it is.

Forums and chat rooms

Many online sites provide forums or chat rooms that enable you to communicate with others who are interested in share trading and investing. Usually notices are fairly short and consist of only a few lines but sometimes they're longer. You can read or post notices and reply to any notices that have been posted. Before you can access these facilities you'll need to register with the site and provide your details. You can also communicate with others using one of the social media sites, such as Facebook, Twitter and YouTube.

Messages are usually filtered to eliminate unseemly language and to ensure authenticity; however, there have been cases where a deception has occurred. Sometimes messages are posted or responded to by company executives but this is unusual.

Tip

The accuracy of any information presented on chat rooms and forums should not be taken for granted.

Recommendations

Some websites give 'buy', 'hold' or 'sell' recommendations for major shares. Sometimes the recommendations are broken down further into categories such as 'strong buy', 'moderate buy', 'buy', 'hold', 'sell' and 'strong sell'. The interpretation of these categories is self-explanatory except for the 'hold' recommendation. This is usually interpreted to mean that if you own the shares you should continue to hold them, as there are no clear reasons to sell or to buy more shares.

Tip

It's been shown that analyst recommendations are biased on the optimistic side, with few sell recommendations. So I suggest you interpret a 'hold' recommendation as a recommendation that if you don't own the shares you shouldn't buy them, and if you do own them you should watch them carefully and be prepared to sell if there's a downturn.

Online broker comparisons

There are many online brokers that you can choose from. While they all provide very similar trading services, costs can differ considerably. There can also be large differences in the amount of useful investor information and facilities provided.

To help you choose which broker you will use for your online trades, there are sites that provide summary details to make it easier for you to make direct comparisons and to choose the online broking service most suitable for you.

Tip

I discuss online broker comparisons in greater detail in chapter 4.

Shareholder benefits

Some companies provide shareholder benefits, usually in the form of discounts on their products. For example, many banks provide a discount rate on loans for their shareholders and some manufacturers of retail goods provide discount vouchers for their shareholders. In some cases, you need to own a certain minimum number of shares in order to qualify for the discount.

You can find out if shareholder discounts apply on some online broking sites and on some public access sites.

Tip
Worthwhile shareholder discounts were more common in the past than they are today. However, it's still worthwhile checking if they apply—particularly if you use (or are contemplating using) the company's products.

Managed funds

Managed funds are an investment product that allows you to invest in a variety of entities by buying into the fund. The types of funds available varies greatly—some examples are:

⇨ general fund that invests in a variety of listed shares

⇨ index fund that invests in all shares included in an ASX index

⇨ sector fund that invests only in shares that are in a specific sector

⇨ special fund that invests only in companies that conform to strict criteria such as ethical investments.

The advantages of investing in a fund are that you can obtain diversification with a single investment and that your investment is managed for you by one or more financial analysts who are alleged 'experts' in their field. The main disadvantage is that the fund charges fees for providing this service, and that—of course—reduces the return to investors.

Rather than issuing shares, funds issue units that you purchase when you want to invest in the fund or sell if you decide to exit the investment. The majority of funds are unlisted; that is, they're not listed with a securities exchange. A minority of funds are listed, and in this case you can trade units in the fund in the same way that you'd trade shares using your broker. If a fund is unlisted you need to apply to the fund in order to purchase units or cash them in. If you want to buy into the fund you'll need to complete the application form in the prospectus and in many case this is available online.

Some online broking sites contain information and prospectuses about managed funds you can invest in with them. Also, some public access sites have this facility. You can search the variety of funds available and obtain up-to-date unit prices for entry and exit of unlisted funds.

Tip

If you want to invest in a managed fund, I suggest that you first look at those that are listed, as it's easier, faster and more convenient to trade these units than if the fund is unlisted.

Self managed superannuation funds (SMSF)

Many investors with substantial capital to invest set up their own superannuation fund, as there are many advantages to doing so. The most cost-effective way of setting up and managing an SMSF is to do so online.

Tip

I discuss the advantages and limitations of a self managed superannuation fund and how you can set up one online in greater detail in chapter 5.

Margin loans

Many online brokers provide a margin loan facility for their customers, especially those affiliated with banks and major financial institutions. A margin loan is a way of increasing your available capital for share investing or trading and it's a special purpose loan where you use an existing share portfolio as collateral for the loan. The catch is that the interest rate for a margin loan will be considerably higher than standard interest rates that apply for other loans such as home loans. Also in the event of a market fall you can get caught out with a margin call if you're highly geared. This basically means that some of your shares will be sold in order to boost your cash balance and this can be unprofitable when prices have turned down.

Tip

If you're considering a margin loan I suggest you don't gear too highly—that is, borrow right up to the available limit—because by so doing you're risking a margin call should the market turn down. A margin loan can boost your profits in a rising market but will generally be counterproductive in a falling one.

Contracts for difference

A contract for difference (CFD) is similar to a margin loan in that it enables you to increase the amount of capital available for investment in shares (or other investment instruments) and thus increase your leverage. With a CFD you don't actually trade the shares or other investment instrument but instead you enter into a contract with a CFD provider for the value of the trade. CFDs have been a growth area of investment and there are now many providers who provide trading in CFDs online.

Tip

Trading in CFDs is a way of leveraging your share investing/ trading profits and will considerably boost your profit if you get it right. But, if you get it wrong, CFD trading will also considerably increase your losses.

Paper trading and investment games

Whether you are new to share investing or an experienced share investor, it's a good idea to test your trading skills and your trading system by paper trading with hypothetical amounts of money before committing real dollars. One way of doing this is to set up a hypothetical portfolio on a website that offers this facility and follow the progress of your portfolio as time goes on.

There are also websites that have trading games that you can play to match your skills against other investors. In theory, the advantage of paper trading is that you can test your ideas or investment strategies without actually committing any funds. You can also change or modify strategies to test the effect that this has on your profits.

Tip

Paper trading is a good way of testing your trading/investment system but a word of caution is appropriate. Paper trading can't simulate your responses under stress so it doesn't necessarily provide an accurate guide to the decisions you'll make when your real hard-earned money is at stake. Research shows that decisions made under stress are often very different to those made in the same situation where there's no stress involved.

Online books and software purchases

Some sites provide links to bookshops where you can obtain a complete listing of all titles held that have any relevance to share investing. Many sites allow you to purchase books, magazines, software and other share investing aids online.

Key points

⇨ There's a great deal of information and many facilities available for online investors that can be accessed using the internet. More detailed discussion of the facilities and information available is given in later chapters of this book.

⇨ It's best to obtain information from Australian websites as they are more directly focused toward our market. Overseas laws, rules and customs relating to trading or investing can be very different from ours.

⇨ There's a huge amount of information and facilities you can access online. It's best not to try to access everything at once but start in a small and simple way and expand your horizons as your experience and knowledge develops.

⇨ Consider using the information in this chapter in conjunction with the list of websites presented in the next chapter to browse and carry out your own research.

chapter 3

Useful websites

In this chapter I'll outline some websites that you may find useful and worth visiting. This is by no means an exhaustive list, as there are many thousands of websites containing share investing information, and if I tried to give a synopsis of them all there'd be no room in this book for anything else. So I've included only the sites that I consider may be useful for Australian investors. I haven't included sites that are discussed in greater detail in later chapters; for example, online broking sites and charting sites.

First I give you a general introduction to the types of share investing sites available on the internet and then I provide a short synopsis of each one to give you a feeling for the site so you can explore further if you're interested. Information about each site and the fees that may be charged for services provided are current at the time of writing—because websites constantly change it's a good idea to check out any sites you are interested in to get the most up-to-date information.

Tip

Many websites have a search facility where you can input keywords or company codes and check available information on the site specific to your area of interest. If your initial search doesn't yield a result try changing the keywords a little.

Types of share investing websites

Broadly speaking, websites can be classified into three main groups:

⇨   user-pay sites

⇨   free sites

⇨   hybrid sites.

User-pay sites

User-pay sites are sites that provide information or facilities accessible only to paying subscribers. This may be a program or trading system that's claimed to produce superior results or periodic newsletters or trading advice (tips). In some cases the fee may be a once-only charge—for example, to undertake a training program—but in other cases there can be an ongoing charge in the form of a monthly, six-monthly or annual fee if you want access to trading tips, advice or newsletters. You can expect to pay a fee if you want to access specialist share investing information or resources available on the internet. After all, an inventor or creator who puts time, effort and expense into creating a product or resource that offers benefits to others is entitled to compensation from those who use this to their advantage. Use of the internet as a vehicle to access the resource doesn't change this—it just makes dissemination of the information or use of the product or service easier and more accessible to a wider audience.

Once you pay and become a subscriber (or customer), you'll most likely need a log in code and password in order to access the information or resource. Fees vary widely from a few hundred dollars to several thousand.

Tip

Sites offering trading systems or software packages often make grandiose claims and provide glowing testimonials but there's usually very little (if any) independent or authoritative verification of these claims. So I suggest caution before subscribing to any website or purchasing any system or resource available online. I believe a better approach is to learn as much as you can about share trading and investing and then formulate your own system or method that you really understand and know how to use. You can always refine and improve your system as you use it or test it and doing so won't cost you anything!

Free sites

Free share investing websites are accessible to anyone at no cost. In some cases you may need to register and provide some personal details including your email address and perhaps use a log-in code and password, but in other cases you don't even need to do this and the site is accessible to the public at large. Some free sites will send you emails on a daily, weekly or monthly basis providing share investing information or trading tips or links to information or facilities you can access.

Setting up and maintaining a website involves a cost, so the question arises: 'why would anyone go to the trouble and expense of setting up a website that can be accessed by anyone free of charge?' This is an intriguing question, and it seems there are several reasons:

⇨ A website can be set up as a vehicle for advertising the business or product or for customer liaison purposes. Most listed companies and securities exchanges maintain a website for these reasons. Websites often provide a 'Contact us' tab where customers or potential customers can provide feedback or information that may be useful for marketing purposes.

⇨ When you register to use a website you're divulging some personal details that can provide valuable marketing information. Even if you can access the site without registering, the number of hits on the site and the trend of the hits is of itself useful marketing information that may have a saleable value.

⇨ Many free websites contain advertisements. These advertisements may be catchy and tempt you to respond, but even if you ignore them they can have a subliminal impact that you mightn't even be aware of. It's rather like a roadside billboard advertising a product that you don't consciously look at while driving by yet it can have a subliminal impact. Sometimes just by inadvertently passing your cursor over the advertisement you'll be linked to it anyway.

⇨ The free information or resources are provided in order to 'get you into the shop' to sample the freebies and hopefully buy at a later stage. It's the principle used by stores that advertise a few super specials to lure you into the store in the hope that you'll make additional purchases.

Tip

If you're not sure whether to register with a site and receive free resources such as newsletters or emails, my suggestion is that you do so. If you get bogged down with too many emails (and they can mount up in your inbox), you can always opt out at a later stage.

Hybrid sites

The distinction between user-pay and free sites isn't as clear cut as it appears at first sight because many user-pay sites may still have lots of free information and facilities provided on the site. However, there's additional, more in-depth information or resources available to paying subscribers only. These sites can be regarded as hybrid sites, and indeed many sites fall into this category.

Tip

Hybrid sites can contain a large amount of useful information and many great resources free of charge, making them worth a visit even if you don't subscribe to the fee-paying resources on offer.

Your choice

Clearly it's entirely your choice whether you want to pay for online information or resources. As I said, an inventor or creator of a facility or resource is entitled to compensation, but at the same time I just can't see the sense in paying for something that's available for free elsewhere. I call this the 'Kinsky Principle':

Don't pay for something that you can get for free.

A corollary of this principle is:

Don't pay for online information or the use of some online facility or resource unless you're satisfied that the following two conditions are being met:

⇨ *you really need the information, resource or facility*

⇨ *there's some benefit from the information, resource or facility you're paying for that can't be obtained elsewhere for free.*

Tip

Before you click the 'buy' button on a website make sure you check the two necessary conditions I've outlined.

Company websites

Most listed companies (and many unlisted ones) maintain a website. A company website can contain much information that can be useful to an investor (or potential investor), including the history of the company, its location, size, products and services, directors and executive officers, financial details, share registry and so on. Typically there'll be a 'Contact us' tab, usually designed with potential customers in mind, but which you can use to obtain share investing information. For example, I've often sent emails to company executives with share investing queries and I usually receive a reply. Needless to say, in larger organisations you're unlikely to get a response from the chief executive officer but you may if the organisation is a smaller one. In any case, it's worth the attempt.

You can obtain the web addresses for listed companies in several ways:

⇨ Have a stab. It is a fair bet that www.'companyname'.com.au will produce a result.

⇨ Check the ASX site where the details of all ASX-listed companies—including web addresses—are given.

⇨ Conduct an internet search using the company name.

Tip

If you're considering investing in a company it's worthwhile checking out their website to get a general feel for the company and its products. You can use the site to contact them directly if you have any queries.

Securities exchange sites

Securities exchanges both in Australia and overseas maintain websites containing useful share investing information particularly relevant to companies listed with the exchange, and these sites are well worth visiting. In Australia most securities are listed with the ASX, so clearly this is the premier site for information relevant to Australian share investors.

Online trading sites

The main purpose of an online trading site is to provide an online trading facility. However, in order to attract customers and increase market share most online trading sites provide heaps of additional facilities and information. The purpose of this is essentially to provide a 'one-stop shop' so customers have all the information they require to make trading and investment decisions without needing to search elsewhere. In many cases, even if you're not a subscriber you can access the site and obtain some useful information.

Share registry sites

Share registries maintain websites that contain relevant shareholder information about shares in companies that use the services of the registry. The site will show each stock and the number of shares in each that you own, dividends paid or shares received in lieu of dividends, and so on. The site may also show prices for the shares in your portfolio and a total portfolio value. To access your information on the site you'll need to register and log in with your registration code and password.

Tip

A share registry site will contain information about the companies that use the share registry only so it's a good idea to note which registry applies to each of the different shares in your portfolio. Then if you have a query, you're able to log in to the appropriate registry.

Forums and chat room sites

There's been a mushrooming growth in the use of social media as a means of human communication, and this also applies to share investing. There are a number of online forums and chat rooms where you can get ideas and information from other investors and post replies or raise queries.

Charting sites

I discuss charting in chapter 9, as charts are an essential aid to share trading or investing decisions. Most online trading sites have a charting facility and there are also several dedicated online charting sites.

Recommendation sites

These are user-pay sites––also known as 'tipster sites'—that provide trading tips or advice on a regular basis. They give their ideas about which shares or sectors to buy or sell and when to do so. Like trading software package sites, these sites are most suitable for investors who don't have the expertise or time they believe they need in order to make profitable trading and investing decisions. Most tipster sites provide free access to some past publications or recommendations to give you an idea of the value of the service they provide. However, be wary of claims regarding profits made in the past, as it's very easy to trade profitably with the benefit of hindsight. Some of these sites offer an obligation-free trial, and if this is possible you might like to give it a go. If this option isn't available, you may be able to evaluate how good the service is by trying to contact other subscribers to obtain their opinions. Probably the best way of doing this is to search forum sites for postings relevant to the service you're interested in. You could also post a notice and hopefully receive responses from subscribers to the service.

Failing all that, you could evaluate the service by subscribing to it for the minimum period possible. When renewal time comes around you can do your sums and decide whether subscribing to the service was a profitable exercise or whether you feel you could have made the same (or more) profit using your own resources and expertise.

Tip

The bottom line is that no matter what advice you get from anyone you're ultimately responsible for your investment decisions. I suggest you try to adopt this mindset rather than believing that others can (or should) make investment decisions for you.

Useful websites

I'll now list useful websites (in alphabetical sequence). I'll concentrate on Australian sites with useful amounts of free information but I've also included some overseas and subscriber sites that can be worth a visit. For subscriber sites, I've given an indication of applicable fees and charges at the time of writing.

Tip

You may feel a bit overwhelmed by the sheer number of sites that can be worth a visit, so I suggest you browse through and bookmark those of most interest to you and when you have time later on, explore at your leisure.

Alan Hull: www.alanhull.com

Alan Hull is an author and presenter of share investing courses and newsletters. Some of the courses are classroom-based and others are online home-study courses, the cost of course depending on the type and length of the course. Alan produces several weekly newsletters, including the *Blue Chip Report, Active Investing Newsletter, Active Trading Newsletter* and *Breakout Trading*

Newsletter. To give you an idea of cost, the *Blue Chip Report* involves a charge of $99 per month (or $990 per annum) and a $49.50 joining fee. You can subscribe to the newsletter or purchase books from the site and you can download for free some reports and sample copies of newsletters.

AMP: www.amp.com.au

The AMP site is useful if you are at the planning stage or if you want general information on investing, financial planning and superannuation. Of course, it is tailored to provide specific information about the financial products AMP offers. However, it does contain lots of useful free articles and information and the site is well worth browsing. The investments section includes a range of investment calculators that enable you to work out details such as your life expectancy, home loan cost comparisons, potential effects of salary sacrifice, how much money you need for retirement and so on.

Australian Financial Review: www.afr.com

This is the website of the Fairfax publication *The Australian Financial Review (AFR)*. You can read a synopsis of articles that have appeared in the *AFR* and this is a useful facility. If you wish to you can subscribe, and cost at the time of writing is $65 per month to access the Monday to Friday editions of the paper, and this fee includes a digital iPad app. You can also receive the weekend edition for $10 per month.

Australian Financial Review Smart Investor:
www.afrsmartinvestor.com.au

This is the site of the AFR's *Smart Investor* magazine. You can access for free articles and information that has appeared in previous editions of the magazine. In order to access articles in the current edition of the magazine you need to be a subscriber. If you want to subscribe to the magazine you can do so online.

Australian Investor: www.australianinvestor.com.au

This site is worth visiting as it has heaps of free resources available, but to access some of them you need to register with your email address and a password. The resources provided include a market wrap (news), movers and shakers, company research, trading tools, as well as a forum where you can post or receive messages. You can get an environmental sector rating for a company and also an analysis report relevant to a company of your choice that's listed on both the ASX and NSX boards.

Australian Investors Association: www.investors.asn.au

This is an independent not-for-profit organisation that provides a network of information, education and support to member investors with online and offline discussion groups and forums, information meetings, seminars and other programs on a wide range of subjects of interest to the self-directed private investor, including SMSFs, estate planning and the like. The association deals with a range of asset classes, including equities, property, hybrids, managed investments and cash. The website has an education section with an events calendar and contains many free online resources, including general investing information, member reviews, newsletters and other information. It is worth a visit.

Membership is $110 for one year or $190 for two years, plus a one-off $20 joining fee.

Australian Securities and Investments Commission (ASIC): www.asic.gov.au

ASIC is charged with enforcing and regulating company and financial services laws. Their site is more useful for companies than for individual investors but there's a wealth of information available that makes this site worth a visit. The site is also linked to the Moneysmart site (see p. 69), which is a more useful site for investors.

Australian Shareholders' Association: www.asa.asn.au

The Australian Shareholders' Association is a not-for-profit organisation that aims to keep tabs on listed companies and ensure that shareholders' rights are protected in issues such as corporate governance, transparency and accountability in relation to company performance, executive remuneration, risk management and dividends. The ASA endeavours to monitor Australian-based companies through direct engagement, the publication of 'voting intentions' and a voting and speaking presence at the company's annual general meeting.

The site is designed primarily for members but it has some free information, including a market summary and a list of upcoming company AGMs and access to a number of company annual reports. You can appoint the association as your proxy to vote on your behalf at the AGMs of all the listed companies in your portfolio. If you have a query or complaint about a company you can contact the association and ask them to look into it.

If you wish, you can subscribe to the association (that is, become a member) and receive a monthly report. There are four levels of membership, with cost depending on the service and whether you want printed or online information. They are: $60 (associate), $115 (green), $125 (classic) and $500 (gold).

Australian Securities Exchange: www.asx.com.au

Email: internet services@asx.com.au

This is a very popular public site and is a 'must visit' for any serious share investor. It contains a wealth of free information about share investing and details of all listed shares (and other investment instruments) with their codes and sector groups. You can search for delisted stocks and obtain a brief explanation for the delisting. The site provides current share prices and share price graphs as well as information about other investment products such as warrants, exchange-traded options, CFDs and futures. You can set up a watchlist of shares you're interested in. The site has a search facility to help you find a broker to fulfil the requirements you specify.

As all announcements applicable to ASX-listed stocks must first be lodged with them, the ASX site is the logical place to search for announcements. There's an education section where you can learn about shares and share investing and there's a sharemarket game. You can register and periodically receive an email with investor updates and also articles and videos written by a number of financial advisers about share investing topics such as trends in the Australian market and benefits of investing in selected shares and sectors; it is worthwhile subscribing.

There's an iPhone app that allows you to keep up to date with the Australian market for free using your smart phone. You can monitor 20 companies of your choice and receive real-time company announcement alerts, view market performance, search for prices and codes as well as some other features. At the time of writing the app was available only for iPhones but an Android app was under consideration.

If you have any queries about ASX-listed shares or share investing in general, you can use the 'Contact us' button to send the ASX an email. I've found this to be a very useful facility that I often use and all my queries have been replied to promptly.

Tip

I suggest you set aside sufficient time to browse through the ASX site and familiarise yourself with all the information and facilities available. It's well worth registering and receiving investor update emails and accessing the reports of interest to you.

Australian Stock Report: www.australianstockreport.com.au

Email: notifications@australianstockreport.com.au

If you register you can get an email sent to you that gives you free access to the latest traders report. This is a useful tool and gives a snapshot of market action and a market commentary. There's also a short video presentation you can view as well as a brief analysis of several stocks in the news. They provide live educational trading workshops and you can access extensive course notes and a number of other interactive features designed to improve your trading outcomes.

You can upgrade and obtain access to the options report, CFDs report, FX report (forex), speculative report and investors report. In order to upgrade you'll have to pay an annual fee which at the time of writing varied from about $700 to $1500.

Australian Taxation Office (ATO): www.ato.gov.au

There are many taxation laws and regulations affecting investors and traders that have a significant impact on net share investing income and profit and also on estate planning. There can be frequent changes to tax laws with changes to government policy and budgets, so if you are to make informed decisions you really need to keep updated. You can obtain lots of information from other websites about tax matters, but clearly the most authoritative source is the tax office itself. On this site you can view legislation, changes to legislation and search for any tax topics of interest.

Tip

The real profit you make from shares is the after-tax profit so you need to be aware of, and keep up to date with, the tax implications of your share trading/investing and estate planning strategies.

Bioshares: www.bioshares.com.au

This site has little free information, rather it gives access to a weekly newsletter providing information and advice about investing in biotechnology and healthcare stocks. The annual cost for 48 issues a year (electronically delivered) is $375.

Black Stump: www.blackstump.com.au

This is a very comprehensive website which contains a master directory of Australian financial websites (and other worldwide ones) with links to them. There's an alphabetical list of financial topics so you can select those of interest as well as some tools and calculators.

This site is a great starting point, although there's so many websites given you can become overwhelmed. Unfortunately, there's no summary of what's available on each site so you need to visit each to see what's on offer.

Building Wealth Through Shares: www.bwts.com.au

Email: colin@bwts.com.au

This is website of Colin Nicholson, who is a well-known Australian share investor and author of many articles and a book on share investing, and who also conducts share investing seminars from time to time. There's an amount of free material on the website, including many past questions and answers in the

'Ask Colin' section, and you can access past newsletters. You can also ask questions that Colin will answer by contacting him by email on the previous page.

There's a members' section that contains more advanced material. Subscription, at the time of writing, costs $44 to join with a $55 per year ongoing charge.

CBS Market Watch: www.marketwatch.com

This is a US site and therefore primarily contains information about US shares and global markets. However, our market is strongly influenced by the US market so this site is worth a visit, particularly when there are topical issues in the US that are having a flow-on effect to us.

Citibank Warrants: www.citiwarrants.com.au

This site is a good one for more advanced investors interested in investing in warrants. It contains some free information about warrants and derivative products and there is also a number of different structured financial products on offer to match various investor profiles and interests.

Clime: www.clime.com.au

Clime is an independent Australian fund manager specialising in value investing. It has two main trading divisions: Clime Asset Management (their funds management business), and MyClime, which provides company valuation and research for its members. The website is worth a visit as it has some useful investing information that you can access, including some short reports and video presentations. If you register you can have investing reports emailed to you and these are worth receiving. If you decide to become a subscriber there are several levels of subscription—costs range from 'Lite' at $345 per year to 'Pro' at $995 per year.

CNN Money/Fortune: www.money.cnn.com

This is a US website of CNN Money and the magazine Fortune, and is claimed to be the world's biggest business website. It's a useful free site with lots of information about US and world markets and you can read articles that have appeared in *Fortune* magazine. There is also some information relevant to the Australian market.

CommSec Direct Funds: www.funds.commsec.com.au

This site is not the same as the CommSec online trading site, although it has links to it. The Direct Funds site provides information about managed funds, super funds and allocated pensions, and you can search for funds to suit your requirements and download prospectuses. You're also able to browse through the information given about the various funds, including their historical performances and risk ratings. Most of the information can be accessed without logging in, but you need to register if you want access to the 'My portfolio' feature.

Cromwell Property Group: www.cromwell.com.au

Email: newsletter@cromwell.com.au
Cromwell is a listed property trust with ASX code CMW. If you're interested in property investment, either directly or via a property trust including a retail investment property trust (REIT), it's well worth checking out this site. If you request it they'll periodically email you a newsletter listing a variety of property investments that you can invest in if you want to. The newsletter also contains some useful share investing information.

Cyberspace Law and Policy Centre: www.cyberlawcentre.org

This site is worth exploring as it's totally devoted to online investing. It's produced jointly by the University of NSW, Monash University and the Australian National University (ANU), and contains totally unbiased information, as these organisations have no direct interest in any share investments. As well as information about online investing, there are many useful links divided into both Australian and international sites under the headings online broking sites, general information portals, financial data and newsletters, financial analysis and trading software vendors, internet discussion sites, publications and reports, and general Australian investing information sites. However, you might find that some of the sites listed are no longer operational or have changed but the site is still well worth a visit.

Daily Share Price: www.dailyshareprice.com.au

This site enables you to set up a portfolio (actual or hypothetical) and have the value of your portfolio emailed to you each day. You can monitor ordinary shares as well as warrants, options and most investment products available for trading on the ASX. This is a completely free service and is a good way of monitoring prices of selected stocks or an actual portfolio on a day-to-day basis simply by receiving an email.

Delisted: www.delisted.com.au

This site is helpful when a stock disappears from the ASX board or from newspaper or magazine listings. Information about delisted companies is often difficult to obtain because the ASX doesn't provide information after an entity is removed from its listings. On the Delisted site there's an alphabetic list of ASX listed and delisted stocks and managed funds and you can also search by entering the code or name to obtain further details. There's also some general information useful to investors so this site is worth a visit. If you are unfortunate enough to hold any permanently delisted stocks or funds you have an additional problem because you're not able to declare losses to offset capital gains with other shares in your tax return until the receivers and administrators have made official declarations and this is often a lengthy process. The Delisted site enables you to sell such shares (at a low nominal price) so you can claim the capital loss and reduce your capital gains tax liability.

Download: www.download.com

This isn't an investment site as such but it's a useful site because you can download for free many software programs needed for online investing such as Adobe Acrobat Reader, search engines and virus protection programs. You can also update your programs to make sure you have the latest versions. You can obtain a free scan of your computer to detect any problems and there's also a list (with reviews) of many mobile phone and iPad apps and other odds and ends. This site is well worth visiting and bookmarking for future use.

Educated Investor Bookshop: www.educatedinvestor.com.au

This is a bookshop catering especially to traders and investors. It has a huge range of titles available that you can purchase online.

Ethical Investor: www.ethicalinvestor.com.au

This website examines the ethical rather than the financial aspects of investment in Australian companies so it's worth a visit if you're concerned about the ethical aspects of share investment. It has a 'corporate monitor' with a database of the environmental and social performance of Australian companies. It also undertakes research on ethical managed funds.

Fat Prophets: www.fatprophets.com.au

Fat Prophets provides share trading advice from Sydney stockbroker Angus Geddes. The site contains some free information but primarily it promotes the tipster service. Subscribers receive daily and weekly emails and alerts; the cost of the annual subscription is $1190.

Fool Australia: www.fool.com.au

The is the Australian version of the worldwide Motley Fool site that claims to educate, amuse and enrich those interested in long-term investing. It has lots of free information about money management and shares with many articles and market reports you can read, so the site is worth browsing. If you register you can receive free investing reports and a daily newsletter. For a charge of $399 you can subscribe for one year to the share adviser service and have trade recommendations about our market and the US market emailed to you. They sometimes also offer discounted rates on their subscriptions.

FNArena: www.fnarena.com

Email: info@fnarena.com
This site is worth a visit because you can register and have an informative free daily market report emailed to you and also a weekly report. The site also contains articles about various companies with a consensus broker recommendation. There

are quite a few articles and reports, some of which are free and others are locked and accessible only to paying subscribers. There's also a link to a monthly 'Australian Super Stock Report' that's a summary of major brokers' and financial advisers' buy, sell or hold recommendations about stocks in their coverage. This is a comprehensive report that covers a large number of the major stocks. If you wish to become a paying subscriber the cost at the time of writing was $360 for twelve months, $197 for six months, and $49 for one month.

FP Markets: www.fpmarkets.com.au

Email: support@fpmarkets.com.au
FP Markets is an online broker but you don't need to trade with them in order to receive a daily market report (one-day delay) that's most useful. It shows upcoming dividends and a corporate calendar as well as a section with companies in the news, and this gives you a synopsis of latest Australian company announcements of importance.

George Cochrane: www.cochrane.net.au

George Cochrane is a licensed financial adviser who offers personal investment advice, including full portfolio management. He also publishes three investment newsletters: *News and Views, Buy 'n' Hold* and *Trading Portfolios*, at costs ranging from $64.90 to $72.60 per month with and extra cost of $25 per year to have them mailed to you. On the website you can view past copies of his newsletters for free and there's also some links to other useful financial websites.

Guppy Traders: www.guppytraders.com

This is the site of Daryl Guppy, a well-known Australian share investor and author of books and articles. He also conducts share investing seminars and workshops online that you can subscribe to. He uses the MetaStock trading software and there is some information about this software on his website. The site also contains some free information about investing and technical analysis. At the time of writing the cost for an annual subscription to his Australian newsletter is $229 and the 14-week internet trading essentials course is $55.

Hot Copper: www.hotcopper.com.au

This site is a very popular forum for Australian shares with many posts each day. In order to place or reply to a post you need to join, but this is free and all you need to do is register. Reading these posts can give you a good idea of the shares that are moving at the moment or have caught the interest of traders and that may be worth investigating if you are interested in speculative trading. Also, you can search for notices posted about any shares you're interested in over a time frame you can specify.

This site is well worth a visit if you want to seek the opinions of others about shares you may be interested in or when you want some ideas about shares that could be candidates for a speculative trade.

InfoChoice: www.infochoice.com.au

This is a great free site that is well worth exploring as it has many calculators and tools on a huge variety of financial topics and allows you to search for financial issues such as the best personal or home loans, best bank account or term deposit interest rates and even car, home and life insurance. There's also a comparison of online brokers — I'll explore this feature in detail in chapter 4.

Inside Trader: www.theinsidetrader.com.au

This is primarily an investment organisation that offers investment advice and tips to subscribers. The annual subscription rate is $199. If you register you will receive a free email with a stock pick of the week and information about director purchases — these are worth receiving.

Intelligent Investor: www.intelligentinvestor.com.au

This is essentially a subscription advisory service that offers advice about share investing, superannuation and funds. There are three levels of membership: 'Compact' for $59 per month, 'Unlimited' for $69 per month and 'Premium' for $109 per month. If you aren't a subscriber you can obtain some free information and a free 15-day trial membership.

InvestoGain: www.investogain.com.au

This site has lots of share investing information about Australian and New Zealand shares and managed funds. You can browse listed Australian companies and managed funds or search for companies or funds by name. There's information about superannuation and a listing of the latest director's on-market share purchases. The site also links to the Delisted site (see p. 64).

InvestSMART Financial Services: www.investsmart.com.au

Email: newsletters@email.investsmart.com.au

This is a Fairfax Media site with lots of good information about shares, floats, dividends, change in directors' interests, broker recommendations, managed funds and other investments. You can read financial articles that have appeared in past Fairfax newspapers, and in the 'Education' section there's a glossary, a learning centre and some tools and calculators. There's a free portfolio manager facility that allows you to monitor your investments.

You can register but it's free and well worth doing because you can periodically receive an email with useful investing information. You can arrange for alerts to be sent to your email address on any day of the week that you nominate and the alert will include prices, announcements and upcoming dividends for shares in your portfolio or watch list.

Investor Words: www.investorwords.com

If you register on this site you can receive a daily email explaining a commonly used investor word or terminology. There's a different one each day, so it's a good way of learning the terminology because you can focus on one term at a time. However, this is a US site so some of the words and terminology are more relevant to the US and not widely used or applicable to Australia. Nevertheless, this site is well worth accessing.

Wiley Australia: http://au.wiley.com

This is the website of Wiley Australia, which owns Wrightbooks and publishes a large range of trading, personal investment and finance books for the Australian market (including this book).

The catalogue includes many relevant titles on share investing, charting and stock analysis. Titles can be purchased online.

JustData: www.justdata.com.au

This is an online shop where you can purchase software for trading, charting and market data (for over 90 exchanges worldwide). You can also purchase Alan Hull's or Daryl Guppy's newsletters.

Lincoln: www.lincolnindicators.com.au

This is the website of Tim Lincoln, who provides an advisory service based primarily on fundamental analysis. There are two services available: Stock Doctor, which scans Australian listed companies for the most financially healthy investment opportunities; and Lincoln Managed Investments, where there's a choice of two managed funds for investors who prefer to have their portfolio professionally managed. At the time of writing Stock Doctor Gold cost $1495 per annum and Stock Doctor Platinum $2095 per annum.

Moneysmart: www.moneysmart.gov.au

This site is an offshoot of the ASIC site and is a very useful site and well worth a visit. The beauty of this site (and the ASIC site) is that the information you receive is totally unbiased and directed toward providing help for investors on a variety of topics, including money management, borrowing, superannuation (including self managed), retirement, investment and scams. There are many tools and resources you can use to help you save money and invest wisely, including a budget planner, compound interest calculator and mortgage switching tools. There's also an unclaimed money section that allows you to search for any unclaimed money such as cash in inactive bank accounts or dividends. This is worth checking as you may be entitled to an unexpected windfall.

Moneybags: www.moneybags.com.au

This site has information about investment books, magazines, newsletters, home-study courses and share investing software that you can purchase online. You can search for available resources on any authors or topics you're interested in.

Money Manager: www.moneymanager.com.au

This site has heaps of information about money management, and even though it doesn't contain any share investing information it's still well worth visiting. It contains comparisons, guides and news and tips for a number of topics, including home loans, term deposits, savings, credit cards, managed funds, personal loans, mobile services and broadband.

Morningstar: www.morningstar.com.au

This website incorporates Huntleys' and contains a lot of free share investment information. There are two levels of membership, namely free membership and premium membership where you become a subscriber and can access Huntleys' *Your Money Weekly* as well as other services such as investment picks for stocks and managed funds. Cost of full membership is $698 with an introductory membership rate of $349.

Morningstar is also a data provider currently used by CommSec and there's a glossary that's a useful reference and worth downloading and keeping on file. You can find it at: http://clientservices.morningstar.com.au/display/Public/Equity+Glossary.

Ninemsn: www.ninemsn.com.au

This is the website of Channel Nine and is worth a visit as it has lots of information and articles about shares and other financial topics that you may find useful. There are tools and calculators as well as general financial information.

Rivkin: www.rivkin.com.au

This was originally Rene Rivkin's website but is now managed by his sons. In its heyday, the *Rivkin Report* was the most popular of all newsletters produced in Australia. There's some information available for free on the site but to access the advisory service you need to subscribe. There are two levels of subscription: 'local' and 'global', at a cost of $37 per fortnight each. There's also an SMSF service available and a broking service with online or telephone trading.

Share Cafe: www.sharecafe.com.au

Email: alerts@sharecafe.com.au
This site has lots of share investing and trading information but you need to register with your email address. The 'Community' tab links to a large forum where you can read and place posts. The 'My cafe' tab allows you to enter your portfolio and set up an alerts list. After doing so you'll be sent an email when a company on your alerts list makes an announcement. There's a brief summary of the announcement with a link to enable you to read the announcement in full if you wish. There's also a link that allows you to read the latest news, research and discussion about the shares.

This is a great free site and I would strongly recommend that you register and avail yourself of the information and the many facilities provided.

Share Scene: www.sharescene.com

This is a large forum site where you can read posts about share trades and the impressions of others. If you register, you can post your own message or query.

Share Trading Education: www.sharetradingeducation.com

This is Jim Berg's website where there's some free share investing information you can access. You can join the club and receive some free reports and newsletters. In order to receive the weekly newsletter you need to subscribe at a cost of $29.95 per month (at the time of writing).

Small Stocks: www.smallstocks.com.au

As the name suggests, this website is a good starting site for the small investor and is worth a visit. It contains a number of articles and posts, a comparison list of software and trading platforms, and also a list of online brokers with links so you can investigate further.

Standard & Poor's: www.standardandpoors.com.au

Standard & Poor's is a US compiler of financial credit ratings and market indices for stock markets and investments throughout the world. It's used by the ASX for compiling market and sector indices (which is why these indices are prefaced by S&P). This website is a useful reference for further information about credit ratings and indices and also includes some general information about Australian investing.

TheBull: www.thebull.com.au

TheBull (originally known as CompareShares) claims to be an independent media company but has several sponsors, including some prominent online brokers. The website contains lots of free information about shares and other trading instruments as is well worth a visit. You can subscribe for free and receive several weekly newsletters and these are well worth receiving.

Traders Circle: www.traderscircle.com.au

Email: admin@traderscircle.com.au

Traders Circle is located in Melbourne and runs a variety of share trading courses at various levels and costs, as well as one about SMSFs. When you complete the Trading Mastery Program you'll receive trade recommendations as an SMS message and email and you can log in to the website to see a video explanation of the recommendation.

Trading Room: www.tradingroom.com.au

This site is part of the Fairfax Digital network and has links to the Invest Smart site. There's quite a lot of useful information and news about shares, managed funds and superannuation so this site is worth a visit. There's a broker comparison table and there's a charting facility where you can obtain yearly and intraday charts. If you register, you can set up a portfolio and watch list. When setting up a portfolio of your shares you can include brokerage, which makes the profit/loss calculation more accurate than one that doesn't include brokerage.

Trading Secrets: www.tradingsecrets.com.au

This is the site of Louise Bedford and Chris Tate, who are authors of many articles and books on charting and share trading. They also conduct training and mentoring programs and courses at a variety of levels, with costs ranging from a few hundred dollars to $6000. You can also purchase their books on this site. If you register you can receive some free resources, including an e-course and access to a monthly newsletter. The website openly states that the free resources are provided so you'll be tempted to enrol in the advanced programs after you've accessed them.

Vanguard Investments: www.vanguardinvestments.com.au

Vanguard Investments primarily provides access to managed funds of many types. The site contains a fair amount of information about managed funds and superannuation and also has several tools and calculators, so it's worth a visit if you're interested in investing in managed funds.

VectorVest: www.vectorvest.com.au

This is a web-based share investing advisory service that analyses shares in several world exchanges and produces buy, sell or hold recommendations. Specialist charting and other software packages are available if you subscribe at a cost of $59 per month or $645 per year for Australian shares.

Wrightbooks: www.wrightbooks.com.au

Wrightbooks is part of Wiley Australia and this website links to the Wiley site.

Yahoo Finance: http://finance.yahoo.com

This is a US site with information relevant to US stocks and investments. As our market often takes its lead from Wall Street, the site can be worth visiting for more in-depth information about US markets—particularly when there's some major change in the US that's having a major impact on global markets.

Key points

⇨ In this chapter I've outlined some of the sites that I consider most useful for an online share investor, but you need to browse the sites of interest to get a good idea of what is available. Remember that sites come and go and are constantly changing so when you access a site some details or charges may differ from those I've described.

⇨ There are many websites that you can access for free and that contain a wealth of information about share investing and trading suitable for all levels of investors, from novice to experienced.

⇨ If you have the time it is worth browsing most of the sites I've listed, but so you don't get overwhelmed I suggest you do so in stages.

⇨ In many cases you need to register, but as registration is often free this isn't a great disadvantage. Of course, you can cancel your registration at any time if you're not happy with the information you're receiving or if you're getting too many emails.

⇨ Some websites offer emails, newsletters and alerts that will be sent to you on a regular basis at no cost and these are usually worth receiving and reading.

⇨ There are many websites that require you to pay a fee for the facilities and information provided. Sometimes this is only a small amount but in other cases it can be big dollars. Remember the 'Kinsky Principle': don't part with your hard-earned money unless you're sure that the resource is essential for you and that it's not available for free or at lower cost elsewhere.

⇨ You can set up watch lists and portfolios online for free and these enable you to easily check the performance of your portfolio and to keep an eye on shares on your radar screen. Your online broker will probably offer this facility but there are many public-access sites that also offer this facility at no cost.

⇨ Consider using the 'Contact us' facility on the ASX site or other sites to obtain specific information you want or to have a query answered.

⇨ You can get opinions from other traders and investors by accessing a chat room or forum, but remember that the advice or information you receive isn't necessarily informed and may be based on personal opinion or rumour.

⇨ There are many proprietary software and trading packages on offer and many established advisory services you can subscribe to that contain trading and investing recommendations. I suggest caution regarding the claims made about past profits as there's usually no independent, unbiased audit of them by a knowledgeable authority. I'm not suggesting fraud but it's easy to declare big profits made with the benefit of hindsight. I suggest a better approach is to develop your own expertise and strategies rather than relying on others. Presumably that's why you're reading this book—so please read on.

chapter 4

Choosing an online broker

In previous chapters I've outlined useful share investing resources available on the web and the advantages of trading online. In this chapter I discuss the costs and resources available with online brokers operating in Australia to help you make an informed decision about the broker that best fulfils your requirements. In the next chapter I'll discuss how you can get set up with your broker of choice so you can trade online once you've made your decision.

If you're already trading online you can use this chapter to widen your horizons and perhaps register with another online broker that offers additional benefits. Usually there's no cost involved in becoming a customer with an online broker so it's not a problem to use different brokers for online trading provided you sell shares in a stock with the same broker you initially used to purchase them.

Tip

You might like to connect to the internet as you read, and explore sites that appeal to you. Most online broking sites provide some free public-access information that makes them worth visiting even if you don't register or trade with them.

The cost factor

Brokers (both online and offline) most often have a brokerage fee structure (including GST) where there's a certain minimum charge in the form of a flat fee for small parcel values (typically below $10000) until you reach a threshold, after which the brokerage is proportional to the parcel value. In some cases there's more than one threshold parcel value; for example, a flat fee for parcels up to $10000, another flat fee for parcels of value $10000 to $25000, and a percentage fee for parcel values above $25000.

In today's competitive society, the first thought in most people's minds when shopping for any commodity or service is: 'how can I get what I want at the lowest price?' With share trading, this question is: 'how can I trade shares with the lowest brokerage charge?' While I endorse this principle as it's really an extension of the 'Kinsky Principle' I outlined in the previous chapter, with share investing other factors apart from brokerage can be very important and need consideration. So it's not just a matter of finding the lowest brokerage fee.

To put it in perspective, suppose you wanted to buy a used motor vehicle and were looking at one for which the asking price was $10000. Would you try to save $10 on the purchase by entering into negotiations with the seller to reduce the price by $10? I think you'd agree that a saving of $10 on an outlay of $10000 isn't worth thinking about, as it represents only 0.1% of the price. Well that's really the situation with online share trading, because the difference in brokerage between the various major online brokers is only about $10 for share trades of value to $10000. The 0.1% difference is really trivial when you consider that most share traders aim to make a capital gain of at least 10% and share investors can obtain ongoing grossed-up dividend yields of at least 7% per year with many shares.

The economics is rather different if you're trading a $500 parcel of shares; in this case a $10 saving is 2% and is far more significant. The economics is also different if you're a frequent trader averaging, say, five trades a day, because a $10 saving per trade is a daily saving of $50 and could be a lot more significant.

To summarise, the importance of the brokerage cost depends on two factors:

⇨ Frequency of trading—how often will you trade? The more often you trade, the more significant is the brokerage charge.

⇨ Parcel value—what's your average parcel value? The smaller the parcel value, the more significant the flat fee. On the other hand, if you trade really large parcel values, a small percentage brokerage difference can amount to significant dollar savings.

Tip

Some online brokers charge a monthly fee too in order for you to maintain customer status and use their site, so you need to check this before you become a customer. You don't want to pay account-keeping fees unless you're a very active trader, in which case the fee could be offset by a reduced brokerage cost.

Your broker wish list

Before you go shopping, it's generally best to have a preconceived idea of what you're looking for in a product; that is, have a list of requirements you've thought about in advance. When shopping for an online broker the situation is no different, and to get what you want it makes sense to first think about your requirements. Then you can conduct a more objective search for a broker to best fulfil these requirements.

Certain essential features are provided by all online brokers and therefore don't need consideration because you can take them for granted. These include:

⇨ Trading data—a trading depth list showing the buy/sell orders at market with prices and volumes (order quantities).

⇨ Order status—this allows you to check the progress of your open orders (orders in market that haven't transacted) as well as your orders that have been processed and completed.

⇨ Trades history—your complete trades history showing all the trades you've made with that broker.

⇨ Account balance—if you have a dedicated bank account or loan set up with the broker, you're able to check available funds in your account at any time. However, you need to remember that cash transfers occur three business days after the day the trade occurred.

⇨ Portfolio—the list of stocks you own with price and value (and often profit/loss).

⇨ Market news—when you log into a broking site you will generally be given an indication of how the market has moved up to the time you log in.

One-stop shop?

The first requirement your need to think about for your wish list is whether you consider that a one-stop shop is important for you. When physically shopping for a number of different products it's very convenient to be able to get all you want at one shop as it saves a lot of time and effort (not to mention cost of transport). With online trading the same idea applies and it saves time and effort to be able to get all the facilities and resources you need for share trading from one site. However, with online trading it's not nearly as important a consideration as when you're physically shopping because computers allow you open a number of websites simultaneously and easily toggle from one to the other—although this may not be so easy if you're using a smart phone to access the internet. If you can easily access a number of sites simultaneously then the range of online facilities provided by your broker isn't such an important consideration because you can use your broking site for trading only and other websites for research.

For example, in my case the charting facilities available on my online trading site aren't an important consideration for me because I use a dedicated site for my charting analysis. Before trading, I log into the charting site where I can access all the charts and technical analysis tools I want (I discuss this further in chapter 9). I then minimise the screen and log into my trading site and toggle between the two sites as I contemplate my trading decisions. In a similar way, I don't require in-depth market analysis from my online trading site because I've registered with several sites that send me emails each day summarising daily market and company action as well as sending me weekly summaries.

Tip

If you're new to online trading, the 'one-stop shop' option is good to start with. As you gain expertise and experience, you can widen your horizons and use more than one site simultaneously when you want to trade.

Features to consider

To help you set up your list of requirements, I've made a list of features for you to consider and that can vary between different online brokers:

⇨ tradeable financial instruments

⇨ brokerage or other fees

⇨ course of trades

⇨ types of orders

⇨ fundamental analysis data

⇨ charting facility

⇨ research tools

⇨ market updates

⇨ alerts

⇨ announcements

⇨ watch list

⇨ recommendations and forecasts

⇨ margin loans

⇨ share packs

⇨ smart phone/tablet app

⇨ customer service.

Tradeable financial instruments

You need to consider the range of financial instruments you plan to trade. All online brokers offer trading in ASX-listed shares and company options (renounceable issues). As a general rule, most online brokers also provide trading of ASX-listed warrants and managed funds. Fewer online brokers provide trading in shares listed on international exchanges or trading derivatives such as exchange-traded options (ETOs), futures, contracts for difference (CFDs), or currencies—also known as foreign exchange rates (forex). So if you want to trade these instruments, you need to ensure your online broker provides the facility for you to do so.

Tip

If you're not an experienced investor the range of tradeable financial instruments available on your trading site won't be of importance because you'll most likely want to trade ASX-listed shares only.

Brokerage and other fees

There are differences in brokerage and fees between the various online brokers. The brokerage cost for each trade is important but, as I've already mentioned, its importance depends on parcel size and trading frequency.

A complication when comparing trading cost (brokerage and other fees) is that some brokers offer discounts for frequent trading. These can take the form of reduced brokerage if you exceed a certain number of trades in a period, or the waiving of fees and charges that otherwise would apply. There can also be additional charges that you may not be aware of until you trade; for example, CommSec charges an additional fee for trades made using a margin loan account that doesn't apply with a conventional account. Also different types of trades may have different brokerage and fee structures applying to them; for example, CommSec charges an additional fee for conditional-order trading that's additional to the normal brokerage.

Tip

As you can see, there are a number of different factors you need to consider when estimating your total trading cost, and an exact apples-to-apples comparison is not easy to make. However, you can come up with a reasonable estimate if you know the type of orders you intend to make, what instruments you intend to trade and how often you plan to trade. (I discuss planning in detail in chapter 6.)

Course of trades

The course of trades is a list of all parcels traded up to the time you access the site, with price and volume for each parcel. The data can be presented as a table or more conveniently as a one day chart (intraday chart). Many (but not all) online brokers provide this facility.

Tip

It's a good idea to check the course of trades before you place an order so you can form an impression of how the share price is moving as this can influence your trading decision.

Types of orders

All online brokers cater for the two most common types of orders, namely limit and market orders. In the past, only a few online brokers would accept conditional orders (such as stop-loss orders) but now an increasing number are doing so. If you want to include these types of orders in your trading strategy you need to ensure your online broker provides this facility.

Tip

Types of orders you can place (including conditional orders) are discussed in detail in chapter 7.

Fundamental analysis data

Fundamental data is the basic current and past financial performance information about a company you need to consider if you're a share investor (rather than a share trader). It includes data, such as earnings per share, dividend per share, level of franking and price/earnings ratio. Most online brokers provide this facility but there can be considerable differences in the amount of data shown and how it's presented.

Tip

Fundamental analysis is discussed in detail in chapter 8.

Charting facility

This facility allows you to access important trading information presented in chart form, including price and volume movements as well as technical analysis tools. Most online brokers provide a charting facility but there can be considerable differences in the types of charts and technical analysis tools available, how they're presented and the extent to which you can customise a chart (for example, draw trendlines or change the time period or type of chart).

Tip

Charting is discussed in detail in chapter 9.

Research tools

This facility allows you to search the website database and obtain a shortlist of shares that satisfy criteria you set. This can be based on fundamental data such as dividend yield or technical analysis data such as moving average crossover points. Research tools are provided on many (but not all) online broking sites.

Tip

The use of research tools can save you a great deal of time and effort when you are looking for shares that satisfy fundamental or charting criteria you specify, so it's a facility worth including in your requirements list.

Market updates

When you trade online you can rest assured that no matter which broker or trading platform you use, all brokers trading ASX-listed financial instruments are treated equally and access the same trading data at the same time. That is, you will see the same orders at market as anyone else with prices and parcel volumes at each price. This data is current and valid at the moment you access the market trading data. When you place an order it will go to market in time priority; that is, first in, first to the market.

However, with data other than trading data (including charts and financial statistics) there can be variations in the time line at which the data is updated. These variations can be as follows:

⇨ Dynamic—the data updates automatically and is completely up to date at all times.

⇨ Real time (live)—the data is up to date when you first access the site but if the data changes while you're accessing the site you won't see the most recent data and you need to use the 'refresh' button in order to do so.

⇨ Delayed—the data is delayed, most often by 20 minutes, so the data you see when you log in is delayed by this amount of time.

⇨ Previous day—data is updated today so it's current at the close of trading for the previous business day.

⇨ Full-day delay—the data is delayed by a full business day. For example, you won't receive the data applying to close of trading on Friday until Tuesday morning.

The differences in the data time lines occur because the more recent the data the more costly it is to obtain. For this reason free websites usually display only delayed, previous-day or full-day delay data and many online brokers offer different trading platforms at different costs depending on the data timeline you specify. Trading data is usually real time, and for other data the delayed-data option is usually the default one. If you want dynamic data you may have to pay a monthly fee, so you need to check this out.

Tip

Always check the timeline of any data you access online and be aware of the implications. Generally speaking, data delays of a day or more aren't critical for fundamental data that's not price-based because the vital statistics released about a company's operations change infrequently. For example, you don't get a blow-by-blow profit update, and changes in company profitability are released only when the company issues a report or makes a formal announcement.

Alerts

This facility provides for SMS or email alerts to be sent to your computer or mobile phone device for shares you nominate and for events you nominate; for example, when the price rises or falls to a certain level or when the company makes an announcement. This facility is not normally included for free in a basic trading package but can be available if you're prepared to pay, either as a fee per alert or a monthly charge. The facility may also be included in a higher cost trading platform.

The importance of this facility depends on how active you are as a trader. Remember that many public-access websites will send you email alerts for free if you register with them, but they will usually be 20-minute delayed alerts and not real time ones.

Tip

I suggest that before you pay for alerts check out the ones available for free. I've found these to be perfectly satisfactory for my share investing and trading requirements.

Announcements

This facility provides a list of the announcements made by the company over the last few months (or other period you specify). In many cases there'll be a link to the ASX site which allows you to read the announcement. Even if you've registered with a website where you've set up an alert list and receive emails when announcements are made for shares on your list, this is a useful facility on your online trading site because it's a time saver. For example, when a share price changes dramatically you should check if there are any announcements that may shed light on the reasons.

Tip

Having an announcements facility on a broking site isn't a vital consideration because all ASX announcements are listed on the ASX website. However, it is a time saver to be able to link up to ASX announcements from your online broking site.

Watch list

Some online brokers allow you to set up a watch list of stocks you're interested in so you can easily keep track of price movements or other changes. In some cases you can also have an email or text message sent to you when one of the companies on your list makes an announcement.

Tip

I don't regard a watch list facility as a major consideration with an online broking site because there are many free websites that provide this facility.

Recommendations and forecasts

Some online brokers provide financial analysts' recommendations and forecasts for major shares. This facility isn't a very important one for me because I prefer to do my own research and because I've found from bitter experience that the recommendations of financial analysts can't be relied on and can be counterproductive if you act on them without thorough research using your own criteria.

Tip

As I've said before, recommendations and forecasts can't be relied on even though there may be a consensus opinion among a number of informed financial analysts. However, they do provide a guide to analysts' opinions.

Margin loans

Many online brokers have a margin loan facility—if not their own they provide it via some other financial service that's affiliated with them. A margin loan allows you to increase your trading capital by using your existing share portfolio as collateral. This can be a good idea in times of rampant bull markets but is fraught with danger in volatile or bear markets.

Tip

The availability of a margin loan isn't an important consideration unless you're an experienced trader with a fairly extensive share portfolio or the market is in a sustained bull phase.

Share packs

Some online brokers have a facility that allows you to purchase a selection of stocks (called a share pack) at discount brokerage. That is, the brokerage for the share pack is considerably less that the brokerage that would apply if you purchased each parcel of shares in separate trades. There's usually a number of different share packs available and the shares in each pack are provided in a list.

Tip

Share packs are an ideal way for a new investor to get exposure to a variety of different shares at a discount rate. So if you're getting started with shares (or purchasing shares as an investment for a child or grandchild), this could be a facility of importance to you.

Smart phone and tablet apps

Another issue you might want to consider is the availability of an app if you're planning to trade online using a mobile device. Many online brokers have free apps for several types of smart phones—as well as Blackberry and iPad apps—that allow direct and convenient access to the site. For example, CommSec offers app capabilities for iPhones, Androids and iPads. Also IG Markets has a free Android CFD trading facility and iPhone app that provide direct market access for CFD trading.

Tip

Clearly, if you plan to use a smart phone or similar device for online trading it's well worthwhile checking the apps that are available with your online broker.

Customer service

A very important consideration is the extent of the customer-friendly personal service provided by your online broker. The chances are that sooner or later you'll want to query an order or some feature of your portfolio, and if so you want to have your query answered promptly and efficiently. The last thing you want is to be connected to an automated answering service or kept in a long queue or to have your email query filed indefinitely in some cyberspace filing cabinet. A broking service should provide telephone contact details as well as an email address and answer your queries in a prompt and efficient manner.

Tip

The customer service provided by an online broker is an important consideration but is one that's difficult to evaluate beforehand—you won't really know how good or bad it is until you actually need to use it. You can try social networking to tap into the experiences others have had with the broker.

Comparing online brokers

Now that I've dealt with the features for consideration in your wish list for an online broker, I'll discuss how you can go about finding a broker to satisfy your requirements. To help you in this search there are several websites that provide a comparison summary of Australian online brokers and these sites are a useful first point of reference. They usually provide a link to the online broking site that you can access for further information. Sites providing a broker comparison service include:

⇨ InfoChoice: www.infochoice.com.au/investment

⇨ Small Stocks: www.smallstocks.com.au

⇨ Trading Room: www.tradingroom.com.au.

There are also sites with a 'find a broker' facility that allows you to nominate your requirements and returns a list of online brokers that fulfil them. The InfoChoice site has this facility as well as the ASX site.

The InfoChoice site provides the following options for broker specification:

⇨ trade products—shares, derivatives and managed funds

⇨ trade method—online or phone

⇨ market updates—dynamic, real time or delayed

⇨ trade features—types of orders you wish to place

⇨ research—profiles and recommendations

⇨ frequent trader discounts.

The ASX site (personal investor link) provides the following options:

⇨ type of broker—advice or non-advice

⇨ trading instruments—shares and more sophisticated instruments

⇨ investment capital—in various dollar amounts

⇨ region—you can nominate any Australian state or territory either metro or regional.

This choice of region is distracting (and I've pointed this out to the ASX) because if you're trading Australian shares online the region in Australia is really immaterial. As I live on the South Coast of NSW, when checking the facility I selected 'NSW Regional' as my region but received an error message. When I selected 'NSW Metro' the site came up with a list of eight brokers (of which one didn't offer online broking).

The information obtained from comparison websites is in summary form and just tells you whether or not a facility is available. The problem with this is that the summary might show that the site provides a certain facility but you won't know the extent of it. For example, the summary may show that a broker provides a charting facility, but you won't be able to determine the types of charts provided or the extent to which charts can be customised. Similarly the summary may show that financial and statistical information is available but you won't know exactly what data is included and how it's presented. Another problem with these summaries is that they don't necessarily apply exclusively to online services. For example, the summary might show that an online broker provides the facility for trading derivatives but in fact this facility may not be available online and is a telephone service only.

Tip

The world of online broking is one of constant change so you can't rely completely on comparison summaries. I've found that they're not always completely up to date with current developments. For example, nabtrade launched an aggressive marketing campaign with reduced brokerage rates and enhanced features, but these weren't updated on many comparison sites when I checked some months later.

Tip

I suggest you use comparison sites to provide an overview only and then access the sites you're interested in for more precise and detailed information. I've included a list of brokers' website addresses at the end of this chapter.

Market share

Online brokers are an example of Pareto's Principle (also known as the 80–20 rule) because a relatively small number of them dominate the market and a larger number have a smaller market share. According to *Smart Investor* in June 2012, CommSec was by far the largest online broker with an estimated 50% market share, followed by E*TRADE with 16%, Westpac 9% and NAB 9%. So you can see that these four brokers accounted for 84% of the business.

Online brokers affiliated with Australian banks

The online brokers with the largest market share are each affiliated with one of the four largest Australian banks. I suspect the reason for this is that when a person is considering online trading or investing, banking customers naturally gravitate to the online broking arm of the bank they normally do business with.

Australian banks affiliated with online brokers are listed in table 4.1 (in alphabetical order).

Table 4.1: online brokers affiliated with Australian banks

Bank	Online broker
ANZ	E*TRADE
Bank of Queensland	BOQ Trading
Bankwest	Bankwest
Commonwealth	CommSec
Macquarie	Macquarie Prime
National	nabtrade
St George	Directshares
Suncorp	Suncorp Share Trade
Westpac	Westpac Online Investing

Tip

The Bull website runs a yearly voting competition where site users can cast a vote over a period of several months to answer the question 'who is the best online broker in Australia?' for various investment instruments. In 2012, CommSec was rated best for shares with E*TRADE being runner-up.

Online share trading accounts

When you buy shares (or another investment instrument), you need to have the cash available in an account the broker can access online. If you purchase you need to have sufficient funds in the account to cover the total purchase cost (including brokerage). When you sell, the broker needs access to an online account into which the net funds can be deposited.

Some online brokers offer incentives to encourage you to set up a dedicated trading account with them or with a nominated bank or financial institution. In most cases you can utilise an existing account for your online trading by giving the online broker authority to access the account for trading deposits or withdrawals.

Tip

To get started with online trading it may be more convenient for you to use an online broker affiliated with a bank or financial institution that already has your custom. As you gain experience with online trading you can explore other options.

Cheapest online broker

As I've said, there are many factors other than broking cost that are important, but as a matter of interest I've looked at the cost of online brokerage for Australian shares. At the time of writing the cheapest was CMC Markets with a brokerage charge of $9.90 or 0.1% (whichever is greater). With this cost structure the trading cost for various parcel values is as shown in table 4.2.

Table 4.2: cheapest brokerage for various parcel values

Parcel value ($)	Brokerage ($)
500	9.90
1 000	9.90
2 000	9.90
5 000	9.90
10 000	10.00
20 000	20.00
50 000	50.00
100 000	100.00

I've included in table 4.3 the three different trading packages offered by CMC to give you an idea of what's included in the trading packages they have available. Remember that the 20-minute delayed data refers only to data other than trading data. Trading data is current and valid at the moment the market is accessed so the 20-minute trading delay doesn't put you at a disadvantage when you trade.

Of the Australian bank sites the cheapest was NAB, who at the end of 2012 reduced their online broking rates so they are as shown in table 4.4 (see p. 94) at the time of writing.

Table 4.3: trading packages available with CMC Markets

Overview	Delayed data	Live (click to refresh) Data	Dynamic Data
	If you don't need access to live data our basic data package gives you ASX pricing delayed by at least 20 minutes	For the more serious online trader, live data gives you up to the second ASX pricing. Click to refresh and see the latest price	The ultimate data package with live, dynamic ASX pricing throughout key pages of the site including depth, watchlists, course of sales etc
Cost	Free	$10 per month	$41.25 per month or free if you exceed $235 in brokerage in the given month
ASX share quotes	20 minutes delayed	Live	Live and dynamic
ASX warrant quotes	20 minutes delayed	Live (Click To Refresh)	Live and dynamic
ASX interest rate security quotes	20 minutes delayed	Live (Click To Refresh)	Live and dynamic
ASX option quotes	20 minutes delayed	Live (Click To Refresh)	Live and dynamic
Watchlists	20 minutes delayed	Live (Click To Refresh)	Live and dynamic
Market Depth	Not Available	Live with full detail	Live and dynamic with full detail
Course of sales	Not Available	Live (Click To Refresh)	Live and dynamic
News and company announcements	Live (Click To Refresh)	Live (Click To Refresh)	Live (Click To Refresh)
SMS and email alerts	Yes – purchase alert credits	Yes – purchase alert credits	Yes – up to 100 free alert credits per day
Research	Yes	Yes	Yes
Charting	Yes	Yes	Yes

Source: CMC Markets Stockbroking.

Table 4.4: NAB online brokerage rates

Parcel value	Brokerage
Up to and including $10 000	$14.95
$10 000.01 to $27 227.27	$29.95
Over $27 227.27	0.11% of trade value

Online brokers in Australia

At the time of writing there were 25 online brokers operating in Australia. The number fluctuates from time to time as new players enter the market or existing ones amalgamate or get taken over. Many provide several different levels of service and trading platforms, each with different facilities and charges, so there's actually more than 30 choices available to Australian online investors. While this amount of choice can be daunting, the benefit is that the highly competitive nature of the market is good news for consumers as features and costs are continually being improved in an effort to gain greater market share. It also means that you're able to choose a broker and trading platform that best suits your trading frequency and the level of sophistication you require.

Following is an alphabetical list of online share brokers operating in Australia (at the time of writing), with web addresses. I've listed the primary site only and not the various trading platforms that may be available with each one. I've listed those providing online trading in shares, but many also provide online trading in more sophisticated financial instruments. In addition to the online brokers there are many offline brokers operating in Australia but I've excluded these.

⇨ Amscot Stockbroking: www.amscot.com.au

⇨ Bank of Queensland Trading: www.boq.com.au

⇨ Bankwest: www.bankwest.com.au

⇨ Bell Direct: www.belldirect.com.au

⇨ CMC Markets: www.cmcmarkets.com.au

⇨ Commonwealth Securities Limited: www.comsec.com.au

⇨ Directshares: www.directshares.com.au

⇨ E.broking: www.ebroking.com.au

⇨ E-Shares: http://e-shares.com.au

⇨ Easy Street Financial Services: www.easystreet.com.au

⇨ E*TRADE: www.etrade.com.au

⇨ FP Markets: www.fpmarkets.com.au

⇨ HSBC Online share trading: www.sharetrading.hsbc.com.au

⇨ IC Markets: www.icmarkets.com.au

⇨ IG Markets: www.igmarkets.com.au

⇨ Interactive Brokers: www.interactivebrokers.com

⇨ Macquarie Prime: www.macquarieprime.com.au

⇨ Morrison Securities: www.morrisonsecurities.com

⇨ nabtrade: www.nabtrade.com.au

⇨ Netwealth: www.sharetrading.netwealth.com.au

⇨ Options Xpress: www.optionsxpress.com.au

⇨ Rivkin Securities: www.rivkin.com.au

⇨ Suncorp Share Trade: www.sharetrade.suncorpmetway.com.au

⇨ Trader Dealer: www.traderdealer.com.au

⇨ Westpac Broking: www.westpac.com.au

Tip

When you become a customer with an online broker offering a number of different data platforms, I suggest you use the default option. The default option won't usually involve additional fees or charges above the normal brokerage charge and will be the cheapest. Unless you're a very active and experienced online trader, I suggest this will be perfectly adequate for your needs. You can always update later on if you feel you'd like to do so.

Making your choice

It's difficult to make a precise evaluation of an online broking site unless you become a customer. Most online brokers have a 'take a tour' or similar feature on their website and this can be a good way of obtaining some idea of the cost structure and facilities provided, but you still won't get a precise idea of the user-friendliness of the site. If there's no registration charge or ongoing monthly charge involved, the best way of finetuning your choice is to register with one or more online brokers that seem best for you. This allows you to access their sites as a bona fide customer and get a more exact idea of the resources available and how data is organised and presented.

Tip

An option you can consider is to use a low-cost online broker for trading but access other websites (either broking or general) for research and information. This strategy allows you to trade at a low cost using a broking website and at the same time access all the information and resources you want from other sites.

Key points

⇨ With so many online brokers and trading platforms available in Australia, you have lots of choice.

⇨ There's a great deal of similarity between online brokers but there can also be appreciable differences in cost structure, instruments traded, types of orders accepted, fundamental research tools and technical analysis indicators, as well as availability of smart phone or tablet apps.

⇨ In order to make an informed choice between brokers you need a 'wish list' of features that you'd like your online broker to provide. I've outlined the ones you may want to consider.

⇨ Many online brokers have dedicated smart phone/iPad apps that allow convenient access to their website using these devices. If you're using them, the availability of such an app may be a key consideration for you.

⇨ To get the lowest overall rate you need a good idea of your average parcel value and how often you plan to trade. Unless you're a frequent trader (particularly in small parcel values) brokerage cost difference may not be a significant factor and other considerations may be more important.

⇨ There are several websites that have online broker comparison summaries with links to each site. Comparison websites are a good way of getting an overall impression but they won't provide the full picture and may not be completely up to date.

⇨ You can access an online broking site and go for a test drive without becoming a customer but if you do this you'll get general information only.

⇨ To finalise your choice of online brokers you really have to 'suck it and see'. In most cases you can become a customer without incurring any costs. This will give you full access to the site and you won't even need to trade.

⇨ In most cases you can utilise an existing account for your online trading by giving the online broker authority to access the account for trading deposits or withdrawals. Some online brokers offer incentives to encourage you to set up specific cash management accounts with minimum deposits.

⇨ Some online brokers charge a monthly fee that's payable even if you don't trade and which can be waived or reduced if you trade frequently. Unless you're a frequent and experienced trader, I suggest you avoid sites or platforms that charge monthly fees (at least initially).

⇨ If no single online broker provides all the facilities you want in the form you want, you can use more than one broker. This is no problem provided you buy and sell the same shares with the same broker.

⇨ While a 'one-stop shop' is the most convenient option, with computers it's easy to have several sites open and to toggle between them while you contemplate your trading decisions.

⇨ Consider using a low-cost online broker for trading but access other websites (either broking or general) for research and information.

chapter 5

Becoming an online investor

Once you've chosen your online broker, you need to set yourself up with the broker so you can trade and invest online. In this chapter I'll look at how you actually do so. I'll also discuss online self managed superannuation as a method of investing, and how to set up to do so. If you're already trading online or have an SMSF, you should be able to skim through this chapter.

CHESS

When you apply to become a customer with an online broker you'll be asked if you want to be sponsored into the Clearing House Electronic Sub-register System (CHESS). Before going any further I'll explain this.

Because you're sponsored into CHESS by a broker, this system is also known as dealer (or broker) sponsorship and you'll be allocated a Holder Identification Number (HIN). This number is the same for all stocks (or other investment instruments) you trade with this broker. You're automatically issued a CHESS holding statement for each stock (or other instrument) you own, which is automatically updated when your holding changes for any reason such as additional purchases, sales or issues of shares (such as you might receive through a dividend reinvestment plan). While there'll be some time delay before the new CHESS statement is issued, this doesn't affect your ability to trade because you don't need the statement to trade.

Issuer sponsorship

Before the CHESS system was introduced all shareholders were issuer-sponsored. When you bought shares you received a statement from the share registry with a Shareholder Reference Number (SRN). This number was the same for all your shares in this particular stock, and for shares in any other stock you were allocated a different SRN. This system still operates today, and if you register with a broker and don't apply for CHESS sponsorship you'll automatically be issuer-sponsored.

Many Australian shareholders still hold issuer-sponsored shares—usually for one of the following reasons:

⇨ The shares were purchased prior to the introduction of the CHESS system.

⇨ The shares were acquired because of demutualisation; that is, when a member-owned organisation, such as a building society, converts to a company owned by shareholders.

⇨ Long-standing shares were acquired as a beneficiary from a deceased estate.

Tip

If you're not sure whether shares you hold are issuer-sponsored or broker-sponsored check the holding statement to see whether your identification number is given as an SRN or HIN.

Advantages of CHESS

CHESS has two main advantages:

⇨ Once you've been allocated your HIN you can place both buy and sell orders almost instantaneously for the same shares (provided that you use the same broker for both transactions). That's to say, you can buy shares and as soon as the order transacts you can place a sell order for the same shares. This is particularly useful if you're a very active trader or prices are volatile and you want to cash in profits or reduce losses quickly. If you're not CHESS-sponsored, you can't sell any shares you buy until the SRN has been allocated to you, and that could take several weeks.

⇨ You have only one number to keep track of for all the shares you purchase using a broker and you don't even need to quote this number when you sell any of these shares (or purchase additional shares in this stock or in any other stock). With issuer-sponsored shares you need to keep track of (and quote) your SRN for each stock when you sell shares because it's a different number for each stock you hold.

Transferring from issuer-sponsorship to broker-sponsorship

If you hold shares you bought or acquired prior to joining CHESS you can easily transfer from issuer-sponsorship to dealer-sponsorship. To do this you need to obtain a transfer form from your dealer sponsor (broker). You then simply fill out the form quoting the shares and the applicable SRN and authorise the transfer. This takes only a few days and doesn't cost you anything. However, it does activate new paperwork, as you'll be treated as a new shareholder for these shares. It's not considered an ownership transfer and there are no capital gains tax implications unless you're transferring shares registered in one name to a different name. If you've acquired shares from a deceased estate, capital gains tax liability doesn't occur at the time of transfer but only at a time when you sell any of the shares.

Tip

It doesn't cost anything to join CHESS and it is one of those rare things in life that has all advantages and no disadvantages. There's no reason not to be in CHESS—unless, for some devious reason, you're trying to make your share transactions more difficult to trace.

Holding statement

When you buy shares you'll be issued with a holding statement sometime later. If you've joined CHESS you'll receive a CHESS statement issued by the ASX, otherwise you'll be issued with a holding statement issued by the share registry. Normally these are paper documents that will be mailed to you free of charge.

When your shareholding changes because you buy or sell shares or receive additional shares in lieu of dividends you'll receive a new holding statement.

Tip

When you receive a holding statement, always check your own records to ensure there's complete agreement between them. You need to investigate any discrepancy immediately.

If you detect any discrepancies, you'll need to lodge a query with the share registry (not with your broker or the ASX).

Using more than one broker

As I suggested in chapter 4, you may wish to open an account with more than one online broker so you can thoroughly check the facilities and services offered. If you use more than one broker with CHESS you'll have more than one HIN. This is no problem provided you buy and sell the same shares with the same broker. This is easy to keep track of because the name of the sponsoring broker appears on the CHESS statement for each stock you own. For example, if you buy shares in Stock XYZ using Broker A then you can't simply sell those shares using Broker B. To do so you need to first transfer the shares by filling out a broker-to-broker transfer form. If you're holding shares you purchased using an offline broker that you'd like to sell online (because it's cheaper to do so), you need to transfer these to your online broker before you can do so.

If in time you decide to deal with only one online broker, you can transfer shares bought using other brokers by filling out a broker-to-broker transfer form obtainable from the broker you're transferring to. If you're transferring all your shares and you're in CHESS with both brokers you won't even need to state the name or code of each stock and the numbers of shares in each—simply indicate that you wish to transfer your entire shareholding. The system can automatically do this and you'll receive new CHESS statements for all shares transferred (at no cost to you). There are no capital gains tax implications from such a transfer.

Tip

If you're currently trading offline you may wish to continue your relationship with your offline broker while establishing an online broking account, so you can get into online trading and test the water before deciding whether or not this is the way you wish to go.

Becoming a client with an online broker

In the old days, to become a client with an online broker you needed to complete a paper application form. While this option still sometimes applies today, with many online brokers you can apply and be accepted entirely online.

If you're applying using a paper application form, you can obtain it in several ways:

⇨ download it from the broker's website

⇨ phone, fax or email the broker and request it

⇨ obtain it from the broker's branch or office; for example, a form for an online broker affiliated with a bank can usually be obtained from a branch of the bank.

When you apply (whether online or with a paper document), you'll need to complete the application form stating relevant personal details. You may be asked to nominate a password that allows you to access the site but you may also have a password allocated to you that you can change later on if you wish.

If you have an existing account with a bank or financial institution affiliated with the broker the whole process is easier as your personal ID will already have been verified. If not, you can still successfully verify your ID using e-verification if you have an Australian passport and tax file number (TFN). Using your address and date of birth, the information is cross-referenced using various databases including the Australian Taxation Office and Department of Foreign Affairs. If the information you provide satisfies the check, you will be deemed as being successfully verified and you'll be able to access the site as a client and start trading immediately. If you don't fulfil these requirements or fail the cross-reference check you'll need to verify your identity by providing 100 points of identification with details such as a certified copy of a driver's licence or other documents. The broker will probably require your signature to be held on file and this will require you to verify your signature by signing a document and including a copy of a signed passport, driver's licence or similar document that has your signature and returning the form by email, fax or post. However, you'll still be able to trade online without this provided you've successfully passed e-verification.

Your share trading account

Some online brokers provide financial incentives to encourage you to open a dedicated share trading account with them or a financial institution they nominate. To open a dedicated account you'll need to provide funds at least equal to the minimum deposit required with your application. In the past this may have been several thousand dollars but nowadays some brokers allow you to open the account with a token minimum deposit. If you don't open a dedicated share trading account with the broker you'll need to authorise cash transfers; that's to say, you need to allow the broker to access the necessary funds so you can pay for shares you buy and also provide an account into which cash can be deposited for shares you sell. This involves quoting a BSB number, account number, branch location and so on.

Once your application has been processed you'll be allocated a customer account number and password and a HIN (assuming you've opted for broker sponsorship). If you're opening a dedicated share trading account, you'll also be given a BSB and account number. The account number will generally not be the same as your online trading account number, but the password may be the same if you so choose. You should also be given phone contact and email details in case you have any questions about your account or experience any difficulties.

Once your application has been processed you're ready to start online trading! At least this is true in theory — but in practice you might encounter some difficulties that may take a phone call or email to sort out.

Tip

If you're new to online trading, I suggest you resist the temptation to trade immediately and do so only after you're read through this book in its entirety. This may prove to be a profitable delay!

Keeping track of your numbers

If you open a dedicated trading account, you'll have quite a few numbers that you need to keep track of and have easy access to, including:

⇨ online account number

⇨ online password

⇨ trading password

⇨ CHESS holder identification number

⇨ trading account.

Online account number

This is the number you use to log in to your online broker's site.

Online password

This is your personal password that you need to log in to your online broker's site.

Trading password

This is a personal password some online brokers require and that you must quote when you are placing a trade order with them.

CHESS HIN

This is the number that will be allocated to you when you join CHESS with your broker.

Trading account

These are the numbers that apply to your trading account (where the actual cash transfers occur) and includes both BSB and account number.

If you're going to use more than one broker you'll have a whole set of these numbers for each one, so you'll have a lot of numbers to keep track of. You may be able to use the same password if you want. In any case, you need a quick, reliable and secure way of accessing these numbers when you need them.

Tip

You may decide to store your numbers on a computer or mobile phone device but this involves some hacking risk. Regardless, I suggest you keep a hard copy in a secure place. It's not a good idea to record passwords, and you probably won't need to do so as you'll know them, but you may want to record the first letter or number as a memory jogger.

Cash transfers

Some brokers require adequate funds in your nominated account before they'll accept purchase orders. Others will provide temporary credit, the amount of which depends on the types of shares you want to purchase. In any event you need to ensure that adequate funds are in your account to cover the total net cost of purchases at the time of settlement.

Settlement and transfer of money occurs three working days after each transaction (T+3 settlement). It's not hourly based but just end of the day. For example, it makes no difference whether you buy shares at 10 am or 3.30 pm on a Thursday, it's regarded as a Thursday trade and you need to have the funds available in your account on Monday night as the cash transfer will occur on Tuesday.

If you buy and sell shares on the same day, you need funds to cover any outstanding net amount only. For example, if you buy shares to the value of $10 000 and sell shares to the value of $8000 on the same day and the brokerage on each transaction is $20, you need $2040 available in your account on day T+3. However, if the buy transaction took place, say, on a Monday and the sell transaction on Tuesday, you need $10 020 in your account on Wednesday night to cover the debit occurring on Thursday. Then on Friday your account would be credited with $7980.

Tip

I suggest you ensure that adequate funds are in your account at the time you place any purchase orders—especially if you're a new customer. If you're depositing a cheque into your account to pay for share purchases (even a bank cheque) it could take up to five working days to clear so you need to exercise caution if you're sailing close to the wind.

Setting up to trade online

I'll now walk you through the process of setting up to trade online. I'll use CommSec as they're the most popular online broker in Australia.

Applying to become a client

You can apply online or else request an application form from:

CommSec
Locked Bag 22
Australia Square
NSW, 1214
Ph: 13 15 19
Fax: (02) 9312 4100

Tip

Although CommSec is affiliated with the Commonwealth Bank, they're separate divisions with little customer interfacing. So a branch of the bank usually won't be able to help you a great deal with any CommSec-related queries. However, I've been informed that steps are being taken to remedy this situation in the future.

Completing the application form

When you complete your application you'll need to provide the details I've mentioned previously and include personal identification (if you're not already a CBA customer). You need to decide whether you'll open a Commonwealth Direct Investment Account (known as a CDIA) that you can use as your online trading account or whether you'll use some other nominated account of your choice. If you open a CDIA account you'll be treated as an 'internet preferred' customer, otherwise you'll be using the 'standard' service. The essential difference between the two is that brokerage is considerably lower on trades made with the CDIA account. If you decide on this option you'll need to open the CDIA account with CommSec. You can obtain a chequebook if you wish and use the account as you would any other account (including online banking).

Tip

It's worthwhile using a CDIA account for your share trades with CommSec in order to get the lower brokerage rates — if you're planning to trade with CommSec I suggest you do so.

Interest

For funds in the CDIA account interest is paid at a rate that depends on the daily balance in the account — the higher the balance the higher the interest rate. The interest rate can be found on the CommSec website and it can vary from time to time and with changes to the official interest rate. Unless you keep a substantial balance in the CDIA account, the interest rate is minimal; for example, at the time of writing for a balance below $10 000 the interest rate was a miniscule 0.01% per annum, and rose to only 3% with a balance of $100 000.

Tip

Interest rates on online trading account balances (both with CommSec and other online brokers) are generally lower than on traditional bank accounts so I suggest you keep a minimum balance in your trading account and transfer funds into and out of your trading account from other accounts as needed.

Trading shares

Once you've been accepted as a CommSec customer you can access the site and trade shares using a computer or smart phone device as CommSec has apps available for these. At the time of writing, CommSec had apps for iPhones, iPads and Android phones but not Windows phones or Android tablets.

If you purchase shares there are five ways you can fund the purchase:

⇨ direct debit from your nominated account (not necessarily a Commonwealth Bank account) on the day of settlement; if you are using this option you don't need to transfer the funds yourself—they will be transferred automatically

⇨ pay over the phone

⇨ pay over the internet using BPay

⇨ transfer funds or deposit money at any branch of the Commonwealth Bank (but remember cheques take time to clear)

⇨ pay online using CBA's NetBank site (if you are a Commonwealth Bank customer).

All CommSec clients are by default given credit on each account to the value of $25 000 for purchases of leading stocks, and $7500 for all others. (CommSec has a list of so-called 'leading stocks' and, as you would expect, these are high market cap 'blue chip' type stocks with some market-leading 'green chip' stocks.) If you want to purchase shares of value beyond these credit limits, a minimum 50% deposit is required before the order will be processed. However, this amount is reduced by the funds available in a CDIA account (if you have one) and the value of your CHESS holdings with CommSec. In other words, the value of your existing portfolio can be used as security for additional purchases. Of course, credit on your account applies only on the day of purchase and until settlement, and you'll still need to have sufficient cash in your account on the settlement date to cover the full net cost of your trades.

Tip

If you're selling shares the net funds will automatically be transferred into your nominated account and you need take no action.

Margin loan accounts

It's possible to extend your available funds using bank credit, known as a margin loan. Essentially a margin loan is one where an existing share or managed fund portfolio is used to provide the necessary collateral. The amount you can borrow depends on the value of your portfolio and the types of shares held—naturally you can get a higher credit with blue-chip shares than with speculative ones.

Most online brokers provide a margin lending facility, including CommSec. The mechanics of setting up a CommSec margin loan account are essentially the same as for any other CommSec account: you need to apply and fill out the application form. You'll be allocated a margin loan customer account number, a trading account number and an HIN with CHESS. If you're using an existing share portfolio as security on the loan, these shares will be transferred into the margin loan trading account and the HIN will be changed. Naturally you'll be charged interest on the daily loan balance and this interest can be found on the CommSec website and it varies from time to time.

If you wish to contact CommSec with regard to margin loan accounts, the details are different as the margin lending facility operates as a separate division. The details are:

Ph: 13 17 09
Fax: (02) 9995 7204

Tip

CommSec charges an additional fee of $10 for margin loan trades over and above normal brokerage, and as there are additional risks associated with margin loans I suggest you don't consider this option unless you're an experienced investor with a good track record of success.

Brokerage

At the time of writing, CommSec brokerage for internet share trades is as shown in table 5.1 (overleaf).

Table 5.1: CommSec brokerage rates for internet share trades

Trade type	Minimum	Above minimum
Internet preferred	$19.95 up to $10000 parcel value	$29.95 up to $25000 parcel value 0.12% above $25000 parcel value
Standard	$29.95 up to $10000 parcel value	0.31% above $10000 parcel value
Conditional	Normal brokerage plus $14.95 up to $40000 parcel value	Normal brokerage plus 0.12% of parcel value

Source: www.CommSec.com.au

CommSec provide additional trading facilities, including:

⇨ phone trading

⇨ trading shares from deceased estates

⇨ one-off trades

⇨ off-market share transfers (such as from one family member to another or privately owned shares into a self managed super fund).

Special rates and conditions apply for these types of trades

Tip

If these types of trades or transfers are of interest to you, I suggest you check out the CommSec website for further information.

Online self managed superannuation funds

An option available to you for investing in shares online is to do so by means of a self managed superannuation fund (SMSF). If you set up an SMSF, your shares will be owned by the fund (that is, by the fund members). An SMSF can have one to four members and each member is a trustee. The members own the fund's assets and (just as with any other managed fund or superannuation fund), an SMSF is controlled by the trustees (of which you'll be one or even the only one). As a trustee you have control over the management and financial decisions of the fund.

The SMSF method of investing is becoming increasingly popular in Australia, and in the 2010–11 financial year nearly $24 billion was invested into Australian SMSFs—up nearly $3 billion from the year before. In June 2012 there were about 443 000 SMSFs, with an average of $800 000 invested in each fund and total assets of almost $440 billion.

Tip

If you're like so many other Australians you may have a busy job and other commitments outside of work and adopt the attitude 'the fees my super fund charges aren't all that great, and I just don't have the time to bother with my own SMSF'. As I'll show soon with some examples, it's amazing how a relatively small saving in fees and charges each year can mount up and make a huge difference to your eventual retirement benefit. So you really need to give an SMSF serious thought, especially if you have a reasonable super account balance.

Legislation

Legislation applying to superannuation has changed over the years and is still in a state of flux as the government tries to come to terms with the conflicting requirements of increasing its income yet at the same time providing substantial taxation benefits to encourage Australians to invest in superannuation. The problem facing the government is that life expectancy rates are continually rising and the Centrelink pension burden for retired persons is rising in lockstep with the aging Australian population. So the government needs to provide substantial incentives to encourage Australians to become self-funded retirees when they leave the workforce.

The Labor government during its term in office up to 2013 tinkered with superannuation legislation as a means of raising more funds and increasing their taxation income. The amount of concessional contributions you can make was reduced, and on 5 April 2013 some sweeping changes were announced to the taxation rates applying to some of the earnings of superannuation pensions. If there's a change in government after the federal election in 2013, it remains to be seen whether a Liberal–National Party Coalition Government will continue to make legislation changes or perhaps repeal those made by the Labor Government.

Tip

Superannuation legislation constantly changes so you need to keep up to date—especially if you have an SMSF (or are thinking of setting up one). The information I give is current at the time of writing but is just a brief outline of what is a very complex area of law. If you want more detailed advice applicable to your own circumstances I suggest you consult a superannuation adviser with expertise in SMSFs.

Why invest in a superannuation fund?

The benefits of using a superannuation fund as a vehicle for share investing are:

⇨ You can build up a nest egg that will provide money that you can access when you retire.

⇨ When you reach your preservation age and retire you can withdraw money from the fund as a lump sum to pay for capital expenditures (such as home improvements, a new car or an overseas holiday), or in regular amounts as a pension income stream to provide retirement income to help compensate for loss of earnings when you no longer work full time.

⇨ Money invested in super receives very favourable tax treatment and the tax saving is money that is reinvested into your super fund to boost the retirement amount.

⇨ You receive the benefit of compounding that really kicks in over the longer term.

⇨ Your money is 'locked away' until you start withdrawing a pension or take a lump sum so you're not tempted to dip into your nest egg. While this is a benefit it's also a limitation should you need to draw down any funds in the account at any time before you retire.

Tip

You may be able to access superannuation funds before you reach retirement age in special circumstances such as severe financial hardship or serious illness, although the conditions of release are very strict.

Why set up a self managed superannuation fund?

The benefits of an SMSF are as follows:

⇨ There can be a considerable saving in fees and charges compared with a super fund managed by an external financial institution controlled by fund managers.

⇨ You have flexibility and control over the fund's investments and you can buy or sell shares (or other assets) as you wish.

⇨ You can transfer shares or certain other privately owned assets into your SMSF, although not all types of personal assets can be transferred to an SMSF. With an externally managed fund you can transfer only cash or roll over a super benefit into the fund.

⇨ Imputation credits on dividends for shares held by the fund are paid directly back into the fund as a cash transfer by the ATO after the fund's taxation return is submitted.

⇨ Profits made by the fund may be taxed at a lower rate than profits made on privately held shares, depending on your marginal income tax rate.

⇨ The potential saving in fees, charges and income tax can be reinvested into your SMSF to provide the benefit of compounding that really kicks in over the longer term and boosts your retirement benefit.

⇨ You know exactly where your money is invested and you can track every dollar of it. When your superannuation is an account set up and managed by a financial institution, your funds are mixed in with those of many others. This makes it very difficult (or impossible) to trace exactly each dollar of income, loss or expense that's attributable to you.

⇨ You can transfer cash into or out of your super fund very quickly (provided you're legally entitled to do so). This is because you directly control the transfers and they can be done electronically. I have found that with externally managed funds there could be a delay of up to a month or so with cash transfers.

⇨ You have peace of mind because the SMSF fund members legally own (and control) the assets of the fund. If your super is in an externally managed fund you don't legally own your share of the fund's assets. You're relying on the trustees to manage your super appropriately and to pay you your entitlement in full when you want to and are eligible to withdraw it. There have been cases in the past where externally managed funds have gone belly-up and fund investors have lost most (if not all) of their retirement entitlement.

Factors to consider with an SMSF

Before you rush into setting up your own super fund you need to consider the following factors:

⇨ The potential saving in fees and charges depends primarily on the amount of super you have (I'll discuss this shortly).

⇨ There's time and paperwork involved in setting up and managing the fund.

⇨ The fund needs to submit an annual taxation return (in addition to your own personal tax return) and there are annual auditing requirements that need to be complied with.

⇨ If there are legislative changes affecting SMSFs, the trust deed may need to be altered and this can involve some cost.

⇨ You control the fund's investments and trading decisions so you need to know what you're doing; you can't rely on the expertise of others.

⇨ You need to maintain accurate financial records (down to the last cent).

Tip

If you're comfortable with investing in shares online, I suggest you'd have no particular difficulties doing so using the structure of an SMSF.

Online and offline SMSFs

You can set up and manage your super fund online or offline just as you can invest in and trade shares online or offline. The benefits of an online SMSF are essentially the same as for shares, and the main one is a considerable saving in fees and charges when you initially set up the fund and in each year the fund is in operation. A possible downside of the online mode is that after the initial documentation has been completed most communication and data files are in electronic form. However, this isn't necessarily a great disadvantage, as you can always make an appointment with a financial adviser or accountant with expertise in superannuation, if you feel you really need a face-to-face discussion.

Tip

If you choose an online SMSF provider and invest in shares, make arrangements with the share registry so that all share documentation for SMSF-held shares is in electronic form. This will save you the hassle of scanning paper documents and converting them to electronic form.

SMSF cost benefits

There are potentially worthwhile cost savings if you set up and manage your own super fund—particularly if you choose the online mode. If your super is managed by an external financial institution they need to recoup their costs, and then some, in order to make a profit. Therefore there'll be management fees and charges that are deducted from any profits made by the fund and that reduce your accumulated pension benefit. Despite the fact that the fund investments are controlled by financial managers with alleged expertise, you may find (as I did) that the profitability of the fund can be lower than the profitability you can achieve using your own share investing expertise. It's particularly annoying to pay fees to others to have your hard-earned money managed by them when their profitability is less than you can achieve yourself.

The greatest saving in fees and charges with an SMSF can be achieved if you choose an online SMSF provider whose fees and charges are on a flat-fee basis rather than in proportion to the asset value of the fund. In a superannuation fees survey (reported in *The Sydney Morning Herald* business section on 6 April 2013), Australians were paying $20 billion in super fees each year with average fees of 1.28% across the whole superannuation system. On the other hand, with an online provider your annual fees and charges can be less than $1000 per year and even as low as about $700.

At the time of writing, the lowest cost online SMSF provider was E-Superfund whose cost structure was as follows:

Set-up fee: nil

Annual fee: $699

ATO supervisory levy: $200 (free for first year)

In addition, there's a charge of $110 per year to prepare an actuarial certificate if required. The certificate is required if a member of the SMSF who commenced a pension still had a balance in their accumulation account at any time during the financial year.

Tip

Fund managers and financial advisers make money from managing your super, and naturally they're reluctant to lose your business. I've seen some analysts reports suggesting that you need substantial funds before it's worthwhile setting up an SMSF. A minimum amount of $200 000 is often quoted but I've seen reports advising that you need at least $500 000 before an SMSF becomes a feasible option. I'll investigate the reality of these statements by looking at the economics of setting up an SMSF in the example that follows.

Example 1

Suppose you set up an SMSF with an online provider and pay $900 a year in fees rather than the average Australian rate of 1.28%. The annual cost saving in fees and charges of the online SMSF mode is given in table 5.2.

Table 5.2: annual cost savings according to SMSF fund balance

Fund balance $	Annual cost saving $
70 000	0
100 000	380
200 000	1 660
300 000	2 940
400 000	4 220
500 000	5 500
700 000	8 060
1 000 000	11 900

Conclusion

When the fund balance rises above the break-even amount, a substantial saving in fees and charges can be achieved. In my example the break-even point occurs when the fund balance is only about $70 000 and that's nowhere near the $200 000 to $500 000 figure often quoted by financial advisers. With a fund balance of less than the break-even amount there'll be no financial benefit in having a self-managed fund unless you can achieve a higher return on investment than that achieved by an externally managed fund. Remember that when your fund invests in shares the return consists of capital gains profits, dividends, and franking credits on dividends.

Tip

If your super is invested in an externally managed fund, make sure you know exactly what fees and charges you're paying. Also look at the return on capital invested by the fund and compare this to what you have achieved (or can achieve) with your privately held shares. You can then do the maths and decide whether setting up your own SMSF can result in worthwhile savings in fees and charges.

Accumulated benefit

An annual saving in fees and charges (as well as a possibly higher return on investment) is money that can be reinvested in your SMSF and gives you a double-whammy of extra profit with time because the benefit of compounding kicks in—especially over the longer term. Let's look at another example to see how this works.

Example 2

Suppose by setting up an SMSF you can save $1000 a year in fees and charges and you can reinvest the cost saving back into your fund and achieve an average return of at least 8% per year over the long term. This is a reasonably conservative return that should easily be achievable by investing in bank shares (or other blue chips) paying a good, steady, fully franked dividend. Indeed between 1982 and 2012, Australian shares gained an average of 12% per annum (despite the 1987 market crash and the 9/11 terrorist attack in the US). So during this time if your portfolio matched the market average there was a potential return of 12%.

I'll now look at a saving of $1000 per year that's reinvested into the fund each year with three investment returns:

- 8% (conservative)

- 10% (realistic)

- 12% (somewhat more optimistic).

The boost to your retirement benefit over the longer term is shown in table 5.3.

Table 5.3: annual cost savings reinvested

Years	$ boost to your super benefit		
	8%	10%	12%
10	14487	15937	17549
20	45762	57275	72052
30	113283	164494	241333

Conclusion

Over the longer term an SMSF has the potential to boost your retirement super by a large amount if you can save in fees and charges and invest wisely. I've based this table on $1000 per year saved, but if you can save $3000 per year the boost to your super balance is three times greater. In this case after 30 years at 10% investment return it would amount to nearly $340 000! After 30 years a saving of $3000 per year invested at 12% amounts to a hefty $724 000 boost to your super!

Tip

My examples show that you shouldn't take at face value the advice of naysayers who try to discourage you from setting up your own SMSF because it's not an economical proposition unless you have a huge fund balance. I suggest that you do your own research and calculations and come to your own conclusions.

Superannuation phases

A superannuation fund can essentially be in one of the following two phases:

⇨ *Accumulation phase:* this is the phase in which (as the name suggests) you're building up your account balance. If you're employed and earn over a certain threshold, your employer is required to invest a proportion of your wages (currently 9% and to be 9.25% from 1 July 2013) into a superannuation account. In most cases you can nominate the superannuation account of your preference, and if you can you can choose your own SMSF. If you wish, you can make additional payments into the account either as a salary sacrifice or as a voluntary personal contribution from your own resources.

⇨ *Pension phase:* in this phase you're starting to withdraw regular income from your superannuation account. To do so you must be at least 55 years old and retired from full-time work or aged 65 or more regardless of work status. The government sets the minimum pension you must withdraw each year as a pension and it rises with your age. You can nominate how you wish to take your pension and it can be in the form of regular withdrawals or a single, annual one.

If you're withdrawing a pension from your super fund, you can still make voluntary contributions into the fund although your contributions will be paid into a different account than your pension account but can be transferred later on. If you're aged over 65 you can only do so if you satisfy the work test that requires you to work at least 40 hours in a single 30-day period during the year. However, this cuts out when you reach age 75, after which you can't make additional deposits into your fund and can only withdraw (as a pension or lump sum).

Tip

If you're in the pension phase but still want to keep building up the balance in your super account, it's best to take the minimum pension and take it as a single payment just before the end of the financial year. At the start of the next financial year you can reinvest the money back into your super fund provided you can satisfy the work rule and are below the age limit.

Concessional and non-concessional contributions

Contributions into your super fund can be one of two types: concessional (before tax) and non-concessional (after tax). The essential difference is that concessional contributions provide taxation benefits that reduce your income tax liability. Concessional contributions, also known as before-tax contributions, include your employer's compulsory superannuation guarantee contributions and any salary-sacrificed contributions that you arrange for your employer to deduct from your before-tax salary. You can make voluntary concessional contributions into your super fund if you can satisfy the 10% rule which states that your employment income is less than 10% of your assessable income. This is most likely to apply if you're self-employed or receive a relatively small proportion of your income from an employer. In order to claim these contributions as a tax deduction you must lodge a notice of intention to do so with your super fund at the time you make the contribution.

Total concessional contributions in any financial year are limited by the government and in past years were capped at $50000 for those aged over 50, but for the 2012–13 financial year the amount was reduced to $25 000. For the 2013–14 financial year the cap continues to be $25 000, although it has been raised to $35 000 for those aged over 60 and for those aged over 50 in the following year (subject to legislation). It remains to be seen what it will be in future years.

Tip

Concessional contributions are a great way to reduce your tax liability so do your homework and use them if you possibly can.

Setting up an SMSF

The most feasible way of setting up and managing your SMSF is to use the services of an SMSF provider. There are many SMSF providers operating in Australia, in both online and offline modes, but you'll save considerably if you choose an online provider.

The funds you need to start your SMSF can come from two sources, namely:

⇨ an existing superannuation account (or accounts), where the balance in the account can be rolled over into your own SMSF

⇨ private investment capital or assets you own that can be transferred into your SMSF subject to certain restrictions; for example, current superannuation law doesn't allow you to roll over residential property owned by a fund member or a fund member's relative into your SMSF.

Tip

Be aware that the transfer of assets into an SMSF from private ownership must be at market value and will involve transfer fees, and in the case of business real property, possible property taxes and stamp duty (there's no stamp duty on share transfers). Any asset transfer could also trigger capital gains tax for you personally as the transfer is regarded as a change in ownership and therefore a capital gains tax event.

SMSF investments

There are many ways your SMSF can invest the assets of the fund—including shares, property and other investment instruments—provided that the investment is an allowed one and is for the legitimate purpose of providing funds for your retirement. Of all the allowed investments, franked shares are an excellent investment instrument because franking credits are automatically deposited back into the fund after the fund's tax return is submitted each financial year.

SMSF costs

As we've seen, one of the main benefits of an SMSF is the potential saving in annual fees and charges that you would otherwise pay to an externally managed super fund. There are two costs you need to consider:

⇨ *Setting up costs:* these are the once-only costs associated with the initial setting up of the SMSF.

⇨ *Ongoing fees and charges:* these are the annual fees and charges associated with maintaining the fund and complying with the all the statutory requirements. This involves the annual preparation and lodgment of a balance sheet, profit and loss statement, members' statements, trustee resolutions and minutes, income tax return and audit.

Tip

When I set up my SMSF online, the setting-up costs were waived. You may also be able to obtain this concession if you shop around. You should also compare the ongoing fees and charges between various SMSF providers before you make a selection.

SMSF providers

There are many providers that will organise the legislative setting up requirements and the ongoing legislative and taxation requirements on your behalf, so all you need to do is complete the necessary documentation they provide you with. At the end of each financial year, you'll need to submit certain financial transaction records including share dividend statements so the provider can prepare the fund's tax return and an auditor can review the fund (if necessary).

Tip

Some SMSF providers operate in the online mode and some in the offline mode; as I've already said, the online mode is the cheaper option where you'll make the greatest savings in fees and charges.

Online SMSF information

There are many websites you can access for further information about all aspects of an SMSF. Some websites are independent and some are set up by superannuation providers. I'll list only four sites that I consider to be very good ones for further research.

Super Guide: www.superguide.com.au
This site is an independent one that contains heaps of information and is well worth browsing. You can subscribe to a free monthly newsletter and email any questions you may have about super.

SMSF Review: www.thesmsfreview.com.au
This site gives a comprehensive listing of SMSF providers in Australia and it has a comparison table that provides an excellent summary of the various providers and lists the set-up fees and ongoing management fees.

Australian Taxation Office: www.ato.gov.au
The ATO site provides a great deal of information about the taxation laws and regulations applying to super in general and SMSF funds in particular.

E-Superfund: www.esuperfund.com.au
This site is clearly focused toward their services as an online superannuation provider but nevertheless contains lots of free information and publications that are worth accessing.

Tip

The sites I've listed are all well worth visiting if you're seriously contemplating self managed super. In particular, I suggest you visit the SMSF Review site before you make any decisions about setting up an SMSF and the provider you will choose.

Key points

⇨ Once you've chosen the online broker (or brokers) you wish to use for your online trading and investing, you'll need to apply to become a client. To do this you need to complete an application with all required details, including personal ID. If you can do this online the whole process is sped up considerably.

⇨ When you apply to become a client with an online broker you'll be asked if you want CHESS sponsorship. I suggest you indicate that you do as it's free and has significant benefits.

⇨ At any time you can transfer shares you own into CHESS with your online broker and this will simplify your account keeping and make it easier to keep track of your portfolio. This is simple and free.

⇨ It may be beneficial to open a dedicated bank account with your online broker at the time of your application. Otherwise you'll need to nominate an existing account where funds can be withdrawn or deposited for your trades.

⇨ Adequate funds need to be available in your account to pay for the net value of any purchases at settlement day (T+3).

⇨ After you've completed and submitted your application, you'll be given an account number and other details that you need to get started. If you complete a paper application form there may be a time delay of a week or more before you're accepted as a client and you're able to trade.

⇨ Interest rates on online trade account balances are generally lower than on other bank accounts so I suggest you keep a minimum balance in your online trading account. You can transfer funds in and out of your trading account from other accounts that pay a higher rate of interest on an as-needs basis.

⇨ Once you've set yourself up with one or more online brokers I strongly suggest that you resist the temptation to trade online until you've read through this book in its entirety. You need to properly understand the nuts and bolts of trading online in order to avoid errors that could prove costly.

⇨ An SMSF can be a very effective vehicle for share investing and if you're comfortable with online share trading and investing you should have no particular difficulty doing so using an SMSF.

⇨ There can be significant cost savings in fees and charges if you set up an SMSF and manage your share investments as a trustee of the fund.

⇨ As a trustee of the fund you control how your super funds are invested and managed.

⇨ With an SMSF you can easily account for each dollar of your super.

⇨ The economics of setting up your own SMSF depends on your choice of provider and the fund balance in your super account. If you choose the least expensive online SMSF provider the break-even point occurs when your fund balance is $55 000. For a fund balance greater than this there can be a significant saving in fees and charges.

⇨ A saving in fees and charges is cash you can reinvest in your SMSF to boost the balance. Over a number of years the benefit of compounding really kicks in and in the longer term can make a significant difference to your retirement benefit.

⇨ Concessional contributions into your fund can considerably reduce your income tax liability. However, there's a capped limit to the amount you can deposit in this way and this can change from year to year.

⇨ Profits from shares invested in super receives a more favourable tax treatment than shares held outside super (unless you're a low income earner). Ensure your SMSF reverts to pension mode as soon as you can legally do so because of the beneficial tax treatment. This requires you to withdraw a pension that must be at least equal to the minimum amount stipulated by legislation and that increases as you age.

chapter 6

Online planning and monitoring

Now you've investigated the online brokers available in Australia, made your choice of the one (or ones) you'll use and have set up to trade online, you'll no doubt be itching to start online trading. Before you do so I strongly suggest that you develop a trading plan, and in this chapter I discuss how you might go about this and what factors you need to include in your plan.

An essential part of your planning is to consider how you will monitor the market, your share trades and the performance of your portfolio. In this chapter I'll also discuss how you can monitor online and check (and hopefully improve) performance.

Methods of online trading

There are essentially two methods of online trading that might be termed the 'impulse method' and the 'planned method'.

Impulse method

The impulse method works this way:

1   You receive a trading stimulus that may come from a number of sources, such as an article you've read on a website, paper or magazine; the advice of an adviser, friend or associate; a

tweet, blog or chat room message; or a radio or television news report.

2   You consider this stimulus to decide whether or not you'll act on it. The amount of consideration you give it could vary from almost none to a thorough investigation of the stimulus using fundamental and/or technical analysis.

3   You act on the stimulus by placing a trade order with your online broker.

Planned method

In the planned method you have a plan that you've thought about and prepared in advance and that you'll follow with all your online trades. The plan has a number of aspects and you'll consider each one before you place an order. When you receive a trading stimulus you'll incorporate it into your plan and act on it only if it satisfies the criteria you've outlined in your plan.

Which method is best?

I suspect most online trades made by personal share traders are made using the impulse method because it's simple, fast and easy. The planned method requires some forethought and time and in the busy world of today most of us (even when retired!) have limited time. Nowadays, access to the market to trade online is so convenient and rapid that there's a real temptation to 'just do it' without much forethought. To emphasise the point I'm making, I'd like to share with you a true-life experience of mine.

Some years ago I bought a cruising yacht that I moored in a bay in Sydney that was very crowded with other yachts and cruisers. One day when leaving my mooring, the particular combination of wind and tide caught me unawares and very nearly resulted in a disaster that by sheer good luck I managed to avoid. When I told a friend of mine (who was a very experienced seaman) about it, he explained that there was a right and a wrong way of leaving a mooring. He then outlined the right way, and I realised that the method was logical and obvious and I didn't understand why I hadn't used it. His reply has stayed with me ever since and is something I often think about. He said:

'You didn't do it because you hadn't thought about it.'

Why am I telling you this? Simply because the lesson I learned that day applies to so many situations in life—and certainly to online trading. When I left my mooring without a planned method, I was like an online trader initiating trades on impulse and without a plan.

Now I'm not suggesting that if you don't have a plan you can't trade successfully. Before I had a plan I successfully left my mooring many times, and there are probably many traders who make profitable impulse trades. But profitable impulse trading over the long run requires a special talent most of us don't have or else a particularly fortuitous run of good luck that can't be relied on. If you want to swing the probabilities in your favour and trade successfully over the longer term, I strongly suggest that you develop a plan that you follow for all your online trades.

Tip

If you want to trade shares successfully without relying on luck, you need a plan that you follow.

Writing down your plan

It's best to have a written plan for each online trade you intend to make. It doesn't have to be a paper document; it could be a document stored on your computer, smart phone or tablet, but it needs to be written. A verbal plan or one that's in your mind isn't really satisfactory for a number of reasons, one of which is that a written plan acts as a checklist so you're less likely to ignore it or not act on all facets of your plan.

Tip

Have a written trading plan and refer to it every time (no exceptions) before you trade online. If you get nothing else from this book except to follow my advice and have a written trading plan, your time reading this book has been worthwhile.

When should you plan?

You don't necessarily need to finalise all details in your plan a long way in advance of placing an online order. But it's most important that you have a written plan and that you fill in all the headings before you press any trade buttons on your computer or smart phone. Indeed, in some cases your trading decision may be influenced by current market action and these can't be planned a long way in advance (or sometimes even a relatively short way as the market can change significantly by the hour).

Your online trading plan

I'll discuss a trading plan applying to shares but your trading plan can apply to other investment instruments such as managed funds, CFDs, options and so on. Your plan should consider three aspects of a trade: entry, monitoring and exit.

Entry

These are the conditions that must be satisfied before you initiate a trade; that is, when you buy shares.

Monitoring

After you've entered a trade you need to keep tabs on your investment, a process known as monitoring.

Exit

It's tempting to ignore the exit conditions in your planning with the idea that you'll think about it after you've initiated the trade. But it's a much better idea to plan the exit before you enter a trade, even if you're buying shares as a long-term investment.

Note: If you've already bought shares without a plan, for these shares your plan can skip the entry conditions and move on to the monitoring and exit phases.

Tip

Don't plan the entry conditions of a trade only—consider also the monitoring and exit phases.

Factors to consider

Factors to consider in your trading plan

⇨ intention

⇨ reasoning

⇨ timing

⇨ price trigger

⇨ duration

⇨ profit target

⇨ parcel value

⇨ number of shares

⇨ order type

⇨ monitoring

⇨ exit strategy.

I'll now consider each factor in detail.

Intention

This is the starting point of your plan where you write down the trade you intend to initiate.

For example, your intention might be:

⇨ Buy a parcel of 1000 XYZ shares.

⇨ Increase my existing holding of XYZ shares by buying an additional 500 shares.

⇨ Sell all my holding in XYZ shares.

⇨ Sell half of my holding in XYZ shares.

Reasoning

This is probably the most important aspect of your plan where you ask: 'why do I intend to initiate this trade?' There could be many reasons why you want to buy or sell shares, including the ones I've listed in the following section.

Buy intention reasons

⇨ My friend (who dabbles in shares) advised me to buy them.

⇨ I read a report about these shares in a financial newspaper (or magazine) and they look good to me.

⇨ On my broking website there was a consensus of broker opinions stating these shares were a 'strong buy'.

⇨ I already have some of these shares and they've been good performers.

⇨ I read posts in a chat room where a number of people recommended these shares.

⇨ I like the business the company is in and I think it's a growth industry.

⇨ The shares pay a good dividend.

⇨ The business the company's in is a growth sector of the market.

⇨ The shares have good fundamentals that conform to my criteria so they look to be worth purchasing as a long-term investment (more on fundamental analysis in chapter 8).

⇨ The chart looks good with the right indications so they look to be a good buy (more on charting in chapter 9).

Sell intention reasons

⇨ I need cash to fund a coming lifestyle event.

⇨ The shares aren't performing as well as I expected and I can see better opportunities elsewhere.

⇨ I want to cash in profits; that is, convert 'paper profit' into money in the bank before the price falls.

⇨ The shares have been unprofitable so I'll cut my losses.

⇨ On my broking website there was a consensus of broker opinions stating that it was time to sell these shares.

⇨ The company has cut their dividend payout so I want to sell the shares and buy higher yielding shares.

⇨ There's been a downturn in the fundamental criteria so there's no longer a reason to hold these shares.

⇨ The chart indicates the price is entering a down turn.

⇨ I've held these shares for some years now and they haven't done much so I'll sell them and invest the proceeds into shares that seem more profitable.

And so on...

The importance of having a written plan will be evident after you write down your reasoning in conjunction with your intention. For example, if you write down as your reasoning that you want to buy these shares because you were advised to do so in a chat room post or a financial tweet or blog, it will focus your mind on the validity of your reasoning. After all, is the suggestion of a friend or total stranger (who may or may not have any financial expertise) really a good reason to act?

Timing

Once you've written down what you intend to do and why you intend to do it, you need to consider when you'll act; that is, turn your planned intention into reality. For example, if you're keen to buy shares in order to get the next dividend, you'll need to time your purchase to transact before the ex-dividend date. On the other hand, if you want to sell them but still get the dividend, your sell order will need to transact on the ex-dividend date or later.

If you specify a share price you can place your order almost anytime with an online broker as most will accept the order on a 24/7 basis, even though the market is closed. For example, you could place an order with your online broker on Sunday afternoon, but your order can't transact until trading commences on Monday morning. However, I suggest you avoid placing orders outside of market hours unless exceptional circumstances apply. There are two reasons I suggest this:

⇨ I believe it's wise to get an idea of general market direction and share price movements before you trade, and that means not trading until the market has been open for some time.

133

⇨ The trading screen you access at, say, 7 pm on a Sunday evening may be very different to the screen when trading commences at 10 am on the following Monday (even though no trading has taken place in Australia in the intervening period). If you act on the information available on Sunday evening you could enter into a trade at an unfavourable price or perhaps make a trade you would not have made had you seen the screen after the market had opened.

There can even be situations when you look at the market depth screen when the market is closed and see apparent nonsense, like bids that are higher than the offers. This means that buyers are prepared to pay more than the price at which sellers are willing to sell! This type of anomaly can occur during non-trading periods as a result of unfulfilled orders in the system or international trading in Australian shares while our market is closed (due to time differences).

It's rumoured that some traders even place 'dummy' orders when the market is closed, knowing full well that the orders can't transact. Then just before the market opens they cancel the orders. Dummy buy orders give the false impression of high demand for the shares and tend to drive bids up, whereas dummy sell orders have the opposite effect.

Assuming that you intend to place an order during a time when the market is open, when is the best time to do so? Usually during the opening period there's a great deal of volatility, but after an hour or two the market usually settles down with clearer trends being established. After the initial jostling is completed you can get a much better impression of the mood and how prices are moving. For this reason I generally avoid placing orders during the first hour or so of trading. The downside to this strategy is that the market could move against you later on and you might have traded at a better price if your order had transacted during the early period. However, I have found that, on balance, it is usually safer to wait some time after market opening before placing orders.

As a small investor I have found that it's very difficult to get a jump on the rest of the market in the hope of pre-empting a significant price move by placing an order before the market opens. The market is an informed one and generally by the time my order transacts the price reaction has already taken place.

Tip

Unless you're desperate to sell, I suggest you don't place orders outside of market opening hours or immediately after the market opens because there's too much initial volatility; it's usually better to wait until the jostling is over and the market settles down.

Price trigger

A trigger is the firing gun that goes off to start a race, and with a share trade it's the price stimulus you'll use to initiate the trade. Some examples of price triggers are:

⇨ Buy at market; that is, the lowest price offered by a seller.

⇨ Buy when the price rises to $x.

⇨ Buy when the price falls to $x.

⇨ Buy at no more than $x provided the share price is rising.

⇨ Buy at market provided the market is rising and the share price is rising.

Tip

It's generally not a good idea to initiate a trade regardless of current price movements. Always consider how the market and the shares are performing before initiating a trade. In particular, avoid placing a buy order when the market as a whole is falling and/or the price of the shares you intend to buy is falling. (I'll discuss this in more detail in later chapters.)

Duration

In your planning you should consider the duration between trade entry and exit. This could vary from just one day (or even less) to indefinitely (that is, you're essentially planning a 'buy and hold' strategy). The duration will depend on the type of shares involved in the trade. If you're planning to make a fast dollar from price movements in speculative shares your planned duration could be very short, whereas if you're looking at 'blue chip' or 'green chip' type shares you'll usually be planning a long-term investment with good annual returns over a number of years.

Profit target

No doubt everyone trades shares with the idea of making as much profit as possible from the trade in the shortest possible time, but that's not a good enough target for a plan. You really need to have some concrete idea of what profit you're hoping to make over the duration of the trade.

If you're buying shares with the idea of making a fast dollar you might aim to make a capital gain of 10% within a week or a month, whereas if you're buying shares as a long-term investment your aim might be to make a combined dividend and capital gain profit of 10% per year for the indefinite future.

Tip

It's been proven by many experiments that humans perform best when striving to achieve a concrete goal that's challenging but at the same time realistic; that is, not too easy and not too hard. Bear this in mind when setting your profit target by considering current and realistic future price movements and dividend payments of the shares involved in the context of the market as a whole.

Parcel value

You need to consider the funds you'll allocate to the trade, making sure you include brokerage. This will depend on:

⇨ your available funds

⇨ minimum brokerage for small parcels if you're considering a small parcel-value trade

⇨ your level of confidence; that is, the amount of risk involved in the trade and how confident you are that the trade will be a profitable one. Clearly the greater your confidence is the greater the amount you'll be prepared to invest in the trade.

Internet brokers (and indeed all brokers) have a minimum charge for orders. Once you exceed the minimum (typically parcel sizes of $10 000 or so) a uniform percentage cost usually applies, so that the cost per share isn't affected by the parcel value. For small parcel values the cost per share is affected by the parcel value, and the smaller the parcel value the higher the cost per share.

To see how this works, let's suppose you are buying shares with a market price of $1.00. Table 6.1 shows the effect of parcel value on the cost per share with an assumed minimum brokerage of $20 (typical online brokerage).

Table 6.1: Cost per share for various parcel sizes at $20 trading cost

Parcel value ($)	Brokerage and GST ($)	Total cost ($)	Cost per share ($)
500	20	520	1.04
1000	20	1020	1.02
1500	20	1520	1.01
2000	20	2020	1.01
2500	20	2520	1.01
3000	20	3020	1.01

Conclusion

This table illustrates that with small orders the cost per share reduces as the parcel value increases. However, the law of diminishing returns means that at a certain point the difference becomes negligible as the cost per share doesn't change (when rounded to the nearest cent). With brokerage of $20 that point is reached with a parcel value of about $1500. You can also see that online trading makes it feasible to trade small orders. This is a great feature if you're a small investor with limited trading capital, or if you wish to dabble in some speculative trading or test a trading system without committing yourself to large amounts of money.

Tip

The parcel value should be inversely related to the riskiness of the trade. That's to say, the higher the risk, the lesser the proportion of your available funds you should allocate to the trade.

Number of shares

When you place an order you'll need to specify exactly how many shares you intend to trade. In the old days the number of shares needed to be a round number such as 1000 or 1200, but nowadays you can place an order for any number of shares you like, such as 1362. For buy orders the number of shares you can buy depends on the share price, your planned parcel value and the brokerage.

Order type

There are three different types of online order you can place, namely:

⇨ market order

⇨ limit order

⇨ conditional order.

I'll discuss these orders in greater detail in the next chapter. Your plan should include consideration of the type of order you intend to place.

Monitoring

Monitoring is the process of keeping tabs on share price action and also sector or general market movements. You can monitor either before or after a trade.

Monitoring before a trade

When you're contemplating a trade, monitoring is important because you don't want to buy shares when the share price is falling and you don't want to sell them when the share price is rising.

Monitoring after a trade

After you've bought a parcel of shares you need to keep tabs on how your investment performs as well as the general direction of the market as a whole. You also need to keep up to date with any announced changes (including declared dividends) that could significantly impact on the value of your shares. It's also a good idea to monitor after you've sold shares to give you an idea of the success of your trading plan.

Monitoring frequency

How often you should monitor this depends a great deal on the volatility of the shares involved in the trade. If they're volatile and speculative shares, you may need to check the market several times during a day but if they're defensive and blue-chip shares once a week should be fine. For blue-chip shares some share investors adopt a 'bottom drawer' approach because after they've bought such shares they forget about them. The name derives from the idea that data about the shares is virtually filed in the bottom drawer of a cupboard where it's out of sight and out of mind. This approach tends to minimise stress and worry but it's not an approach I recommend; you really need to have a good monitoring system in place for all shares in your portfolio whether they be speculative or blue chip in nature.

Methods of monitoring

Your monitoring can be manual (you do it yourself) or automatic (you set up an alert system such as a price or announcement alert sent to your computer or phone). This can be free or you may need to pay a fee (particularly if the alert is sent to a mobile device).

Some examples of each are given here.

Manual monitoring

⇨ I'll check the price of the shares I'm contemplating trading three times today.

⇨ I'll check the price (and announcements) at close of market every day.

⇨ I'll check the price (and announcements) once a week on Saturday mornings.

⇨ I'll check the price (and announcements) once a week on Saturday mornings and also look at the share price chart.

Automatic monitoring

⇨ I'll arrange for an alert to my mobile phone (or computer) if the share price rises to $x or falls to $y.

⇨ I'll arrange for an alert when the company makes an announcement.

Tip

Even if you monitor manually, I suggest you consider setting up automatic monitoring for most (if not all) of your shares but especially the most volatile ones. Reasons you might not want to do so include if you have many shares and you're getting swamped with too many alerts each day or you're paying for the alerts and the cost is becoming significant.

Online watch list

When you have a number of different shares you're contemplating trading you can set up an online watch list. This enables you to keep track of the prices of shares you nominate with a single website entry and is a time-saving facility usually provided on online broking sites and also on some public-access sites.

A sample of a typical watch list is shown in figure 6.1 and should be self-explanatory.

Online portfolio monitoring

Your online broker will maintain a portfolio for shares you hold and bought using the broker. It will automatically update with current prices and values. The updating can be real time, 20-minute delayed or in some cases at the completion of trading each day with values based on the last day's sale price. When you sell shares the sold shares will automatically be deleted from your portfolio. If you've joined the DRP and receive shares in lieu of cash dividends the portfolio will automatically be updated to show your new shareholding after the shares are allocated to you.

Some public-access sites also offer a portfolio facility that can be used for real or hypothetical portfolios. If you use such a site for your actual portfolio clearly the site will not be aware of your trades and you'll need to update the portfolio manually when you trade shares or receive shares through a DRP.

Your online broking portfolio may automatically show the buy price for each stock, but if this isn't the case you'll need to insert buy prices manually. You can do this using the 'edit' function in the portfolio facility. With buy prices included the portfolio will show the profit/loss for each stock, usually in both dollar terms and as a percentage of your initial investment.

Figure 6.1: sample watch list

Shares										Remove
Select	Security	Exchange	Watch set	Open	High	Low	Current price*	Volume	Last close	
○	➡ DORAY MINERALS LIMITED (DRM) ORDINARY FULLY PAID	ASX	21st Dec 2012	$0.775	$0.780	$0.775	$0.775	414,493	$0.780	
○	➡ GALE PACIFIC LIMITED (GAP) ORDINARY FULLY PAID	ASX	21st Dec 2012	$0.280	$0.280	$0.275	$0.275	217,645	$0.280	
○	➡ INCITEC PIVOT LIMITED (IPL) ORDINARY FULLY PAID	ASX	21st Dec 2012	$3.300	$3.300	$3.240	$3.260	7,739,876	$3.270	
○	⬅ JACKA RESOURCES LIMITED (JKA) ORDINARY FULLY PAID	ASX	21st Dec 2012	$0.205	$0.210	$0.205	$0.205	431,928	$0.200	
○	➡ STARPHARMA HOLDINGS LIMITED (SPL) ORDINARY FULLY PAID	ASX	21st Dec 2012	$1.240	$1.245	$1.225	$0.205	560,700	$1.235	
○	⬅ TREASURY GROUP LIMITED (TRG) ORDINARY FULLY PAID	ASX	21st Dec 2012	$4.990	300	$4.960	$5.300	53,865	$4.960	

*Security prices are delayed by least 20 minutes and are indicative only.

Source: investsmart.com.au

You're also given a total for the portfolio; that is, the total current market value and total profit/loss. However, your online portfolio won't show profit/loss for shares sold as these are deleted from your portfolio after sale. Also, it won't include cash dividends or brokerage. For these reasons your online portfolio as it appears at the end of a financial year can't be used for income tax purposes or for calculating your annual profit or loss or percentage return on investment. Nevertheless, an online portfolio is a very useful summary that allows you to easily keep track of your shareholding and I often refer to mine (usually at least once a week).

A sample online portfolio (from the CommSec site) is shown in figure 6.2. Going from left to right the columns are:

1   *Code:* the code for the stock.
2   *Available units:* the number of shares available for you to sell (should you want to). This is equal to the number of shares you own unless you have an open sale order for shares in this stock (that is, an order placed but not transacted), or if you've traded shares in this stock in the last three days. (Remember settlement takes three days.) The term 'units' is used rather than 'shares' because, strictly speaking, trusts and managed funds issue 'units' rather than shares and the term 'unit' covers both.
3   *Purchase price:* the price you paid for the shares when you bought them. This price won't be accurate if your total shareholding consists of different parcels purchased at different times and at different prices, or with differing allocation prices when you receive shares through a DRP. In such cases, you can insert an approximate average price to make your profit/loss figure more reasonable but this will be a profit estimate only.
4   *Last sale price:* latest price at which the shares traded.
5   *Market value:* the last sale price multiplied by the number of units.
6   *Profit/loss:* the difference between last sale price and purchase price multiplied by the number of units.
7   *Profit/loss percentage:* the profit/loss divided by market value and expressed as a percentage.
8   *Change $:* the change in share price today compared to yesterday's close. It will be positive or negative depending on whether the price rose or fell.

Figure 6.2: sample portfolio

| Share Holdings | | Thur 20 Dec 2012 12.07 (Sydney time) | | | | | | |
Code	Available Units	Purchase $	Last $	Market Value $	Profit / Loss $	Profit / Loss %	Change $	Change Value $
ABC	5,900	2.58	3.1	18,290	3,068	16.77	0.04	236
ANZ	4,335	19.53	24.8	107,508	22,845	21.25	0.02	87
ASL	6,121	2.65	2.52	15,425	−796	−5.16	0.04	245
ASX	275	31.05	31.15	8,566	27	0.32	0.01	3
BEN	5,789	7.49	8.48	49,091	5,731	11.67	0.035	203
BKN	6,154	5.54	5.4	33,232	−862	−2.59	−0.02	−123
BLD	1,889	0	4.37	8,255	8,255	100.00	0.01	19
BPT	21,367	1.24	1.505	32,157	5,662	17.61	−0.02	−427
CBA	1,940	51.36	61.51	119,329	19,691	16.50	0.03	58
FWD	2,613	7.776	9.78	25,555	5,236	20.49	0.025	65
MND	600	22.4	23.41	14,046	606	4.31	0.015	9
NAB	1,350	23.44	24.88	33,588	1,944	5.79	0.03	41
NCM	378	23.56	22.49	8,501	−404	−4.76	−0.05	−19
STO	550	10.85	10.72	5,896	−71	−1.21	−0.04	−22
SUN	1,598	8.47	10.3	16,459	2,924	17.77	0.02	32
TLS	2,600	3.91	4.35	11,310	1,144	10.11	−0.02	−52
TTS	8,076	2.85	2.95	23,824	808	3.39	0.01	81
WAT	3,550	1.05	1	3,550	−178	−5.00	0	0
WBC	1,436	22.46	25.97	37,293	5,040	13.52	0.02	29
WES	845	29.35	36.61	30,935	6,135	19.83	0.04	34
WOW	1,088	24.56	29.49	32,085	6,364	16.72	0.02	22
Total				634,897	92,171	14.52		519

Source: www.CommSec.com.au

9   *Change in value:* the change in value compared with yesterday's close, and is the price change multiplied by the number of units.

Online portfolio charts

A useful feature of the CommSec site is that you get a visual impression of the balance of your portfolio value with pie charts showing the breakdown by both stocks and sectors. A typical chart is shown in figure 6.3 (note that this chart doesn't apply to the same portfolio given in figure 6.2). On a computer screen or smart phone or tablet they're coloured for easier identification.

Figure 6.3: typical portfolio charts

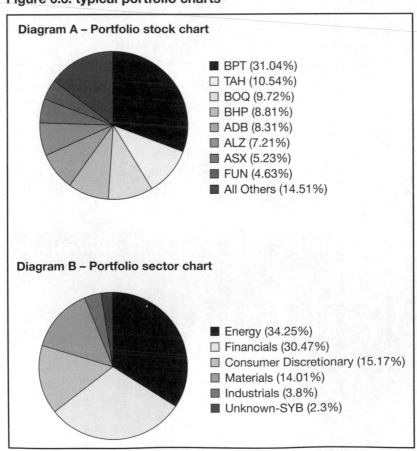

Diagram A – Portfolio stock chart

- BPT (31.04%)
- TAH (10.54%)
- BOQ (9.72%)
- BHP (8.81%)
- ADB (8.31%)
- ALZ (7.21%)
- ASX (5.23%)
- FUN (4.63%)
- All Others (14.51%)

Diagram B – Portfolio sector chart

- Energy (34.25%)
- Financials (30.47%)
- Consumer Discretionary (15.17%)
- Materials (14.01%)
- Industrials (3.8%)
- Unknown-SYB (2.3%)

Source: www.CommSec.com.au/Paritech

Exit strategy

Unless you're a short-term trader there's a great temptation to ignore the exit strategy in your trading plan and regard it as something you'll think about later on after you see how the shares perform. The exit decision is usually the most difficult one to make because if you've bought shares that are profitable you won't want to sell them, and if you've made a trade that's showing a loss it's really tempting to hang on in the hope that there'll be a change in fortunes and your loss will eventually turn into a profit. That's why you need to consider an exit strategy as part of your trading plan because it makes the selling decision less emotional and easier to make when you need to make it.

Some examples of an exit strategy are:

⇨ I'll hold the shares indefinitely provided the price remains stable or rises and the dividend yield remains above a%. I'll sell if the price starts to trend down and reaches $b or the dividend yield falls below c%. (This is fundamentally a modified buy and hold strategy.)

⇨ I'll sell all the shares if the price falls to $d (loss minimisation strategy).

⇨ I'll sell half the shares if the price falls to $e and the other half if the price falls further to $f (two-tiered loss-minimisation strategy).

⇨ I'll sell all the shares if the price rises to $g (profit-taking strategy).

⇨ I'll sell half the shares if the price rises to $h and the other half if the price rises further to $i (two-tiered profit-taking strategy).

⇨ I'll place a stop-loss order at 10% below the purchase price and adjust it upward if the price rises to 10% below the end-of-day market price but I won't adjust it downward if the price falls.

⇨ I'll place a profit-stop order at 10% above the purchase price.

⇨ I'll hold the shares for three months and if the price doesn't rise to my target profit level of $j by this time I'll sell them.

Trading frequency

I've outlined the factors I consider important in a trading plan for each online trade you intend to make. However, as well as having a plan for each intended trade you should have an overall plan for your trading frequency; that is, how often you intend to trade. I assume you're not a full-time day trader, so you need to consider how often (on average) you intend to trade online.

There are three possible scenarios for your trading frequency:

⇨ undertrading

⇨ overtrading

⇨ optimum trading.

Undertrading

You undertrade when you don't trade often enough, usually for two main reasons:

⇨ You hang on to unprofitable shares for too long. It's a classic trap you can fall into when you indulge in wishful thinking hoping that a loss will turn into a profit provided you exercise patience and wait long enough.

⇨ You don't take profits when you can and before long your profit evaporates or turns into a loss.

An extreme case of undertrading is a buy and hold strategy because with this strategy you place buy orders only and no sell orders for the shares. This strategy is often criticised as an extreme case of undertrading, but on the other hand studies have shown that it can be a very successful one. After all, if the shares are performing to your expectations there's no logical reason to sell them. A buy and hold strategy could also be appropriate if you have a good monitoring system in place so you're alerted should circumstances change significantly and holding these shares is no longer an appropriate strategy.

Tip
Consider a buy and hold strategy only for shares that continue performing to your expectations.

Overtrading

You overtrade when you switch in and out of trades too often. While you might believe that trading frequently will make you more profit, studies show that usually the result is you end up paying a lot more in brokerage and you make less profit. Also, you spend too much time trading rather than using your available time for research and planning.

Overtrading is a trap that's easy to fall into because trading online is so cheap and convenient, and because most traders believe you need to trade frequently to be successful. However, research in both Australia and the US has shown that this idea isn't borne out in practice and indeed the opposite is more often true. For example, studies comparing women and men as share investors found that women (on the whole) were more successful than men. The two main reasons for this were:

⇨ women trade safer and less speculative stocks than men

⇨ women trade less often than men.

Tip

Avoid the temptation of trading online too often simply because it's so cheap and convenient.

Optimum trading

Clearly there's a balance between undertrading and overtrading that occurs when you're making the optimum number of trades to maximise profitability. This is shown diagrammatically in figure 6.4 (overleaf).

Tip

Keep figure 6.4 in mind when planning your online trades and try to strike a balance between undertrading and overtrading. Apply a disciplined approach to avoid the temptation to trade too often or, on the other hand, becoming apathetic or indulging in wishful thinking so you trade too seldom.

Figure 6.4: optimum trading frequency

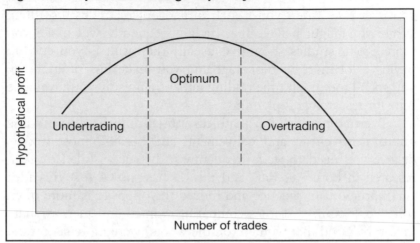

Following your plan

As I've said, I suspect that the majority of online trades are initiated without a plan. Even when you do have a plan, you won't necessarily follow it unless you adopt a very disciplined approach. Indeed, you could say that planning is the easy part; the hard part is following the plan through thick and thin.

Human action can result from careful and logical consideration of all relevant factors or simply as a result of an emotional stimulus. Psychological research shows that the conflict between rational and emotional considerations occurs with all our decision making, and all too frequently emotion overrides rationality. For example, you might trade in the expectation of making a short-term profit but instead the trade goes pear-shaped and you're making a loss. In your planning you've considered this and have a planned exit strategy to minimise losses. However, when your exit condition is reached you don't follow your plan because emotion overrides rationality. You justify abandoning your plan with thoughts such as: 'If I sell now I'll make a loss but if I hold on for just a bit longer the price could rise again and I'll make a profit', or 'the price drop is probably a temporary one and will reverse', or 'I bet the current price is the lowest that will be reached and I don't want to be a mug and sell at the bottom of the market'.

When you look at it dispassionately you'll realise that th thoughts are really nothing more than wishful thinking. Fr personal experience I've found that the sharemarket has a way of ignoring my wishful thinking and goes its own merry way regardless of what I hope (or think) might occur.

Tip

The hardest part of planning your online trades is sticking to your plan. The less emotional you are about your trades the more successful you're likely to be.

Key points

⇨　You can trade online using the impulse method or planned method.

⇨　The most reliable method of online trading is to follow a plan you've thought about before initiating any trades.

⇨　Your plan should be written and not just some idea in your mind.

⇨　Your plan should consider three aspects of trading: entry, monitoring and exit.

⇨　In the entry aspect of your plan you need to write down what you intend to do and why you intend to do it.

⇨　Your plan should include the duration of the trade and the profit target you want to achieve during this time.

⇨　Your profit target should be realistic and take into account overall market performance. It's counterproductive to set unrealistically high targets that most likely won't be achieved, or to set targets that are too low so you miss out on the really good profits you could have made.

⇨　You can place a number of different types of online orders and your plan needs to consider which is the most suitable for the trade you're contemplating.

⇨ Your planned parcel value depends on the funds available to allocate to the trade and should be inversely proportional to the riskiness of the trade.

⇨ Take into account the minimum brokerage charge if you're planning low parcel value trades.

⇨ Parcel value dictates the number of shares you can purchase at the price you'll be paying.

⇨ You should plan an exit strategy for all trades before you initiate the trade.

⇨ You need to plan the method and frequency of your monitoring when you're considering a share trade and after you've purchased shares.

⇨ Consider automatic monitoring (particularly for speculative trades) by arranging for emails or SMS messages to be sent to your computer or mobile phone device base on price limits or when announcements are made.

⇨ In some cases (particularly for low-risk blue- or green-chip shares) you might plan a buy and hold strategy, but it's still a good idea to plan an exit to the trade if there's an unforseen change in fortunes.

⇨ Because online trading is so easy there's a temptation to overtrade in the belief that more trades will result in higher profits. This belief isn't substantiated in practice, and overtrading usually results in less profit.

⇨ There's a happy medium between undertrading (holding for too long) and overtrading, and you should plan for an optimum trading level.

⇨ Preparing a plan is relatively easy; sticking to the plan is the hard part.

⇨ Try to be rational rather than emotional when you trade and don't allow wishful thinking to override your planned strategies.

chapter 7

Trading shares online

In previous chapters I've outlined the different online brokers operating in Australia and how you can set up a trading account so you can access the trading facility to enable you to trade online. I've also discussed the planning I recommend you undertake prior to placing any orders, and the importance of planning an exit strategy for all your trades. I've also discussed the monitoring you should undertake before or after you've traded. Finally, I've discussed trading frequency and the two traps you can easily fall into: undertrading and overtrading.

In this chapter, I'll discuss the process of online trading; that is, the types of orders you can place online and how you do so. I'll look at online trading ASX-listed shares using CommSec for my examples, but the same basic principles apply to the trading of any other instrument with any online broker placing orders with any securities exchange.

Buying and selling

When share trading originated, buyers and sellers met at a common location (usually a coffee shop) and negotiated the trade as a private treaty (contract) between them. Later, share trading exchanges were developed where agents (brokers) acting for the buyers or sellers met and negotiated the trades. This took place on the trading floor and it was a very busy (and noisy) place. With the advent of computer technology, in Australia (and most of the world) trading floors became obsolete and most trading now takes place using an exchange trading software platform that matches buyers and sellers. The ASX trading platform is the ITS (Integrated Trading System) that all brokers can access to place trades, regardless of how their customers have contacted them or the software or trading platforms they provide for their customers.

The old trading floor was very similar to an auction room—a place where buyers and sellers met and competed so the buyers bought the shares they wanted at the lowest price they could obtain from competing sellers, and the sellers were able to sell their shares at the highest price offered by competing buyers. Even though share trading today is computerised, the basic principle remains the same and trading is essentially an auction between competing buyers and sellers, where trades occur when there's agreement between them about price and quantity.

Tip

There's no law preventing any person or organisation from entering into a private treaty with someone else in order to exchange or trade shares. In particular traders with high-value trade parcels often bypass securities exchanges and negotiate trades by private treaty. Recently, so called 'dark pools' have arisen; these are private exchanges operating outside the requirements of securities exchanges thereby avoiding paying exchange trading fees. As reported in Smart Investor *(May 2013) some large brokers now participate in the pools, including CommSec and E*TRADE.*

Bids and offers

The price a buyer is prepared to pay is known as the **bid** and the price a seller is prepared to accept is known as the **offer**. Interestingly, this terminology isn't necessarily the same as in everyday life where a buyer might say, 'I'll offer you $x'. In share trading the buyer's offer is always known as a bid.

The difference between the closest bids and offers is known as the **spread** and it can be as little as a fraction of a cent or as much as 20 cents or more.

Liquidity

For some shares there are lots of buyers and sellers, with bids and offers in the system at all times, so many trades occur each trading day (high volume) and this is known as high liquidity. Most shares listed with the ASX have high liquidity; however, for some shares there are few bids and offers in the system and few trades occur on a daily basis, and indeed no trades at all may take place for a day or two (or even longer). This is known as low liquidity and the shares are considered to be illiquid. These shares are usually the less well known ones or those where almost all the shares are owned by a small number of shareholders (often corporations).

As you might expect, with liquid shares there's usually a very low spread, whereas with illiquid shares the spread can be high.

Tip

Unless you have particular reason to trade them, I suggest you avoid illiquid shares. They are too difficult to trade at the price you may want when you want to do so.

Parcel value

If you want to place a sell order you can do so for any number of shares you own whatever the parcel value. However, if you own low-value shares—say 1000 shares that last traded for 1.5 cents each—you need to consider that the proceeds from the sale will be $15, and if the minimum brokerage is $20, to sell the shares will cost you more than you'll receive. If you want to buy some more shares in a stock you already own you can buy any number for any parcel value, but remember that the smaller the parcel value the greater the effect brokerage has on increasing the actual cost per share. If you want to buy some shares in a stock you don't already own there's a parcel limit size of $500; the order won't be accepted if the parcel value is lower than this.

Tip

Small parcel-value shares are a nuisance as the brokerage on a trade can make the trade a counterproductive exercise. Also, small parcel-value shares are a nuisance in your portfolio and also to the share registry.

Tick

The tick is the smallest price increment allowable by the ASX trading system for bids or offers and it varies according to the share price. At the time of writing, tick sizes are:

⇨   0.1 cents for share prices up to 10 cents

⇨   0.5 cents for share prices from 10 cents to $2.00

⇨   1 cent for share prices over $2.00.

For example, you can bid or offer 51.5 cents but you can't bid or offer 51.6 cents or 51.8 cents because for prices between 10 cents and $2.00 the tick increment is 0.5 cents.

Trading data

The majority of online brokers provide 'real time' trading data, rather than the 20-minute delay data common on public-access sites. In some cases the trading data available is 'dynamic data' that is automatically updated each time a trade takes place. If this is the case, it will be obvious because you'll see the screen change as each trade takes place on the exchange. More commonly, real-time data is available and it's current only at the exact time at which you access it.

Tip

If your broker is providing real-time trading data you may need to refresh the screen periodically in order to keep tabs on the latest trades.

Trading hours

ASX trading hours for normal trading are 10 am to 4 pm Sydney time on business days, and this is when normal trading takes place.

However, three hours before the market opens brokers can enter orders in the system but these won't transact until the market opens. There's also a short period of 10 minutes after the market closes when brokers can adjust or cancel orders. Remember that most brokers will accept your order at any time subject to certain conditions but the order won't transact if the market is closed.

Tip

As discussed in chapter 6, I suggest you don't place orders outside of normal trading hours (for the reasons I gave).

Order processing

The ASX trading system matches buyers and sellers, and trades occur when there's agreement between them about quantity and price. If there is more than one buyer or seller at a certain price, orders are transacted on a first-in–first-out (FIFO) basis. When there's no agreement on price but instead there is a difference (spread) between the closest bids and offers, orders are listed in price order sequence.

Tip

If you really want your order to jump the queue you can up the ante by the minimum tick amount and that will move your order above the top bid if you're buying or below the lowest offer if you're selling.

Email confirmation

Your online broker should give you the option of receiving an email confirmation of your order. This ensures that your order has been received by the broker and will be acted on according to your instructions. It also ensures that there's no foul up of any sort and that you're both in complete agreement about all the order details.

Tip

Arrange email confirmation of all your orders and ensure you check your emails after you place an order.

Contract note

When you enter into any legal trade it's regarded as a contract and there are legal implications. With shares, after the transaction occurs your broker will produce a contract note as documentary proof of the contract. With online brokers this is usually in electronic form and if you want a hard copy you'll have to print it. After the order transacts you should receive email confirmation with the contract note as an attachment.

Tip

It's a good idea to keep a hard copy of all your contract notes and to file them in date order. However, if you opt to keep only the electronic version make sure you keep a copy in an external memory device so you'll still have it in the event of a computer malfunction.

Order purging

When you place an online order that doesn't transact it won't stay in the market indefinitely and may be purged (either by your online broker or by the ASX). Expiry periods for orders vary with the type of order and with each online broker, but are commonly 20 or 21 trading days. Orders can be purged for other reasons, such as trading halts, takeovers or the shares going ex-dividend during the order period.

Tip

If you're unsure about the currency of any order, you can check by clicking the 'Order status' or similar tab on your online broking website.

Multiple-parcel order transacting

Usually your order will transact as a single parcel but that's not always the case. For example, suppose you place an order to buy 10 000 XYZ shares at a certain price. Let's say there was a seller for 4600 shares at this price. In this case your order will partially transact and you'll buy 4600 shares. The balance of your order for 5400 shares will remain open (and might not transact) unless another seller enters the market willing to sell XYZ shares at the same price. If this seller has 5400 or more shares for sale, the balance of your order will transact. In this case you've bought 10 000 XYZ shares in two parcels. However, if the seller has only 4000 shares to sell, you'll buy another parcel of this size, leaving a balance of 1400 shares. If another seller enters the market, the balance of your order will transact, thus fulfilling your order in three parcels.

When a single order transacts in more than one parcel, each parcel is regarded as a different transaction so each will be listed separately on the contract note. If the trades occur on different days, there'll be separate contract notes for each transaction. In such cases, there'll be different dates of acquisition (for buy trades) or disposal (for sell trades) and this can have capital gains tax implications.

CHESS (or the share registry) will automatically amalgamate parcels and your CHESS statement (or SRN statement) will show your total shareholding. Also, with most online brokers you won't pay additional brokerage (compared with buying the shares in a single parcel), provided you haven't changed any details (prices or quantities) from those in your original order.

Tip

In some rare cases, brokerage may be charged on a 'daily transaction' basis rather than on a 'per transacted order' basis. In such cases additional brokerage will apply when a single order transacts in separate parcels over separate days, so ensure you obtain an up-to-date fee structure if you are contemplating using a broker who's not using a conventional fee structure.

Order status

You're able to check the progress of your orders at any time by entering your online broking website and checking the current order status. You'll see details of any outstanding orders that haven't transacted. If your order doesn't transact, most likely you've specified a price outside of the current trading range and there are no sellers at your bid price, or no buyers at your offer price.

Amending or cancelling your order

Current order status or outstanding order status screens will have links that will allow you to amend or cancel your order if you wish to. I know of no broker (online or offline) who charges a fee for amending or cancelling an order not transacted. However, if you amend an order by changing the price or quantity after partial transaction, the amended order will be treated as a new order and will incur additional brokerage.

For example, suppose you place an order to buy 10 000 XYZ shares at $1.00. You obtain 5000 shares at this price but then the price rises to $1.10 and shows no indication of dropping back. You now feel there is little chance of obtaining the additional 5000 shares at $1.00 so you raise your bid to $1.10 and your order now transacts. In this case you'll have to pay full brokerage on each parcel.

Unfulfilled trades

If your order doesn't transact, three things could occur in the future:

⇨ Your order will transact at some time in the future as prices change.

⇨ Your order will pass the time-lapse date and will be automatically cancelled.

⇨ Your order will be cancelled (purged) if some change occurs. For example, your order will automatically be purged if the shares go ex-dividend while your order is still in the market. Automatic purging will also occur if you're trading contributing shares or options that pass through the expiry date before your order transacts or if there's a takeover or change of code or major restructuring of the company.

Tip

In your planning you should include a strategy for orders that don't transact. I suggest you don't leave orders in the market for more than a few days, particularly if the order involves speculative shares. If you cancel an order, you can re-evaluate it in the light of recent share price and market movements and re-examine whether indeed you still wish to proceed with the trade.

Example 1

You place a buy order for a parcel of shares but the price rises and your order doesn't transact. You leave your order in the market. A few days later the price reaches a peak, then starts to fall, soon reaching your bid price and now your order transacts. The result is that you've bought shares in a falling market—generally not a good strategy! Often the price will continue to track down until you note, with dismay, that you've bought the shares at a higher price than you could have had you cancelled your initial order and placed a new buy order at a later date after the share price had bottomed out.

The same type of scenario can occur when you place a sell order and leave it in the market when price tracks down. After a time, the shares recover and start tracking upward. Soon the price rises to your offer, at which point your shares are sold. The result is that you have sold your shares in a rising market—generally also not a good strategy! You've missed the additional profit you could have made as a result of the continuing price rise.

Tip

I suggest you don't leave an unfulfilled order in the market for an extended period unless you have very good reason to do so.

Trade price

Essentially buyers can bid whatever price they wish to pay and sellers can offer whatever price they want to obtain, but a trade won't occur unless agreement is reached between them. Agreement can be reached in two basic ways:

⇨ The buyer increases her bid price or decides to accept the seller's price.

⇨ The seller reduces his offer price or decides to accept the buyer's price.

Which of these will occur depends on the competition between buyers and sellers. The number of shares bid determines the demand and the number of offers determines the supply. According to traditional economic theory, the price will rise when demand (bids) exceeds supply and the price will fall when supply (offers) exceeds demand. This is illustrated in figure 7.1.

Figure 7.1: market price

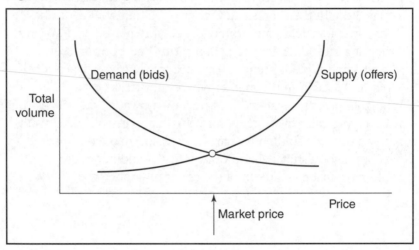

This theory is borne out in practice every day in the stock market and explains why share prices rise and fall. The price of a share rises when demand (bids) exceeds supply (offers) and falls when supply (offers) exceeds demand (bids). Buyers and sellers frequently change their bids and offers and they enter or leave the market periodically, so supply and demand are dynamic. This can cause the share price to change constantly, moving up or down as trading progresses.

Tip

You should always check the bids and offers at market before you place an order.

Trading transparency

Trading using a securities exchange is transparent; that is, anyone can access the trading platform and view the bids and offers in the system. You can also see the last trade price and how trade prices have moved throughout the day; that is, the trading history (known as the course of trades).

Just like in a public auction, transparency is a very important factor in share trading using an exchange as it allows everyone to see what everyone else is bidding or offering.

Tip

Just like an auction, share traders are influenced by other traders, so trade prices don't necessarily change in a way that's consistent with the intrinsic worth of a share but rather according to the mood of the market.

Key prices

There are five key prices of importance to traders. These are:

⇨ opening price: the price for the first trade of the day

⇨ last sale price: the price of the most recent trade

⇨ high price: the highest price reached

⇨ low price: the lowest price reached

⇨ closing price: the price of the last trade for the day.

Tip

Apart from the opening and closing price, the other prices can change constantly during a day's trading and sometimes dramatically. Naturally, the closing price won't be available until after the market has closed for the day.

Price variations

During the course of a day's trading there are many possible price change scenarios, including:

1   the price rises all day so the closing price is the highest price

2   the price falls all day so the closing price is the lowest price

3   the price rises, then falls
4   the price falls, then rises
5   the price rises, falls, then rises again
6   the price falls, rises, then falls again.

And so on…

These scenarios are illustrated in figure 7.2.

Figure 7.2: some daily price scenarios

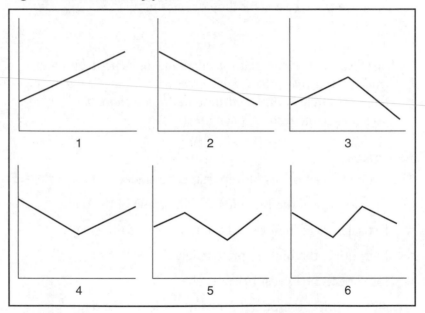

Tip

You might expect that the price moving in one direction all day (scenarios 1 and 2) is the most common one, but usually it's not. It's more common for prices to move both up and down during the course of a trading day. As well as prices changing in various ways during the course of a day's trading, they can also change in these ways (or others) over the longer term. This can become a trend, and I'll discuss trends in chapter 9.

Volume

When you look at daily share price variations, you need to also check volume as it can be an important factor. To see why, consider the following example.

Example 2

Trader A has 10 000 shares he wants to sell and Trader B has 500 shares she wants to sell. Buyers are in the market but the price they're offering is 5 cents below the last sale price. If Trader A decides to accept the buyer's bid, this will cause a profit drop of $500. On the other hand, for Trader B, accepting the buyer's bid will cause a profit drop of only $25—that isn't much at all in the total scheme of things.

Consequently, while Trader A will baulk at selling his shares with a price drop of 5 cents and incurring a $500 loss, Trader B will more happily accept the bid price and suffer the $25 loss.

The point of this example is that traders with relatively small numbers of shares to trade will often enter trades at prices significantly away from the last market price and thereby cause a relatively large share price change. (Remember that a share price is the price of the last trade.) These small-volume share trades result in share price changes that aren't really significant because the volume and trade value are relatively small.

Tip

When checking trade price movements you should consider volume in conjunction with price. Price movements on low volumes aren't nearly as significant as those that occur with high volumes.

Gaps

It would seem reasonable that yesterday's closing price would be today's opening price but that's not always the case—today's opening price may be either higher or lower than yesterday's close. This is known as a gap, which may be either up or down.

I've illustrated up and down gaps in figure 7.3, overleaf (Y = yesterday's close and T = today's open).

Figure 7.3: up and down gaps

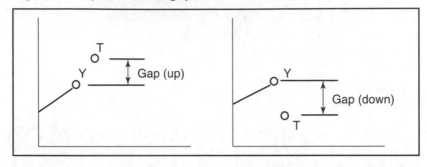

Gaps may have a number of causes, which may include the following:

⇨ There's some change (or rumour of a change) that becomes known when the market's closed.

⇨ Today is the ex-dividend day—the shares will almost always gap down by the amount of the dividend and usually also the value of any franking credits.

⇨ Trading in the shares takes place on overseas exchanges while our market's closed. In particular we tend to follow the trend set by the US market (Wall Street). Also remember that some Australian companies have shares listed on overseas exchanges as well as in Australia and the shares can trade while our market is closed.

⇨ World events that occur while our market's closed influence global markets and affect our market when it opens.

Tip

Small gaps aren't usually significant and are caused by normal fluctuating supply and demand in the market, but large gaps are usually significant and you need to investigate their cause.

Price spikes

Sometimes a share price will spike up or down dramatically during a day's trading, as shown in figure 7.4.

Figure 7.4: price spikes

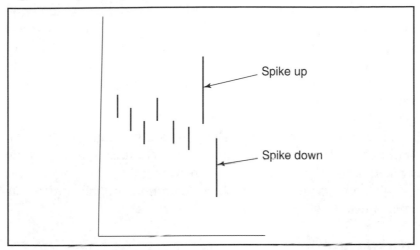

Price spikes are usually triggered by an announcement of a major impending change or rumour of such a change. Very often there's irrational optimism or pessimism about the change, and in such cases after the price spikes (either up or down) there'll be a subsequent correction as traders realise that prices have gone too far one way or the other. If it's spiked up, profit taking inevitably occurs as sellers scramble to cash in quick profits before the price falls, and if it's spiked down, buyers scramble to buy at a bargain price before the price bounces upward.

Tip

Beware of dramatic price spikes or gaps—they're danger signals for the inexperienced and it's usually best to stay away until there's a subsequent price stabilisation.

Order types

In chapter 6 I mentioned the three different types of online orders you can place when you want to trade shares, namely:

⇨ market order

⇨ limit order

⇨ conditional order.

There is actually a fourth type of order I didn't mention, and that's a short-sell order. Normally you place a sell order to sell some (or all) of the shares you own and all brokers will accept this order. With a short-sell order you place an order to sell shares you don't own with the intention of buying them at a later time, and in this way trading profitably in a falling market (not just a rising one). Many online brokers (including CommSec) won't accept short-sell orders.

If you want to profit in a falling market you can also do so by trading CFDs (contracts for difference), or futures or options with brokers who offer trading in these instruments.

I'll now look at the three common online orders in greater detail.

Market order

You place a market order when you agree to trade at the market price. That's to say, if you want to buy, you accept the lowest offer available for the shares, and if you want to sell you accept the highest bid.

The advantage of a market order is that the trade will transact very quickly (literally within a second or less) so there's no dilly-dallying and you can get on with whatever else you want to do, secure in the knowledge that you've traded the shares. It also means that you'll buy at a good price if the price rises and sell at a good price if the price falls.

The disadvantage of a market order is that you won't buy at a good price if the price falls after your trade or sell at a good price if the price rises after your trade. At the very least, for a buy order your bid will be above the highest current bidder and match the lowest offer. Similarly for a sell order your offer will be below the lowest current offer and match the highest bid.

Tip

If the market's liquid, the price difference when you place a market order won't usually be much and shouldn't be a very important consideration. It's usually not worth missing a trade by holding out for a very small price difference, and by placing a market order you're assured of the trade.

Using a market order

If you want to buy shares in a liquid stock at a time when the price is rising, a market order would be appropriate. The spread would most likely be small and you could safely place a market order knowing that you'd buy the shares at the last sale price or at a small premium to it. The market order would place you at the top of the list of buyers and in most cases your order would transact very quickly.

However, if the price is falling it would generally be prudent to wait before placing a market buy order—unless you have good reason to believe that the price has bottomed out and that the falling price is only a temporary aberration. Of course, if you wish to sell, all the opposite conditions apply and a market order to sell in a rising market is unwise, whereas it's the best strategy in a falling market, so you can offload quickly before the price falls further.

Tip

It's generally best to avoid placing a market sell order in a rising market or a market buy order in a falling one.

Limit order

You place a limit order when you specify a price limit, which is the highest price you're prepared to pay if you're buying and the lowest price you'll accept if you're selling. In a sense, you're ignoring the market and taking the attitude, 'I don't really care what others are doing, I'm setting my price and if I can't get my price I won't trade'. The advantage of a limit order is that you're setting your price, so you know exactly what price you'll get if the trade proceeds and the exact total value of the trade. You'll buy at a lower price than you'd get with a market order if the price falls to your limit, or sell at a higher price than you'd get with a market order if the price rises to your limit.

The main disadvantage of a limit order is that you're not assured of the trade. This means that you need to keep monitoring the market and keep tabs on the trades and your order status for some period after placing the order. It also means that you could miss out on the trade completely if the price moves away from your limit and doesn't return to it. If you want to trade later on, you'll probably have to amend your order and specify a new price that may be a far less favourable one.

Tip

Be aware that if your price is too far away from current price action, your broker may reject the order (as it will be regarded as unreasonable), or if the order does go to market it will be way down in the queue and may not show up on the market trading screen.

Example 3

You want to buy shares and trades are taking place at around $1.20, so you bid $1.18, hoping to pick up the shares at a good price if the price weakens. However, the price rises during the day and closes at $1.22. Next day, the price gaps up and the shares open at $1.25 and trade all day at around this price. Now what are you going to do? You have to decide if you'll amend your bid or leave your order as is. If you don't amend your order and the price continues to rise you'll miss out on the profit you could have made had you initially placed a market order and bought the shares for $1.20 or maybe $1.21.

Tip

If you place a limit order, you need to monitor the market closely and be prepared to amend your order quickly if the price moves away from your limit.

Conditional order

As the name suggests, a conditional order is one that won't be sent to market when you place it but at some later time and only then if some conditions you've specified are met. These conditions are known as 'trigger' conditions—a descriptive name because your order won't 'fire' unless the trigger is activated. So when you place a conditional order you need to specify the trigger conditions as well as the price and volume of shares you're planning to trade. Naturally, you can't place a conditional market order but only a conditional limit order.

The four most common types of conditional order are:

⇨ rising buy

⇨ falling buy

⇨ rising sell

⇨ falling sell.

I'll now discuss these orders.

Rising buy

Your buy order will trigger only if the price rises to your trigger price that's above the current trade price. The purpose of this order is to ensure you'll buy in a rising market.

Falling buy

Your buy order will trigger only if the price falls to your trigger price that's below the current trade price. The purpose of this order is to buy the shares you want at a lower price than the current market price.

Rising sell

This is also known as a 'profit stop' order. Your sell order will trigger only if the price rises to your trigger price that's above the current trade price. The purpose of this order is to take profits when your planned profit target is reached.

Falling sell

This is also known as a 'stop loss' order and it's the most common type of conditional order. Your sell order will trigger only if the price falls to your trigger price that's below the current trade price. The purpose of this order (as the name suggests) is to stop further losses if the price continues to fall.

More advanced conditional orders

Some online brokers offer more advanced conditional orders, including the following variations.

Price and volume order

In your trigger conditions you specify a minimum cumulative trading volume for the day as well as price. The idea of this is to ensure your order isn't triggered on low-volume trades that can cause unsustained price spikes.

Price and volume with delay

This is similar to a basic price and volume order except that you also specify a time delay after the market opens or a time period before it closes. The idea of this order is to prevent your order being triggered during the flurry of trading activity that usually occurs at opening and closing times.

Trailing sell

This is a stop-loss order with the trigger price automatically revised upward at the end of each day's trading if the price moves upward.

Trailing buy

The trigger price to buy is automatically revised at the end of each day's trading if the price moves (upward or downward) but doesn't reach the trigger price.

Straddle sell

You place both a trailing stop-loss and profit-stop simultaneously. The idea of this order is to allow you to take profits if the price rises to your profit target or stop losses if the price falls to your stop-loss point.

Buy then sell

You can combine any of the conditional buy orders with a straddle sell. Naturally, the sell orders won't go to market unless the buy order triggers first.

Tip

I suggest you don't place more sophisticated conditional orders until you become experienced with the simpler types.

Specifying trigger conditions

Conditional orders are more complex than conventional orders because you need to specify trigger conditions in addition to the normal price, volume and expiry limits. Specification of the trigger conditions requires greater financial expertise and knowledge of market trends. Even if you're planning to use the most common type of conditional order—that is, the stop-loss order—you need to carefully consider the trigger price in relation to current market price, the price you originally paid for the shares and your planned exit from the trade. If your trigger price is too close to the current market price (last trade) your order will most likely be rejected and you'll receive a message to this effect from the broker.

There are literally hundreds of different systems for setting stop-loss triggers, with varying degrees of complexity and claimed superiority. I've seen no factual evidence that a more complex system produces better results than a simple one. I use a simple 10% down from the purchase price when setting my stop-loss trigger as I've found that this works as well as any more complex system I've tried. Using the 10% down stop loss, if you buy speculative-type shares for $1.00 hoping for quick capital gains, you set your stop-loss trigger at 90 cents and exit the trade with a 10% loss if the price drops rather than rising as you hoped. On the other hand, if the share price rises to $1.10 and looks like continuing the upward trend, you can reset your trigger to $1.00, so at worst you'll exit the trade breaking even (apart from brokerage).

Note: I look at the charting aspects of loss and profit stops in the next chapter.

Tip

If you plan to use conditional orders, start out with simple criteria for setting your trigger points. You can advance to more complex criteria as you gain experience and feel there are benefits in doing so.

Should I use conditional orders?

There's no clear cut answer to this question as conditional orders have both advantages and disadvantages that I'll now outline.

Advantages

⇨   Conditional orders provide additional flexibility compared with ordinary limit or market orders and allow you to plan more sophisticated trading strategies.

⇨   Conditional orders such as stop-loss orders or profit stops allow you to minimise losses or crystallise paper profits.

⇨   You don't have to constantly monitor the market for the stocks you're interested in. Conditional orders allow you to essentially 'set and forget'. This is very useful if you have a busy job, or if there are any other times when keeping close tabs on the market is impractical (or impossible).

⇨   After you place a conditional order the emotion tends to be taken out of future trading decisions relating to that trade and you don't need to agonise because the trade will or will not transact depending on market forces. And the less emotional and the more disciplined you are about your trades the greater the likelihood of success.

Disadvantages

⇨   You can't place conditional orders (or all types of them) with all online brokers and not all offline brokers accept them either.

⇨   In times of rapid market movement, particularly when prices gap from one day to the next, conditional orders may be ineffectual as prices can shoot above or below your trigger limit and the trade won't transact. For example, you set a stop-loss trigger price of $1.02 and a limit price of $1.00 on a day when the shares are trading at $1.10. Next day, the shares open at $0.98 so your stop-loss order doesn't transact and your intention to sell on a price fall is ineffectual.

⇨   Often the market moves dramatically just after opening (as banked-up orders are transacted) and just before close (as day traders exit positions). A conditional order (without time delay) may be triggered at such times and at a price that doesn't hold up during normal trading activity.

⇨ Sometimes a conditional order will result in you selling at the very lowest price or buying at the very highest price (or close to them). This can occur when there's a significant price jump or fall during a day's trading that's only a temporary one but sufficient to trigger your order.

⇨ Many brokers (including CommSec) charge a fee in addition to brokerage for conditional orders and this considerably increases your trading cost.

Conclusion

You can see that the decision whether or not you should place conditional orders depends on several factors. While conditional orders (particularly stop-loss orders) seem a logical way to reduce losses and therefore increase profits, there's no factual evidence that this actually happens in practice or that use of other types of conditional orders actually increases overall trading profitability.

If you're not an active trader or you simply can't (or don't want to) monitor the market continually, conditional orders can be useful, especially if you're trading speculative shares. If you're an investor following a disciplined trading plan and regularly monitoring your investments, you're generally better off placing ordinary limit orders for your trades instead of conditional orders. If you're not short-term trading or have some blue-chip or green-chip stocks in your portfolio that pay good dividends and that have been good long-term investments there may be no point in setting conditional sell orders. After all, you don't want to sell good shares just because the market is going through a jittery phase unless some significant adverse change occurs that causes you to re-evaluate the investment.

Tip

If you're unsure whether to use conditional orders, it might be a good strategy to set them on a few of your more speculative stocks and monitor results; that is, did setting the conditional order improve or reduce your profitability? After some time you'll be in a better position to decide whether or not you want to use conditional orders on a regular basis.

Market screen

All online brokers provide a screen that shows the bids and offers (price and volume) at market for listed shares at the precise moment you access the screen. To progress to the market screen from the default home screen you need to enter the code (usually a three-letter one) for the shares.

Tip

Although share codes are usually capitalised, you don't need to use capital letters in order to access the market screen for the shares.

The default market screen with most online brokers shows real-time data, and you need to refresh the screen from time to time otherwise it won't show the most recent action. The screen shows bids and offers at market only and won't show conditional orders held by brokers that haven't yet triggered.

As well as current bids and offers, the market screen usually provides a summary of key trading data including opening price, high and low prices attained and trading volume.

Tip

Some online broking sites (including CommSec) have a default time disconnect so if you don't do anything within a reasonable time period you may be disconnected and you'll have to log back in again.

Typical market screen

An example of a market screen for a liquid stock—ANZ Bank (ANZ)—taken from the CommSec site is shown in figure 7.5.

On the CommSec site (as is typical with many online trading sites) 10 prices only are displayed on the screen. These are the buy and sell orders at prices closest to the last sale price and not necessarily a complete list of all orders at market. Some online brokers display 15 or 20 bid and offer prices and others show all (unlimited). Displaying 10 prices only isn't really a disadvantage because the orders not displayed are so far away from the current price action that they'll have no effect on current trading unless there's a dramatic change in market price.

Figure 7.5: market screen

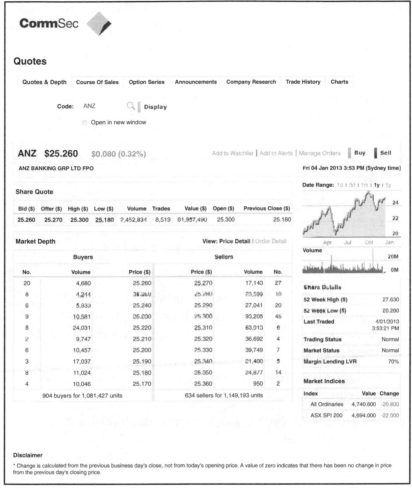

Source: www.CommSec.com.au

Interpreting the market screen

The market screen is very important when you're contemplating a trade so I'll now discuss it in some detail using figure 7.5 as my example.

At the very top of the screen the code (ANZ) is shown with the latest trade price ($25.26) and next to that the latest price change compared to yesterday's close is shown in dollars ($0.08) and as a percentage (0.32%). On the CommSec screen the price variation is shown in green if it's higher than yesterday's close and in red if it's lower. In this case it's in green so the price has risen.

On the next line is the name of the company and the time and date, in this case ANZ BANKING GRP LTD FPO Fri 04 Jan 2013 3:53 PM (Sydney time). The FPO notation after the name stands for fully paid ordinary shares.

Below the header information on the screen is a trades summary. Reading from left to right the trades summary shows you:

⇨ Bid ($25.26): the current highest price a buyer is prepared to pay.

⇨ Offer ($25.27): the current lowest price a seller is prepared to sell.

⇨ High ($25.30): the highest trade price so far today.

⇨ Low ($25.18): the lowest trade price so far today.

⇨ Volume (2 452 834): the total number of shares traded so far today. It's the number of shares bought or sold, as the number of shares bought must be exactly equal to the number of shares sold.

⇨ Trades (8519): the total number of trades in ANZ shares so far today.

⇨ Value ($61 957 490): the dollar value of all trades in ANZ shares so far today.

⇨ Open ($25.30): the price of the first trade today.

⇨ Previous close ($25.18): the price that ANZ shares closed at on the previous day (Thursday 3 January).

You can see that if you add today's price change of $0.08 to previous close of $25.18 you get $25.26 which is the latest trade price today.

Tip

ANZ Bank shares are liquid because many trades occur each day. As is typical of liquid shares, the spread (difference between highest bid and lowest offer) is very small—only

*1 cent for a share selling for over $25.00, which is only 0.04%.
If you access the trading screen for some other share and it
shows a small number of trades, and few buy or sell orders on
either side, with a comparatively large spread, this indicates
the shares are illiquid. As I mentioned in previous chapters,
it's best to avoid trading these unless you have a very good
reason to do so.*

Market depth table

Underneath the trades summary is the market depth table, which
is divided vertically into two. On the left hand side are the buy
quotes (bids) and on the right hand side the sell quotes (offers).

Looking at the bids, the first column tells you the number of
separate buy orders at each price. Next comes the total quantity
and finally the price is stated. The offer side is the same, except
that the order is reversed.

In this case you can see there were 20 buy orders for 4680
shares at a price of $25.26 and 27 sell orders for 17143 shares at
$25.27. The next line shows the next closest buy and sell orders
and so on as you move down the orders further away from the
current price action. At the bottom of the market depth table
is a summary of the total number of bids and offers at market.
This includes all those shown in the market depth table as well as
those that aren't shown—remember that CommSec displays only
10 bids and offers whose price is closest to current market action.
In this case the summary shows that there were a total of 904
buyers for 1081427 shares and 634 sellers for 1149193 shares.
The high number of bids and offers confirms the high liquidity of
ANZ shares.

Tip

*You will sometimes see the order quantity shown as 0/u which
indicates an order for an undisclosed quantity. Such orders
can be placed on large parcel values (at least $500000) and
are used when big traders don't want to reveal the number of
shares they want to trade. If you see this type of order you can
assume that if the price reaches the specified limit the order
will soak up a huge number of shares.*

Other information

On the CommSec site other information about ANZ shares is shown to the right of the market depth table. Firstly, there's a one-year price chart that gives you an impression of how the price of ANZ shares has trended over the last year. Below the price chart is a volume chart. I won't discuss these charts in detail here as I'll look at charting in some depth in chapter 9. The chart shown is too small and coarse to show the short-term trend in detail; however, you can see that after reaching a high in October the price fell for a while and now appears to be rising again.

Below the chart are some price details for the year to date which show ANZ shares reached a high of $27.63 and a low of $20.26. You're also shown the exact time of the last trade and market and trading status, both of which were normal. Below that is the LVR (loan to valuation ratio), which for ANZ shares is 70%; this is of relevance only if you're using a margin loan to buy the shares.

Finally below this information two market indices are given and these give you an idea of market action today. I'll discuss indices in detail in a later chapter, but you can see that today the market trended down. So ANZ shares bucked the market trend as they rose in value today.

Tip

This information given on the right of the market depth table is unique to CommSec and won't necessarily be shown on other broking sites, which may show other information or none at all.

Order specification

When placing an order you need to specify the number of shares you wish to trade, the parcel value and which of the three types of order you wish to place. As I suggested in the previous chapter, this should be part of your written trading plan and you should be referring to your plan as you contemplate placing the order.

Placing market or limit orders

If you've decided to now go ahead and place a market or limit order (go from thought to action) you need to progress from the market screen to the trading screen. On the CommSec site all you need to do is click on the 'buy' or 'sell' links shown at the top of the screen above the time and date and you'll progress to the trading screen.

A typical trading screen from the CommSec site is shown in figure 7.6A. In this case the shares are Telstra (TLS).

Figure 7.6A: trading screen

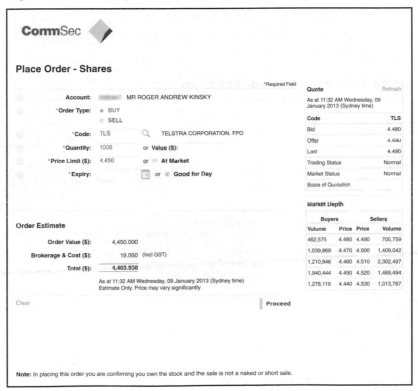

Source: www.CommSec.com.au

To place your order you need to enter the required details as follows:

⇨ *Buy or sell:* click on the appropriate one. If you've accessed the screen by clicking the 'buy' link on the market screen the trading screen will default to the buy setting but you can still change that to sell if you want to.

⇨ *Quantity or value:* you can enter the number of shares you want to trade or else the trade value. In figure 7.6A you can see I've placed a buy order for 1000 TLS shares. In figure 7.6B I've placed a buy order for TLS shares with a trade value of $5000. The software has calculated the number of shares to produce closest to this trade value and in this case it's 1123 shares. This won't work with market orders; you must specify a price before the software will calculate the number of shares for the trade value you specify. However, once you know the number of shares you can amend the order and change it to a market order if that's the type of order you wish to place.

Figure 7.6B: trading screen specifying value

Source: www.CommSec.com.au

⇨ *Price limit or market:* if placing a limit order you need to enter your price limit, or you can simply click the market order button if placing a market order. In this case, I've specified a price limit of $4.45.

⇨ *Expiry date for your order:* the CommSec default order expiry is 30 days but you can also choose 'good for day'. A calendar is provided so you can specify another order duration if you wish. In this case, I've specified 'good for day'.

Tip

I suggest you specify 'good for day' duration for all your orders or else don't leave your order at market for more than a few days.

Order estimate

Once you've filled out your order details an order estimate will be shown at the bottom of the screen showing the dollar value of your parcel, the brokerage fee and the total net parcel value. Note that if you place a buy order brokerage is added to the cost and if you place a sell order brokerage is deducted from the proceeds.

Tip

If you place a limit order the order estimate will be precise, but if you place a market order the order estimate won't be precise because the exact trade price of the shares can change if the market is moving rapidly before your order transacts.

Order transaction

To send your order to market you now need to click the 'proceed' button on the bottom of the screen. This will progress you to an order confirmation screen as shown in figure 7.7 (overleaf).

Figure 7.7: order confirmation screen

CommSec

Place Order - Shares

Details of your order instruction are shown below for your approval and confirmation.

Account:	███████ - MR ROGER ANDREW KINSKY
Order Type:	BUY
Code:	TLS
Description:	TELSTRA CORPORATION. FPO
Quantity:	1000
Price Limit ($):	At Limit (4.450)
Expiry:	Good for Day

Order Estimate

Order Value ($):	4,450.000	
Brokerage ($):	18.140	(excluding GST)
GST ($):	1.810	
Total ($):	4,469.950	

As at 11:35 AM Wednesday, 09 January 2013 (Sydney time)

Please check all details carefully before proceeding with this instruction.
This instruction will be actioned on the market only when trading in the security is open.

Change I Cancel   ▌ **Submit Order**

Note: In placing this order you are confirming you own the stock and the sale is not a naked or short sale.

Source: www.CommSec.com.au

This screen gives you the opportunity to review all details of your order, and outlines the contract you're about to enter into with your broker. If you click 'confirm' your order will now go to market, but if you're not completely satisfied you can click the 'change' or 'cancel' link. If you confirm the order it should transact very quickly if you've placed a market order. If you've placed a limit order it will go to market and be contained within the market screen that will change to reflect your order. Whether or not it transacts quickly (or at all) depends on how close your specified price is to the latest trade price and how quickly the market is moving.

Tip

Some brokers require an additional trading password before they'll accept your order.

Placing conditional orders

Some brokers (including CommSec) won't let you place conditional orders until you've read the PDS that details information about the various conditional orders available and the terms and conditions applying to them. Then you need to answer a short quiz in order to ensure you have a reasonable understanding of this. Once you've successfully negotiated these hurdles you're able to place conditional orders in the future without going through the procedure again.

To place conditional orders, you'll need to enter a dedicated area of the website. On the CommSec site you click on the trading link and then the conditional orders link which takes you to the screen shown in figure 7.8 (overleaf).

You then need to select from the options available or enter the required details as follows:

⇨ *Trigger type:* select from the four available options: falling sell, rising buy, falling buy or rising sell.

⇨ *Code:* enter the code of the shares you're planning to trade.

⇨ *Trigger price:* specify your trigger price.

⇨ *Trigger volume:* this is an optional condition where you can choose not to have your trigger fire unless your specified cumulative trading volume is reached.

Figure 7.8: typical conditional order screen

Source: www.CommSec.com.au

⇨ *Active option:* this is an optional condition that allows you to enter the time of day after or before which your order will be active for that day.

⇨ *Order details:* enter the normal details for a limit order; that is, the price and volume of the shares you want to trade and whether you want the order to be good for the day only or you choose the default expiry (20 trading days).

After you've completed these details, you'll be given an order estimate and you can proceed with the order by clicking on the 'proceed' tab or you can clear the order if you aren't satisfied with the estimate.

Amending a conditional order

If your conditional order doesn't transact within a reasonable time, you can amend or cancel it if you want to. This won't cost you anything if you've chosen the 'fee for transaction' option rather than the 'fee for placing order' option. With conditional orders, you're most likely to want to amend your trigger conditions if the market moves in a direction contrary to your expectations. In particular, you can reset a stop-loss trigger higher should the share price rise rather than fall.

Tip

It's a good strategy to reset a stop loss upward if the price rises, but you shouldn't revise it downward if the price falls. There's no point in using a stop-loss order if you don't stick to your original intention when the price falls.

Predicting short-term price changes

Naturally, if you want to buy or sell shares on a particular trading day, you'd like an idea of how prices might trend on the day before you place the order. One way of doing this is to use economic supply and demand theory in conjunction with the market screen by comparing buy and sell order quantities. If you look at the market screen for ANZ shown in figure 7.5 (see p. 175) and compare buy and sell quantities closest to the last sale price, you can see that there were buyers for 4680 shares at $25.26 and sellers for 17 143 shares at $25.27. The considerable excess of sell orders indicates the price is unlikely to rise above the last sale price of $25.26 and will most likely fall. Another clue is that the shares reached a high of $25.30 at some point, and because the last trade was at $25.26 the price must have fallen back from the high. The two closest bids to the last sale price were for a total of 8924 shares (4680 + 4244), whereas the two closest offers were for a total of 40 742 shares (17 143 + 23 599). That is, there was more than four times supply than demand at prices close to the last sale price. This reinforces the expectation that, on the balance of probabilities, the price is unlikely to rise and indeed is more likely to fall.

Another way you can get an idea of how the price is trending is to look at the course of trades. You can access this screen from the 'Quotes and research' tab on the CommSec site. A typical course of trades for TLS shares is shown in figure 7.9.

The CommSec site defaults to the last 20 trades but you can access the complete course of trades history on the day if you wish. For a liquid stock, such as TLS, after some time there'll be many trades and the complete course of trades can be a lengthy document. A more practical way of viewing the course of trades is to look at an intraday chart that displays the data in chart form. I'll discuss these charts in chapter 9.

On the CommSec course of trades data various notations are used in the 'Condition' column such as CX and NXXT. These conditions aren't of significance to you as they indicate whether the trade has taken place between two CommSec clients rather than between CommSec clients and the clients of another broker.

Figure 7.9: course of trades

Tip

It's a good idea to practise your skill at picking short-term market price movements by viewing the market screen and course of trades and making a prognosis, then checking an hour or two later to see whether your prognosis was correct.

Possible mistakes

When you trade online it's possible for mistakes to occur. Of course, it's possible to make a mistake with any method of trading but some mistakes are more likely when you trade online, basically because you're on your own and don't have a broker or share adviser with whom you can discuss your proposed trade and to check your trade details.

Possible mistakes that can occur with your online trades include:

⇨ trading the wrong shares

⇨ trading the wrong amount

⇨ trading at the wrong price

⇨ trading at the wrong time

⇨ your order not going to market

⇨ overtrading

⇨ exceeding your available funds

⇨ your order transacting at the wrong time

⇨ selling fewer shares than you intend.

Trading the wrong shares

When you trade shares you need to identify the shares with the three-letter code that identifies those shares, so if you happen to type in the wrong code you'll trade the wrong shares. However, this is a very unlikely mistake because when you type in the code most service providers show the name as well as the code. Therefore you should be alerted in case you happen to get the code wrong.

Trading the wrong amount

When trading shares you have to state both quantity and price, so if you inadvertently type in a wrong number the amount of shares in the order could be different to what you intended. This error is most likely and particularly unfortunate if you inadvertently add or omit a zero in the order quantity. This is most likely to occur if you're trading a large quantity of low-value shares (such as 250 000 shares at 3.5 cents each).

The best way of avoiding this error lies in the planning of your order, where you should plan both the number of shares you intend to trade and the value of the trade. In my example, 250 000 shares at 3.5 cents gives a trade value of $8750. If your order value came to $875, you'd know you'd omitted a zero, and if it came to $87 500, you'd know you'd inserted an additional zero.

Tip

Before you submit the order you should carefully check the total parcel value.

Trading at the wrong price

If you place a market order, the price is determined by market forces as the broker will attempt to buy at the lowest possible offer price and sell at the highest possible bid price. However, if you place a limit order, you decide the price and you need to state it when you place the order and it's possible that you could make a mistake when doing so. However, this type of mistake is unlikely as your online broker should send you an error message if your order price is too far away from the current market price and so be unlikely to transact in the foreseeable future. If you do happen to make a favourable mistake (such as too high a sell price, or too low a buy price), the only effect will be that your order won't transact unless the market moves significantly in a direction favourable to you—in which case your mistake could end up being a profitable one.

Trading at the wrong time

All details of your order may be correct but the timing of your order can be unfortunate. For example, you buy shares and the price subsequently falls or you sell shares and the price subsequently rises. Although you'll no doubt tell yourself that you've made a mistake, it isn't really one because no matter how careful you are this will happen from time to time. So you need to resign yourself to the fact that you can't get it right all the time and make every order a winner. Rather what you need to do is maximise your successes and minimise your failures, and to do this you need good planning before you place orders and to use technical analysis with trend identification (combined with fundamental analysis for longer term investments).

Tip

Use good planning based on fundamental and technical analysis to swing the probabilities in your favour. I'll discuss these types of analysis in following chapters.

Your order not going to market

It's possible that your order doesn't actually go to market; that is, it doesn't transmit from your computer (or mobile device) to the market. This could be because you inadvertently don't press the 'send' (or similar) button, or because of a glitch in your computer (or online device), or a glitch in your internet access system, your online broker's system or the securities exchange system.

While this error can occur, it's most unlikely, but nevertheless you need to exercise vigilance to ensure that your order does actually reach the market as soon as you confirm it and that it transmits in exactly the way you intended. The best way of doing so is to set up your communication system so that you receive email confirmation of your order from your broker as soon as your order is received by them.

Tip

After you've placed an order, check your emails immediately and ensure that your order has been received and accepted by the broker and that all details of it are correct.

Overtrading

As mentioned in chapter 6, because it's so cheap to place online orders you can make the mistake of overtrading. I won't discuss this further here but please refer back to my discussion of trading frequency in chapter 6.

Tip

While it's not profitable to hang on to shares that are going downhill you should continue holding shares when the price is rising, or even if the price is stable but they pay a good dividend. Be aware of the trap of overtrading and ensure you include consideration of trading frequency in your planning.

Exceeding your available funds

This is a buy order mistake that occurs should the total cost of your order (including brokerage) exceed your available funds. In some cases your broker's trading system may ignore the order and send you an error message but in other cases your order will process and you'll be required to quickly top up your funds. In the worse case, if you don't do so within a certain time the shares may be sold by the broker and you'll be liable for any cost deficit. To avoid this mistake you need to be aware of the fee structure and carefully calculate the total cost before submitting the order and ensure you have available funds to cover the cost of a buy order at settlement date.

It can get tricky when you sell shares and use the proceeds to cover all or some of the cost of a buy order. Remember that the cash for the sell transaction will take three business days to go into your account so you have to allow for that time delay. Also be aware that there can be a time delay if you're transferring funds from a bank account or depositing a cheque into your online trading account. I found out (to my great surprise and concern) that a bank cheque from the Commonwealth Bank took five business days to transfer into my CommSec trading account!

Tip

When transferring funds into your trading account you need to exercise vigilance to ensure the transfer occurs in time to cover the total buy order cost on settlement day.

Your order transacts at the wrong time

This is a mistake that can occur when you place a market order or a conditional order that doesn't transact because your price is away from the current market action. You leave your order in the system (and you may even forget about it, as I once did), and then get an email at some future date advising you that your order has transacted. In light of market action in the intervening period you realise that you didn't really want the order to transact and indeed you wouldn't have placed the order today with your most recent knowledge.

Tip

Make sure you follow up all orders that don't transact within a planned time period. Amend or cancel the order—don't leave it in the system for any appreciable length of time.

Selling fewer shares than you intend

When you want to sell all your shares in a particular stock there's a trap you can easily fall into if you've joined the DRP. This trap can arise because there's a delay of a month or so between the cut-off date for the payment of the dividend (ex-dividend date) and the actual date at which the dividend is paid—which in the case of the DRP is paid in shares. When you place the sell order you check your records and place your sell order to sell all the shares you're holding. All good, and the order transacts; however, if you've placed your sell order after the ex-dividend date you're still entitled to the dividend. Sometime later you get a dividend statement for a relatively small parcel of shares allocated to you under the DRP. These shares are more of a nuisance value than benefit (to both you and the share registry) because there's no point holding a small parcel and because selling a small parcel is relatively costly and may hardly be worthwhile.

Avoiding this trap

To avoid this error, there are two things you should do:

⇨ Before placing a sell order for dividend-paying shares you should always check the ex-dividend date. If you've joined the DRP be aware that you're entitled to the dividend in shares even if you sell after the ex-dividend date and ensure that your dividend share entitlement is included in your sell order quantity.

⇨ Always check your online portfolio with your online broker before you submit a sell order and make sure you know exactly the number of shares you hold or that you're entitled to.

Tip

Before placing a sell order always check the ex-dividend date and also confirm your shareholding by checking your online portfolio for the precise number of shares you hold.

General strategy for minimising the risk of online trading mistakes

Online trading mistakes are most likely to occur when you're rushing because you have limited time, or because the market is moving rapidly and you want to trade quickly, or when you're distracted by background noise or movement. I suggest that before you trade online you set aside the time you need and you sit down in a quiet place that's free from background noise or distractions. You should know exactly what you're intending to do—preferably in the form of a written trading plan that you refer to.

Tip

I find it's a good idea to make a cup of tea or coffee and sip slowly while mulling over your online trade. Provide yourself with a pencil or pen, a clean sheet of paper and a calculator, and don't rush—a few minutes here or there is unlikely to make that much difference!

Key points

⇨ Before you place any online orders, have a copy of your trading plan with you, and refer to it and stick to it.

⇨ Obtain email confirmation of your order and check it to ensure all details are correct.

⇨ If your order doesn't transact within a reasonable time period I suggest you review it and amend it or withdraw it.

⇨ If your order doesn't transact it may be purged.

⇨ Your order won't necessarily transact in a single parcel but you won't be charged additional brokerage unless this is part of the brokerage fee structure, but that's uncommon.

⇨ You can amend or cancel any type of order at any time and you shouldn't be charged additional brokerage unless this is part of the brokerage fee structure, but that's uncommon.

⇨ The market screen allows you to compare supply and demand. It's generally not a good practice to buy when there's an excess of sell orders around the last trade price or to sell when there's an excess of buy orders.

⇨ In addition to the market screen, course of trades data or an intraday chart can help you get a feel for the direction of the market.

⇨ Consider volume in addition to price movements as price changes on small volumes are often unsustainable.

⇨ The two most common types of orders are limit orders and market orders, and you're likely to use these for the majority of your trades. If you place a market order, your order will usually transact very quickly, but a limit order will transact only when the price reaches your limit.

⇨ Conditional orders (particularly stop-loss orders) are tools that you may wish to use, but they have both advantages and disadvantages. There's most likely a fee payable in addition to the normal brokerage.

⇨ Short-sell orders are a special type of order that's not available with many online brokers. If you want to profit in a falling market it's best to use CFDs or options.

⇨ Avoid placing orders when the market is closed unless you have special reasons. It's also usually a good strategy to wait a while after market opening before placing orders, as this allows time for the market to settle and for you to get a feel for market direction in general, or for that of any particular share you're contemplating trading.

⇨ Pay special attention to gaps and spikes before you place an order.

⇨ It's possible to make a mistake when you trade online. There are many possible mistakes that can occur, so you need to exercise vigilance. Make sure you take adequate precautions to ensure your order is correct in all details and that it transacts when you want it to. I've suggested several strategies for minimising the risk of mistakes. The best strategy of all is to ensure you plan your orders before you place them, and to allocate the time and find a quiet environment where you can concentrate without distractions.

chapter 8

Online fundamental analysis

In this chapter I'll describe fundamental analysis, which is part of a long-term approach to share investing based on the philosophy that if the basic foundations of a business are sound the business should do well in the long run and therefore so will the share price. I'll discuss how to obtain the fundamentals from the internet and how to interpret them and thereby improve your share investing profitability.

Using fundamental analysis

You use fundamental analysis when investigating shares as a medium or long-term investment. There's no point using it for short-term or speculative shares you plan to buy and sell quickly. Fundamental analysis doesn't help you get the timing right by picking the best times or prices to enter or exit a trade, but instead looks at long-term prospects based on the fundamentals of business. When you become a shareholder you're actually a part-owner of the business, and before you invest in any business for the longer term you need to ensure the business is a sound one.

Tip

The terms 'earnings' and 'profit' are key fundamental statistics but they actually mean the same thing.

Obtaining fundamental data

One approach that can be used to obtain fundamental data is the one you'd most likely use if you were thinking of purchasing a business. You would, no doubt, conduct an on-location investigation—talking to the management, customers, staff and suppliers, examining the books of account, financial records, projected sales and earnings, and so on. From this investigation you could form a very good impression of how good the business was and what its likely prospects were. Clearly, for the average stock market investor this approach isn't feasible, although it may be possible for large institutions, such as major stockbrokers or financial advisers, to do this.

For the average share investor the internet comes to the rescue because you can obtain the important fundamentals you want online. There are numerous websites that provide fundamental analysis data for shares you're interested in — please refer to chapter 3 where some of the most useful ones are listed. However, your online broker should also provide most of the data and this will usually be the most convenient source for you. I'll use the CommSec site for the fundamental data in my examples.

Tip

If you want to delve deeper into the derivation and significance of fundamental data, please refer to my book Teach Yourself About Shares.

Types of fundamental data

There are essentially two types of fundamental data relevant to a business:

⇨ general

⇨ financial.

General data

This is data such as:

⇨ Size of the business: is it small, medium or large?

⇨ Directors and managers of the business: who are they and what is their track record?

⇨ How long has the business been in operation and how long has it been a listed entity with shares?

⇨ What are the products of the business and how well are they accepted or well known in the marketplace?

Financial data

This is data such as:

⇨ revenue (or turnover) from sales of products

⇨ cost of producing and supplying products

⇨ the earnings (profit) or loss

⇨ capital invested in the business

⇨ assets and liabilities (both short term and long term).

Accounting periods

Company directors can make announcements at any time — indeed listing rules require that any key changes affecting a listed company are made available promptly to all investors. In Australia there are two official accounting periods for which all relevant financial data are compiled and published. Dividends (if any) are also paid to shareholders at the conclusion of each of these periods. These periods are:

⇨ interim period: the first six months of the financial year

⇨ final period: the last six months of the financial year.

Naturally, full-year data is the sum of the two and gives the financial performance for the total year. Most financial statistics will default to the full-year result unless stated otherwise.

Tip

Most Australian companies use a financial year ending 30 June but this isn't always the case so you need to check.

Reporting periods

As well as the official accounting periods, exchange listing rules may require a listed entity to compile financial information that must be submitted to the exchange by specified dates. In the case of the final report, this report is usually called the 'preliminary final report'. In addition, the company directors may issue trading and profit update announcements at any time when it's evident that some major change in the financial data is likely due to changing circumstances.

Tip

Financial reports — both official ones and directors' updates — provide a guide to company financial performance, and announced changes can have a major impact on the share price.

Types of financial data

Financial data can be presented in a number of ways:

⇨ total amount

⇨ per-share basis

⇨ as a ratio (or percentage)

⇨ snapshot

⇨ historical

⇨ dynamic

⇨ future.

Tip

When you examine financial data, make sure you know which of the above applies.

Total amount

The total amount is simply the total dollar value. For example, a company may report earnings of $a million for the financial year, or sales of $b million.

Per-share basis

The per-share basis is the total amount divided by the number of issued shares. For example, the earnings can be shown as $c per share and sales as $d per share.

> *Tip*
>
> *From a share investor's viewpoint, data calculated on a per-share basis is a more meaningful statistic than a total amount.*

As a ratio (or percentage)

Many financial statistics are expressed as ratios (or percentages) because a single value on its own doesn't provide a basis for evaluation or comparison. For example, the total dollar profit doesn't provide a good comparison of the profitability of one company compared with another because of size differences. Earnings are dependent on the size of the business—clearly the larger a business, the more profit it should make (in dollar terms). More meaningful earnings statistics can be obtained by dividing the profit by the value of the assets or by the shareholders' equity, thus giving the return on assets or return on equity. These are usually converted to a percentage by multiplying by 100. The percentage return on assets or equity are far more meaningful statistics that allow you to make a fair comparison between businesses of differing sizes.

> *Tip*
>
> *You get a better comparison between businesses of different sizes when you examine statistics that are expressed as a percentage (or ratio).*

Snapshot

As the name suggests, a snapshot statistic is one that applies to a given point in time only—usually the end of an accounting period. For example, a balance sheet shows snapshot statistics such as assets and liabilities at a point in time and doesn't provide data on how they have changed in the past or are changing at present.

If snapshot data is based on official financial reports, remember that official reporting periods are every six months. It usually takes several months to compile the data, so by the time it's published it's already several months out of date. This means that when you look at financial data based on a previous financial period it could be more than six months out of date. A lot can change in a time period of this length. This sometimes explains the dramatic collapses of companies (even large ones) that appear to come 'out of the blue' as they're not evident in the published financial information.

Tip

Despite comprehensive financial regulation by both the government and securities exchanges, some companies have been found guilty of 'cooking the books' or massaging financial results to make them look better through 'creative accounting'. It's unlikely that sound blue- or green-chip companies engage in these practices, and you can feel confident that their announced results are a true reflection of actual results.

Historical

Historical data is data compiled for a number of past accounting periods. Examination of historical data enables you to form an impression of trends; that is, how the data has changed with time. I'll look at this in greater detail a little later in this chapter.

Tip

It's most important to look at trends as well as snapshots. That's a reason why IPOs are more risky because there are no past statistics as a publicly listed company that allow you to form an impression of trends.

Dynamic

Dynamic data is data that's constantly changing. Each day a company is in business fundamentals change, but this won't be reflected in many financial statistics because they're compiled at specific periods of time and don't allow you to see what's changed since the last reporting period. However, some statistics, such as the price/earnings ratio, are dynamic because they're based on share price. Because the share price can constantly change, this statistic will be a dynamic one and change with each change in trade price.

Tip

A dynamic statistic such as the price/earnings ratio will change with each change in share price, but remember the change reflects the change in share price only and not any dynamic change in earnings.

Future

Share investors and traders are interested in past performance but they're even more interested in future performance. To help you to get an idea of likely future performance, financial analysts estimate some future financial statistics and these are published on some websites.

Tip

Just because a forward estimate appears on a credible website (such as your online broker's site), it doesn't mean that the estimate will be reliable. No-one can predict the future with any certainty and financial advisers are no exception.

Financial fundamentals that affect a share price

For a share investor, the most important fundamentals are those that are significant drivers of the share price. There are many financial fundamentals that affect a share price but the main one is the company profitability as measured by earnings per share (EPS). It's true that the dividend yield is also of major importance to many investors and may be an important factor driving a share price, but the fact of the matter is that a company can't pay a good dividend unless it's making enough profit to be able to do so. If a company continues to dip into cash in the bank or sell assets to pay dividends, that company will eventually go bankrupt. It's just the same as if you use an existing bank account to fund your expenses but don't deposit any more money into the account—eventually you'll run out of money.

While investors look at current and historical earnings, in reality these provide a guide only—what drives a share price is primarily investors' perceptions of future EPS. Therefore, we can state a vital principle underlying share price changes:

A share price is likely to rise when a change occurs that investors perceive will result in an increase in EPS and it will fall when investors perceive the change will cause a decrease in EPS.

Tip

Today's investor cannot profit from yesterday's earnings so future earnings potential is far more important than current or past earnings.

Facts and rumours

We'd all like to think that we (and other investors) make rational trading decisions based on sound factual data, and there's a theory called the efficient market theory that says this is how the market works. However, this theory has been largely discredited because it's been found that perceptions about the future are often based on rumour or hype and have little factual basis. This is particularly true regarding the more speculative types of shares. However, the price of any share is likely to change when news (or rumour) of a change first hits the market, and this is often well before any official announcement is made.

Despite all attempts to stamp out insider trading, it is inevitable that some people have access to privileged information and this often filters down and affects the market well before the information is officially released. Subsequently, when an announcement is made and the information becomes official and is known to all, the market may react in the opposite way to what would appear logical. For example, a favourable announcement such as an increase in earnings may result in a share price fall on the day it is made, and vice versa! This usually occurs because the information has already been pre-empted by the market and factored into the share price, which rose in the period prior to the announcement.

Tip

If you're an investor rather than a short-term trader, I suggest you ignore rumours and try not to get caught up in market hype but rather adopt a more sensible and logical approach to your trades.

Fundamental data on the CommSec site

The data on the CommSec site is provided by the data provider Morningstar. You can access the fundamental data on the CommSec site by entering the company code and then clicking the 'Company research' tab. The following major links are provided:

⇨ key measures

⇨ forecasts

⇨ financials

⇨ company info

⇨ announcements

⇨ analysis

⇨ peer analysis

⇨ dividends

⇨ directors

⇨ corporate calendar

⇨ shareholders

⇨ warrants

⇨ research library

⇨ charts.

Key measures

This is a summary of the main financial details you'll be most interested in. I'll discuss this screen in greater detail shortly.

Forecasts

This summary contains some historical information such as earnings surprises (that is, the extent to which actual results conformed to market expectations) and also a panel of analysts' views in categories ranging from 'strong buy' to 'strong sell'.

Tip

A forecast (even the best one) isn't necessarily an accurate prediction of the future. Indeed I once found that a share rated as a 'strong buy' by most analysts turned out to be a lemon within a short time.

Financials

This is a most important screen as it provides historical financial information over the last 10 years of the company's operation. Naturally, if a company hasn't been in business for 10 years the screen will show a lesser number of years. The top section of the screen shows the 'per share' statistics (unless otherwise stated) and below this other vital financial information is shown in total.

Tip

This screen is a most valuable one as it allows you to see trends as well as current important financial data.

Company info

This screen provides useful summaries about the company that are vital to fundamental analysis. It gives information such as who's the chairperson, the company address, phone number, website and whether or not there's a DRP in operation for dividends. There's also a short business summary that outlines the business the company is in and a company strategy that outlines some key data and plans the company has for future profit growth. There's also a link to a PDF file 'company wrap' that provides a one-page summary including key financial details and a chart, and that's well worth a look.

Tip

If you're interested in longer term investing, the information given in this screen is most valuable. It's also well worth checking out the 'company wrap' as this provides an excellent one-page summary.

Announcements

This screen allows you to see company announcements. The default value is the last 10 announcements but you can also choose 'all' or view announcements over a period you specify. There's a 'price sensitive' column where announcements that are considered to impact market price are ticked. If you wish to read the announcement you'll need to click on it.

Tip

In some cases if you want to read the announcement you'll be directed to the ASX site. Look at the length of the announcement as some of them can be many pages long and it can be very time consuming to read all of them. You can simplify your research by looking only at those that are marked as price sensitive.

Analysis

This screen provides historical earnings per share, as well as segment performance and details of geographical income breakdown.

Peer analysis

This screen provides a comparison of key financial statistics of the company compared to others in the same sector.

Dividends

This screen provides interim and final dividend details for the last three years, including ex-dividend dates and pay dates.

Tip

When you're contemplating buying or selling shares that pay a substantial dividend, it's most important you check the ex-dividend date of the next dividend. If the dividend hasn't yet been declared you can get a good idea of the likely ex-dividend date from past ex-dividend dates.

Directors

This screen lists present and past directors of the company, present company executives and details of the number of shares held by each of them.

Corporate calendar

This screen provides dates (or estimates) of when key financial reports will be released.

Shareholders

This screen gives you an idea of the major shareholders in the company and their relatively recent transactions in buying additional shares or selling some of the shares held.

Tip

When major shareholders buy or sell a significant proportion of their shares this transaction should also appear in the company announcements. A significant increase in the number of shares held by major shareholders generally bodes well for the share price whereas substantial selling could herald (or accompany) a fall in share price.

Warrants and research library

In order to access these screens you need to be a premium subscriber.

Charts

This screen links to the CommSec charting facility. I won't discuss this further here as the next chapter explains charting in some detail.

Key measures

I'll now look in greater detail at financial data obtained online from the CommSec website (that they call 'Key measures'). I'm using as my example the company Flight Centre (FLT). See figure 8.1.

Figure 8.1: key measures for FLT

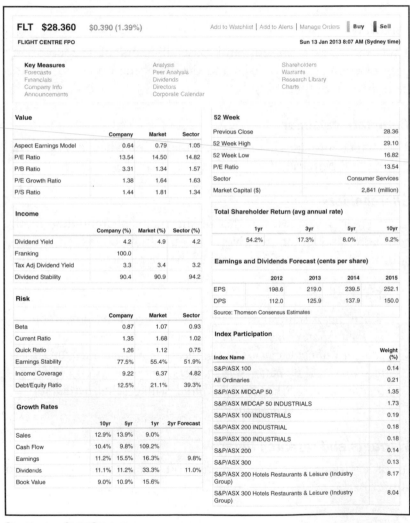

FLT $28.360 $0.390 (1.39%)

Add to Watchlist | Add to Alerts | Manage Orders | **Buy** | **Sell**

FLIGHT CENTRE FPO

Sun 13 Jan 2013 8:07 AM (Sydney time)

Key Measures
Forecasts
Financials
Company Info
Announcements

Analysis
Peer Analysis
Dividends
Directors
Corporate Calendar

Shareholders
Warrants
Research Library
Charts

Value

	Company	Market	Sector
Aspect Earnings Model	0.64	0.79	1.05
P/E Ratio	13.54	14.50	14.82
P/B Ratio	3.31	1.34	1.57
P/E Growth Ratio	1.38	1.64	1.63
P/S Ratio	1.44	1.81	1.34

Income

	Company (%)	Market (%)	Sector (%)
Dividend Yield	4.2	4.9	4.2
Franking	100.0		
Tax Adj Dividend Yield	3.3	3.4	3.2
Dividend Stability	90.4	90.9	94.2

Risk

	Company	Market	Sector
Beta	0.87	1.07	0.93
Current Ratio	1.35	1.68	1.02
Quick Ratio	1.26	1.12	0.75
Earnings Stability	77.5%	55.4%	51.9%
Income Coverage	9.22	6.37	4.82
Debt/Equity Ratio	12.5%	21.1%	39.3%

Growth Rates

	10yr	5yr	1yr	2yr Forecast
Sales	12.9%	13.9%	9.0%	
Cash Flow	10.4%	9.8%	109.2%	
Earnings	11.2%	15.5%	16.3%	9.8%
Dividends	11.1%	11.2%	33.3%	11.0%
Book Value	9.0%	10.9%	15.6%	

52 Week

Previous Close	28.36
52 Week High	29.10
52 Week Low	16.82
P/E Ratio	13.54
Sector	Consumer Services
Market Capital ($)	2,841 (million)

Total Shareholder Return (avg annual rate)

1yr	3yr	5yr	10yr
54.2%	17.3%	8.0%	6.2%

Earnings and Dividends Forecast (cents per share)

	2012	2013	2014	2015
EPS	198.6	219.0	239.5	252.1
DPS	112.0	125.9	137.9	150.0

Source: Thomson Consensus Estimates

Index Participation

Index Name	Weight (%)
S&P/ASX 100	0.14
All Ordinaries	0.21
S&P/ASX MIDCAP 50	1.35
S&P/ASX MIDCAP 50 INDUSTRIALS	1.73
S&P/ASX 100 INDUSTRIALS	0.19
S&P/ASX 200 INDUSTRIAL	0.18
S&P/ASX 300 INDUSTRIALS	0.18
S&P/ASX 200	0.14
S&P/ASX 300	0.13
S&P/ASX 200 Hotels Restaurants & Leisure (Industry Group)	8.17
S&P/ASX 300 Hotels Restaurants & Leisure (Industry Group)	8.04

Source: www.CommSec.com.au

I'll now step you through the data as it's presented. Note that for some of the data on the left hand side of the screen CommSec has three headings: Company, Market and Sector. The company data is relevant to the particular company (in this case FLT), the market data is for the market as a whole, and the sector data is for the particular sector the company is in, which for FLT is Consumer Services.

Value

Aspect earnings model

This ratio is the current share price divided by the intrinsic share value, as determined by a model used by Morningstar. A ratio less than 1 indicates undervaluation and a ratio greater than 1 indicates overvaluation. For FLT you can see that the ratio is 0.64 which is considerably less than both market and sector values, indicating that, according to the valuation model, FLT is undervalued. This indicates that there's potential for the price to rise above the current last trade price of $28.36.

P/E ratio

Known also as 'PE', this is the share price divided by the earnings per share. It provides a measure of price value or 'fairness' as reflected by earnings. That's to say, the higher the P/E the more 'expensive' the share and the lower the P/E the less 'expensive'. For FLT, the P/E is 13.54, which appears fair value as it's a little below both market and sector P/Es.

P/B ratio

The P/B ratio is the ratio of the current share price divided by the per-share book value of the assets. A ratio of 1.00 means that, theoretically, in the event of liquidation, share investors would break even as the assets per share equals the share price. For most shares, this ratio is usually greater than 1.00 because investors look toward the profit-generating ability of the assets and this should be greater than the asset value itself. For FLT, the P/B ratio is considerably higher than the market or sector ratio, indicating that the company is seen by investors as being capable of generating high profits from their assets.

P/E growth ratio (PEG)

A difficulty with using P/E to evaluate the 'fairness' or value of a share price is that it's based on past earnings. As we have seen, investors are far more concerned about future earnings prospects than history.

A way of taking the future earnings growth prospects into account is by means of the P/E growth ratio (also known a PEG), which is the P/E divided by the expected growth in earnings per share (EPS).

Using this ratio, the 'fairness' of a P/E is evaluated as follows:

⇨ Fair value stock: PEG = 1 (approximately)

⇨ Underpriced stock (good value): PEG < 1

⇨ Overpriced stock: PEG > 1.

The PEG for FLT is 1.38, indicating that the shares are overpriced relative to forecast earnings. However, the P/E is not unreasonable considering that it's less than both the market and sector values.

P/S ratio

The P/S ratio is the share price divided by the sales per share. Like PEG the lower it is the 'fairer' the value. For FLT it's 1.44, which seems reasonable as it's lower than the market average and only just a little higher than the sector average.

Income
Dividend yield (yield)

The yield is the annual dividend per share divided by the share price and converted to a percentage. It's equivalent to interest on the capital a shareholder receives by purchasing the shares at their current price. For FLT this is 4.2%, which is reasonable as it's equal to sector yield but is less than market yield.

Tip

Dividend yield is based on the share price and is a dynamic statistic as it depends on the share price. A rising share price will reduce the yield and vice versa.

Franking

Franking is the percentage imputation (or franking) credits investors can claim on their tax return for dividend income, and it can vary between 0 and 100%. For FLT it's 100%, which is the best outcome for an investor as it provides the maximum tax rebate (offset) possible.

Tip

100% franking is also known as 'fully franked'.

Tax adjusted dividend yield

This is the after-tax dividend yield investors on the top marginal tax rate of 48.5% will receive after paying tax on their dividend income. It takes into account the imputation credits associated with the dividend. Investors on a lower tax rate will receive a higher after-tax dividend yield than is indicated by this statistic.

Tip

I consider the most important yield statistic to be the grossed-up yield as this allows you to compare yields from different shares on a true 'apples to apples' basis. Unfortunately, CommSec doesn't provide the grossed-up yield and you'll need to calculate it for yourself by multiplying the yield by the grossing-up factor (as described in chapter 1).

Dividend stability

Dividend stability is a percentage that gives an indication of the stability of the dividend based on the last 10 years' performance of the company (or less if the data isn't available). It's the number of times the dividend has been cut, multiplied by the average size of the cut. Dividend stability can have a maximum value of 100%, indicating that there's never been a cut in dividend. For FLT it's 90.4%, which is good and about equal to the market average but a little less than the sector average.

Risk

Beta

Beta is a measure of price volatility and it's calculated by a rather complex statistical regression method that I won't go into. The bottom line is that the beta value provides an estimate of the volatility of a share price relative to the overall market (as indicated by a sample number of stocks). A beta greater than 1.00 indicates higher volatility than the market as a whole, whereas a beta of less than 1.00 indicates lower volatility. Clearly for a long-term investor a low beta value indicates a relatively safe investment with low likelihood of dramatic changes in share price. For FLT the beta value is 0.87, which indicates that the price of FLT shares has been relatively stable in the past.

Tip

Logically you'd expect the market beta to be 1.00, but actually you can see it's higher. Clearly this must be due to the way the algorithm calculates beta and the stocks that are included in the sample when market volatility is calculated.

Current ratio

The current ratio measures the immediate financial viability of a business; that is, the ability of the business to repay its immediate debts. Current ratio is calculated by dividing current assets by current liabilities.

'Current assets' essentially refers to short-term assets that can be readily converted into cash, as opposed to long-term assets—such as land and buildings—that aren't so readily converted into cash. Similarly, 'current liabilities' are liabilities or debts that need to be repaid in the short term. For example, a long-term loan is a liability but not a 'current liability', whereas the interest due on the loan each month certainly is a current liability.

A current ratio of greater than 2.00 can be regarded as healthy but the higher the better. A value less than 1.00 is decidedly unhealthy. For FLT the current ratio is 1.35, which isn't as high as investors would like and below the market average of 1.68 but higher than sector average of 1.02.

Quick ratio

The quick ratio is regarded as the acid test of financial viability. It is similar to the current ratio except that it's calculated by excluding inventories from the value of current assets—the idea being that when the chips are down, inventories owned by a company may not readily be converted to cash as there mightn't be any buyers! The quick ratio will always be less than the current ratio but it should be greater than 1.00. For FLT the quick ratio is 1.26, which is good and better than both the market and sector averages.

Earnings stability

This is a measure of the stability of the growth of earnings from year to year expressed as a percentage. The maximum figure of 100% represents maximum stability and earnings that go up (or down) by the same percentage each year. A low figure means the company's earnings are more volatile and vary significantly from year to year. It's calculated with a minimum of four years of data, two of which can be forecast earnings per share. You can see that for FLT the stability figure is 77.5%, which although less than 100% is considerably better than both market and sector values.

Income coverage (IC)

This term on the CommSec site is a little confusing as it really should be 'interest cover'—it's a measure of the indebtedness of a company and, in particular, how well it can cover the interest payable on loans from its profits. It's calculated by dividing EBIT (earnings before interest and tax) by the interest payable on loans, and includes non-operating income but excludes abnormal profits or losses.

A high IC figure (anything greater than about three) can be considered comfortable. Anything much lower than this indicates that too much of the company profits are used to pay interest on loans. This isn't a good situation because it means that there are insufficient funds left over from the profits to put into reserves or to distribute to shareholders.

For FLT interest cover is 9.22, which is a high figure and above market and sector averages. This indicates that the company has a low level of long-term debt and can comfortably cover interest on loans from earnings.

Debt/Equity (DE) ratio

DE is calculated by dividing long-term debt by shareholders' equity and converting to a percentage. Like income cover, the

DE ratio is a measure of the indebtedness of a business. It's also known as gearing, and companies with a high DE are said to be highly geared. DE measures the amount of capital in the business obtained by loans (loan capital) compared to the amount provided by shareholders and reserves (equity capital).

As a rule of thumb, a DE less than 100% is comfortable but a DE significantly higher than 100% indicates a highly geared company that's obtaining a large amount of its capital through loans. For FLT it's 12.25%, which is a very comfortable figure and lower than both market and sector values.

Notes:

⇨ IC and DE both measure the amount of debt (or the gearing) and they inversely correlate with one another—a highly geared stock has a low IC and a high DE.

⇨ Long-term debt is basically loan capital (that is, interest-bearing debt) and doesn't include business creditors (short-term, non-interest-bearing debt).

Tip

Experience shows that highly geared businesses are usually the first to go under should there be a downturn in the economy and they take the longest to recover (if indeed they do). Hence, IC and DE are measures of risk, and a low IC and a high DE indicates a stock that is more risky than one with a higher IC and a lower DE (particularly in the same sector).

Growth rates

Here the CommSec site shows the growth in sales, cash flow, earnings, dividends and book value (assets) over the last 10 years, 5 years and 1 year. Also earnings and dividend forecasts are shown. The growth rates give you a snapshot summary of changes in these important financial statistics but you can get a better picture by looking at the actual historical data (as I'll do shortly).

Moving now to the right hand side of the screen you can see how the share price has changed over the last 52 weeks and an indication of the sector. The market capitalisation (market cap) is also shown.

Market capitalisation

Market capitalisation is a very widely used statistic because it gives an indication of the size of a business relative to others in terms of the amount of dollars invested in it. Market capitalisation is calculated by multiplying the number of issued shares by the share price.

Market capitalisation is related to the size of Australian companies in the following way:

⇨ micro: less than $10 million

⇨ small: $10 million to $100 million

⇨ medium: $100 million to $1 billion

⇨ large: $1 billion to $10 billion

⇨ major: more than $10 billion.

You can see that the market capitalisation of FLT is $2.841 billion which makes it a large company.

When a share price falls rapidly it might be reported in the media that 'investors wiped $10 million off the value of the company.' This announcement means that the market capitalisation dropped by $10 million.

Tip

Market capitalisation provides a guide to risk. This is because the more speculative (and risky) shares are associated with businesses that have a low market capitalisation, whereas blue- or green-chip shares have high market caps.

Total shareholder return

The total shareholder return is the total return (capital gains and dividends) a shareholder would have received who bought the shares at their closing share price 1, 3, 5 or 10 years ago. It's calculated pre-tax, so doesn't include the value of imputation credits. You can see that over the last year and the last three years FLT was a good investment, and at none of the four time periods would an investor have lost money on the shares.

Tip

Total shareholder return provides a good guide to the likely profitability of a share investment. Shares that have given shareholders good returns in the past are most likely to continue doing so in the future.

Earnings and dividends forecast

This is a forecast of earnings and dividends per share at the end of each financial year for the next three years. The forecasts have been provided by an external analyst, in this case Tompson Consensus Estimates. You can see that for FLT an increase in both earnings and dividends has been forecast.

Tip

As an investor, you want to see an increase in EPS and DPS in future years as these drive the share price. Bear in mind, however, my previous tip about forecasts. In particular, I wouldn't place too much reliability on a financial forecast going forward for more than a year as a lot can happen in the world of business and economics in two or three years' time.

Index participation

In the next box you can see the indices in which the FLT is included and the extent of the inclusion. I'll discuss indices further in a later chapter but you can see that FLT constitutes only 0.21% of the All Ords (S&P/ASX 500) but makes up over 8% of the industry sector—in this case Hotels, Restaurants and Leisure.

Tip

Index participation is related to the market cap, and the larger the market cap the greater the index participation.

Company historicals

As I've already said, it's important to look at historical data as well as current data, and the future is far more important than the past. However, historical data provides an excellent way of forming an impression of the most likely future performance. We use this principle in everyday life; for example, we refer to a person's track record (in all aspects of life) to assess the likelihood of them performing well in the future. The same principle applies to company performance, and while historical data isn't infallible it provides the most reliable indicator of future results.

Tip

While it's not foolproof, there's no doubt that a good, reliable track record is a very good indicator of future performance.

End-of-financial-year historical data for the last 10 years is given on the CommSec site in the 'Financials' link. There are two tables: the top table entitled 'Company historicals' and the bottom one entitled 'Historical financials'.

There's a lot of data in these tables and you probably won't want to examine all of it in detail but you can look along the lines to form an impression of trends over time.

Tip

The historical data shown in figure 8.2 (overleaf) is end-of-year data and therefore can be considerably out of date when you access it. For example, for FLT, figure 8.1 (see p. 208), shows a one-year total shareholder return (at 13 January 2013) of 54.2%, whereas figure 8.2 shows a total shareholder return at the end of 2012 of −8.3% — a huge difference in a period of just over six months! This difference is because FLT shares had a big price rise from 30 June 2012 to 13 January 2013, when the share price rose from $18.93 to $28.36 — an increase of 50%.

Figure 8.2: historical data for FLT

Company Historicals

Per Share Statistics	2003/06	2004/06	2005/06	2006/06	2007/06	2008/06	2009/06	2010/06	2011/06	2012/06
Sales ($)	6.61	8.24	9.22	10.31	10.29	14.43	16.84	17.55	18.10	19.74
Cash Flow (cents)	138.8	195.4	124.6	130.0	211.8	401.1	-12.6	241.3	161.8	338.5
Earnings (cents)	76.4	89.4	71.9	84.5	96.6	146.5	98.0	138.8	170.8	198.6
Dividends (cents)	43.5	61.0	50.5	52.0	66.0	86.0	9.0	70.0	84.0	112.0
Franking (%)	100	100	100	100	100	100	100	100	100	100
Capital Spending (cents)	-43.3	-63.6	-54.3	-38.1	-43.1	-125.0	-79.5	-20.3	-47.4	-55.1
Book Value ($)	3.94	4.51	4.10	4.35	5.10	6.07	6.13	7.12	7.41	8.57
Shares Outstanding (m)	93.3	94.0	94.5	94.5	94.5	99.6	99.6	99.8	100.0	100.0
Avge Annual PE Ratio(%)	28.6	23.1	24.2	14.1	15.9	15.7	11.2	11.9	12.9	9.9
Relative P/E (%)	216.7	163.7	159.8	100.8	108.4	100.9	105.8	93.3	97.4	81.0
Total Return (%)	-17.5	-11.2	-22.6	-26.4	100.3	-9.7	-45.9	94.6	34.7	-8.3
+/- Market (%)	-16.4	-33.6	-47.3	-50.6	70.0	2.4	-23.7	80.9	22.5	-1.3
+/- ASX sector (%)	--	--	--	--	--	--	--	--	--	--
Net Interest Cover	-16.98	-33.83	-10.57	-12.43	-11.42	-15.90	-7.57	40.58	-38.87	-28.22
Net Gearing (%)	-91.2	-47.5	-52.8	-49.5	-81.7	-95.6	-92.6	-102.1	-109.0	-107.9
Debt/Equity (%)	9.3	13.3	13.6	17.2	15.6	26.6	20.9	25.1	22.7	12.5
NTA	2.14	2.72	2.52	2.27	2.94	1.95	1.92	3.07	3.95	5.04
Market Cap (m)	2,053	1,797	1,323	938	1,814	1,660	862	1,659	2,161	1,894
Dividend Yield (%)	0.0	5.3	3.6	5.2	3.4	5.2	1.0	4.2	3.9	5.9

Historical Financials

	2003/06	2004/06	2005/06	2006/06	2007/06	2008/06	2009/06	2010/06	2011/06	2012/06
Revenues (m)	605.9	774.3	870.2	974.6	1,120.8	1,410.3	1,677.7	1,768.5	1,822.3	1,988.6
Operating margin (%)	21.0	20.5	16.5	15.1	16.2	17.3	8.8	14.5	15.9	16.6
Depreciation (m)	-21.8	-25.8	-32.8	-25.0	-26.7	-34.5	-47.9	-40.7	-37.6	-37.6
Amortisation (m)	-9	-13	-13	-11	-9	-10	-12	-13	-12	-13
Income tax rate (%)	31.6	32.5	36.5	33.4	30.6	32.8	5.5	29.5	34.4	31.1
Net Profit Before Abnormals (m)	70.0	84.0	67.9	79.9	105.1	143.2	97.6	139.9	171.9	200.1
Net Profit (m)	70.0	81.9	67.9	79.9	120.8	143.2	38.2	139.9	139.8	200.1
Employees (thousands)	0.0	6.4	7.5	0.0	0.0	0.0	0.0	0.0	0.0	0.0
Long term debt (m)	30.8	15.0	15.0	27.0	27.0	60.2	76.0	85.0	68.6	62.0
Shareholders Equity (m)	367.6	424.2	387.4	410.9	482.0	604.8	610.7	710.7	740.6	857.1
Return on capital (%)	19	22	20	21	23	25	17	20	24	24
Return on Equity (%)	19.0	19.8	17.5	19.4	21.8	23.7	16.0	19.7	23.2	23.3
Payout Ratio (%)	57	68	70	62	68	59	9	50	49	56
Return on Investments(%)	19.0	19.8	17.5	19.4	21.8	23.7	16.0	19.7	23.2	23.3

Source: www.CommSec.com.au

Company historicals

Of all the data given in this table, the two of greatest importance
to you (as a potential investor) are the EPS and DPS. If you want
to get a better idea of trends in these statistics you can chart them
using an Excel spreadsheet (or charting software), as I've done in
figure 8.3.

Figure 8.3: FLT EPS and DPS

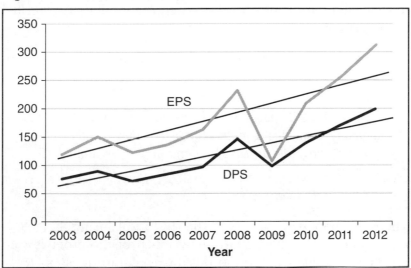

On this chart I've inserted trendlines and you can see that both EPS and DPS have been trending up over the last 10 years despite a small drop in 2005 and large drop in 2009.

Tip

Investors love to see a continually rising EPS and DPS and shares with this type of track record will usually be at a premium price, particularly if the forecast EPS and DPS are also expected to increase. Any decrease in these values from those expected (or forecast) is usually punished severely by the market with a drop in share price that's often dramatic.

Historical financials

There are several important statistics given in this table, but those of greatest importance to investors are the return on capital and return on equity.

Return on capital (ROC) is the profit (after tax) divided by the capital employed by the business expressed as a percentage, and gives a measure of how well the company is utilising its capital to generate profits.

Return on equity (ROE) is the profit (after tax) divided by the shareholders' equity expressed as a percentage, and gives a measure of how well the company is utilising shareholders' funds to generate profits. Note that the shareholders' equity isn't related to the share price but is calculated as:

$$Equity = Assets - Liabilities$$

Tip

ROC and ROE should both be positive, showing that the company is making a profit. The higher they are the better, but they should be at least 10% and preferably around 15% or more.

Payout ratio

The other important statistic in the historical financials table is the payout ratio, which shows how much of the profit is paid out to shareholders in the form of dividends. In the short term, shareholders want a high payout ratio because that means that they are receiving a good slice of the company's profits. However, in the longer term it's important for a business to reinvest some profits so the business can keep its assets in good condition and keep up to date with changes in technology.

Tip

A high payout ratio increases dividends but the ratio shouldn't be too high as that would indicate the business isn't retaining sufficient profits for reinvestment.

Fundamental criteria for purchasing

Having obtained and studied the fundamental data available online, the question is: 'what use is it to me as an investor (or potential investor)?' As I mentioned in chapter 6, when planning and monitoring a long-term share investment, fundamental criteria are of great importance and should be incorporated into your plan. One way of doing this is to formulate a 'health test' where you set out the fundamental benchmarks you plan to apply when considering a share trade. The name 'health test' is descriptive as shares can either pass the test and be considered healthy, or fail the test and be considered unhealthy.

The criteria you select depend on the proposed duration of your trade and whether you're looking for both capital gains and dividends or just capital gains. Your health test can include a large number of fundamental criteria, or just a few of the ones you consider most critical.

Tip

In addition to fundamental criteria your health test should also include chart indications — to be discussed in the next chapter. If you're short-term trading, fundamental criteria have little relevance and your trading decisions will be based almost entirely on technical analysis (charting), but for longer term investing fundamental criteria are of great importance.

Short health test for purchasing

If there are a large number of candidates on your list of prospective shares a short health test is most useful for a preliminary screening as you can quickly scan through the various candidates and eliminate those that fail the test. Below is a suggested list of criteria that you can consider as a short health test for longer term investing in shares.

⇨   Return on equity (ROE) and return on capital (ROC) > 15% and increasing (or steady).

⇨   Price/earnings ratio (P/E) close to the sector average and preferably in the range of 10 to 20.

⇨   Earnings per share (EPS) rising over the last two (or three) years.

⇨   Grossed-up dividend yield > 5%.

Full health test for purchasing

If you include too many criteria in your full health test you may have difficulty finding shares that satisfy all criteria as perfection in the real world is difficult to obtain. You may find shares that pass the test on most criteria, but not all. You then need to consider the deficiencies and the reason for them and whether they're sufficiently important for you to eliminate the shares as candidates for your portfolio. Below is a suggested list of criteria that you can consider for longer term investing of shares as a full health test.

⇨ The business has been operating as a listed company for more than three years.

⇨ The business has a stable and well-respected board of directors.

⇨ Market capitalisation > $100 million.

⇨ Return on equity (ROE) > 15% and trending up (or steady).

⇨ Return on capital (ROC) > 15% and trending up (or steady).

⇨ Earnings per share (EPS) > 8% and rising over the last two (or three) years.

⇨ Annual shareholder return (including capital gains and dividends) > 10% for the last year and also over the last three years.

⇨ Grossed-up dividend yield > 5%.

⇨ Dividend reinvestment plan (DRP) is available.

⇨ Payout ratio < 0.8.

⇨ Interest cover (IC) > 3.

⇨ Debt to equity ratio (DE) < 100% (preferably < 80%).

⇨ Current ratio (CR) > 1.

⇨ Price/earnings ratio (P/E) close to the sector average and preferably in the range of 10 to 20.

⇨ Price/earnings growth ratio (PEG) < 1 (or close to 1).

⇨ Price volatility as measured by beta < 1.3.

⇨ Earnings stability > 55%.

Tip

I suggest you prune my list of suggested criteria for your full health test by choosing those of most importance to you.

Fundamental criteria for selling

After purchasing shares you should monitor them on a regular basis. I suggested ways of doing this online in chapter 6 and your monitoring system should be included in your planning. After the purchase transaction you need to consider the fundamental criteria for your exit strategy. If you've purchase shares because they've passed your fundamental criteria health test you don't have a good reason to sell unless changes occur which mean that they no longer pass your health test and there are other shares you could purchase that will pass the test.

Perhaps you don't want to sell at all and you plan to continue to hold the shares over the long term, but it can be very unprofitable to continue to hold shares if the fundamental indications turn down. The first alert you'll get is when a stable or rising share price suddenly falls and doesn't correct; that is, when a downtrend first appears on the price chart (to be discussed in the next chapter). Unfortunately, confirmed changes to fundamental criteria are usually slower to appear, and by the time they do it may be too late to exit at a favourable price. In some cases there may be company (or other) announcements indicating that unfavourable changes are occurring (or are about to occur) and you may be able to act promptly.

The changes to fundamental criteria that could be a reason for selling include:

⇨ significant reduction in earnings compared with forecast

⇨ loss of a major customer

⇨ significant reduction in the dividend

⇨ significant reduction in the level of franking

⇨ abandoning the DRP

⇨ pending significant litigation

⇨ significant assets writedown

⇨ major competitor entering the market

⇨ changes to legislation or licensing arrangements that could have a major impact on profits.

Tip

It's generally unprofitable to hold shares after the company experiences a significant downturn in fortunes and the share price drops accordingly. However, you need to exercise some restraint to avoid knee-jerk reactions as the sharemarket often overreacts to adverse changes and punishes the share price unduly.

Key points

⇨ Fundamental analysis is most important for longer term share investing and has little relevance for short-term trading.

⇨ The internet is a wonderful resource that allows you to obtain fundamental data for any listed shares from the comfort and convenience of your own home. Your online trading website should provide this data but there are also many public-access sites that do so.

⇨ Fundamental data can be compiled in a number of ways, including the 'snapshot' method that looks at the data at some point in time and the 'historical' method that shows historical data over a period of time (for example, the last 10 years).

⇨ Historical data allows you to form an idea of trends as well as current statistics.

⇨ When examining historical data it can be very useful to chart the data so you can obtain a visual impression of the trend. Most spreadsheet programs (such as Excel) have a charting tool that you can use for this purpose.

⇨ Of all fundamental data, the important figures are earnings per share (EPS); return on equity (ROE); and the fairness of the share price as indicated by the P/E ratio. Also dividend per share (DPS) and dividend yield (DY) are important if you require a regular income from your shares and aren't looking for capital gains profits only.

⇨ Ratios are usually more meaningful to investors. For example, the dividend yield (dividend divided by share price) is far more meaningful than dividend per share as it's similar to interest on money invested.

⇨ Some fundamental data is based on share price, and because the share price constantly changes the data will also change with each change in price. For example, dividend yield and P/E ratio are based on share price and a rising share price will reduce the dividend yield and increase the P/E ratio (and vice versa).

⇨ Investors are more interested in the future than in the past and if you can access forecast statistics then these are well worth examining. However, you can't rely on their accuracy.

⇨ I suggest you formulate a 'health test' based on the key financial statistics of most importance to you. I have presented criteria you can consider including in both a short health test and a full health test based on sound fundamentals when you're considering a shares purchase.

⥲ If shares pass your health test in most areas but fail in some, you need to probe further to try to find the reasons for the shortcomings so you can decide whether these shares are still worth considering.

⇨ In your trade planning you should include consideration of a trade exit strategy. For longer term trades this should include adverse changes in important fundamental data that could be a reason to sell.

⇨ Changes in fundamentals can be slow to appear as they often do so only when the company makes a report. However, there are clues to impending changes and you need to monitor shares you hold or are interested in purchasing so you can be alerted when these occur.

⇨ A most significant clue to impending adverse changes to fundamentals is when a share price starts to drop and doesn't correct.

chapter 9

Online charting

In chapter 8, I discussed fundamental analysis—an important method of analysis for investors interested in medium to long-term investing as the method allows you to make trading decisions that are based on sound fundamentals. For short-term trading, fundamentals aren't of great importance as traders aren't interested in shares with good metrics; they're interested simply in buying and selling shares to make a capital gain—and the faster the better. For these traders, the significant tool is technical analysis; that is, analysing charts to detect trends and to predict likely future price movements.

Nevertheless, charting analysis is also important for longer term investors because, regardless of the length of time of the investment, it's not fruitful to buy shares when the price is falling or to sell shares when the price is rising. In this chapter I'll outline the basics of charting—if you want a more comprehensive treatment I suggest you refer to my book *Charting Made Simple*.

Tip

If you're a longer term investor you should use charting (technical analysis) in conjunction with fundamental analysis.

Why use charts?

The main benefit of charting is that it allows you to analyse share prices and other important metrics easily by visual inspection rather than by trying to analyse them when they're presented in numerical or tabular format. The old saying 'a picture is worth a thousand words' is very true when it comes to share charting. As well as looking at data presented in chart form, many tools have been devised that help you to analyse the chart so you can detect trends and changes in trend and thereby make better predictions about the future. These tools are known as technical analysis tools, or indicators. I'll discuss some of the most important of these later in the chapter.

Tip

If you want to delve deeper into technical analysis, consider joining the Australian Technical Analysts Association (www.ataa.com.au), a not-for-profit association that has the primary aim of promoting the use of technical analysis to enable members to become more effective traders and investors. Membership is open to anyone with an interest in technical analysis or the desire to learn more about it. At the time of writing the cost was $30 to join with an annual membership fee of $260. The association holds monthly meetings as well as an annual conference. Their site contains some free information that you can access, including articles about technical analysis, and there's a link to ASX charts.

Obtaining the charts online

You can obtain many charts and technical analysis indicators from the internet. You have many choices, including:

⇨ your online broker's site

⇨ free public-access sites containing some charts

⇨ free public-access dedicated charting sites

⇨ subscription charting sites.

Your online broker's site

Online brokers provide charts and most also provide some technical analysis tools, the extent and number of which varies with each site (and platform). E*TRADE has traditionally been the leading online broker technical analysis site, but because of the increasing competition between online brokers many others have upgraded their charting platforms and there's been a steady increase in the types of charts they provide and the number of indicators you can access. CommSec has a reasonable charting facility suitable for analysis at a basic level. You can access the charts from the home page by inserting the code of the shares you're interested in and then clicking on the 'charts' link near the top of the page.

Tip

When you've accessed a chart on the CommSec site you can access the chart of any other shares from the charting page by inserting a new code and clicking on the 'display' button.

Free public-access sites containing some charts

There are some free sites that you can access that provide charts and indicators, including the ASX and Trading Room sites, but the charts on these types of sites are usually at a basic level. (Please refer to chapter 3.)

Free public-access dedicated charting sites

There are two free dedicated charting sites that provide a wide range of charts and sophisticated technical analysis indicators and these are the Incredible Charts and Big Charts sites

Incredible Charts: www.incrediblecharts.com

This site has many valuable charting features and gives you free access to different types of chart and technical analysis indicators too numerous to list. In order to use the site you must first register and download the package. I keep the site icon on my desktop, and after you've downloaded the package you can do the same. Thereafter, to access the site all you need to do is click on the icon and you'll be taken directly to the log-in page. As well as a wealth of technical analysis information and facilities, in the 'Help' section of the site there's lots of helpful information as well as an explanation of technical analysis terms and indicators.

When you first access the site your default chart can be the All Ords index (XAO), but then you can call up any stock or index you want by inserting the appropriate code. You're able to customise charts for any time period you nominate or in any of the many formats available, and you can plot technical indicators of interest to you below the main chart. Once you've customised the format of your charts, that format will be retained and you don't need to re-customise every time you log in to the site — a valuable and time-saving feature. However, you can change the format any time you wish to do so. You're also able to insert trendlines or support and resistance lines on all charts.

When you place the cursor over any point in a chart the details of that day's trading (OHLC prices) appear at the bottom of the screen, and this is a most useful way of quickly checking prices or market or sector index values at the close of trading for any date in the past.

You can also obtain a free weekly email written by Colin Twiggs (who manages this site in Australia). Incidentally, this is the only site where you can access an indicator known as the 'Twiggs Money Flow', which he claims is a more reliable indicator than the more widely available 'Chaiken Money Flow'.

You can subscribe to the 'Premium service' and this gives you access to additional data as well as the 'Pro Charting' software. The cost at the time of writing was $19.95 per month for Australian stocks and indices.

Tip

The Incredible Charts site is a wonderful site and one I use constantly. I suggest you register and download the package, and, after doing so, allow yourself sufficient time to fully explore all the features available on the site and to set up the indicators you want. I'm constantly amazed by all the free resources available on the site that subscription sites charge big dollars for!

Big Charts: www.bigcharts.com

This site is also a free site you can access for technical analysis. It is a US-based site but it does have a database of listed Australian stocks. You can access Australian stocks and indices simply by including 'au:' in front of the Australian code. Unlike the Incredible Charts site, you don't need to register or download software. By simply visiting the site you have free access to a huge collection of charting and technical indicators, too numerous to mention.

The data is automatically updated for you so your charts and indicators are up to date. There are three versions of charts available: basic, advanced and interactive. In the 'interactive' mode you have the option of customising the charts and including indicators of your choice. You can store your customised settings, so next time you access the site the charts will automatically appear in the format you have selected. There's also a 'Chart help' that you can use for guidance if required.

This site doesn't have as much information or as many technical indicators as the Incredible Charts site, but it is very convenient to access as you don't have to register or download a package.

Subscription charting sites

There are many subscriber sites that you can join by paying a fee (joining fee and/or ongoing fee) that have proprietary charting packages available. These are often claimed to have some special or superior features not freely available.

Tip

Full-time and serious traders often use subscription charting packages but I suggest you don't get lured in by the promise of superior returns claimed unless you're convinced that the free charts you can access don't provide all the metrics you want and in the form you want them.

Price charts

The most common chart used for any share investing or trading is the price chart, which shows share price vertically against time horizontally. If there's a change in the share code (for example, after a major restructuring), the chart may go back only as far as the time at which the new code was listed.

Tip

Sometimes a zoom function is available in charting packages, and this is very useful as it allows you to draw a chart over a certain time period and then zoom in and expand to focus on a shorter time period within the graph.

Time axis

Most charting software allows you to customise the axis and vary both the time period and time scale.

Time scale

The default time scale on most charts is a time division of one day, but a time division of one hour is used on one-day or intraday charts. For long-term charting, you may want to choose a weekly time division because this produces a chart that's less cluttered.

Time period

The default time period on most charts is one year but you should be able to vary this from as little as one day, one week or one month, to as much as 10 years or even all data. The 'all data' period will go back as far as data exists for the shares and this will depend on how long the shares have been listed. The time period you use should match your trading/investment timeframe. Since charts appear so quickly on your computer, and because it costs nothing to obtain them, there is no reason why you can't look at a multiplicity of time periods for any shares you're interested in. If you're short-term trading choose a short time period (say, one to three months) but if you're in it for the long haul, choose a longer time period.

Tip

A good approach, and one I often use, is to start off with a weekly time scale over a time period of several years, then look at a daily scale over one year and finally over a six-month period to zero in on the most recent trends.

Price axis

You can't change the price range on the price axis because it's automatically chosen to fit into the available space. For example, if the price varied from a low of $1.10 to a high of $2.40 then the price axis would probably start at $1.00 and go to $2.50. However, you may be able to change the type of scale as two types are available, namely the linear and logarithmic scales.

With a linear scale, all the divisions are the same distance apart. For example, a price change from $1 to $2 would look the same on a linear scale chart as a price change from $10 to $11. On a logarithmic scale the divisions are spaced logarithmically—they get closer together as you go up the y (or vertical) axis. The distance between $0.1 and $1 is the same as the distance between $1 and $10. The main advantage of this is that the same relative or percentage price movement is the same vertical distance on the chart. As a share investor you know that a price change from $1 to $2 results in far more capital gain than a price move from $10 to $11. Indeed, the change from $1 to $2 provides a hefty capital gain of 100%, whereas a change from $10 to $11 gives a far more modest 10%. The difference between these would be clear on a logarithmic chart but not on a linear chart.

The same percentage increase over each time period produces a curved upward line on linear scale chart (this is the effect of compound interest) but this line will be a straight line on a logarithmic scale chart. In technical analysis, trendlines are usually drawn as straight lines so it's theoretically better to use a logarithmic scale. A logarithmic scale option is available on the Incredible Charts site, but not many other sites provide it. The good news is that if the price change isn't too great there won't be a significant difference in your interpretation of a chart drawn using a linear rather than a logarithmic scale.

Tip

If the logarithmic scale option is available, by all means try it and see if you can detect any significant difference compared with the same chart using a linear scale.

Intraday charts

If you choose a time period of only one day for your chart, you'll create a special type of chart known as an intraday chart. As I mentioned in chapter 7, before you place any online orders it's a good idea to check daily price action by accessing course of trades data. Rather than studying a mass of numbers, a better way is to call up an intraday chart. An intraday chart for Telstra (TLS) taken from the CommSec site at 1.42 pm (Sydney time) is shown in figure 9.1.

Figure 9.1: intraday chart

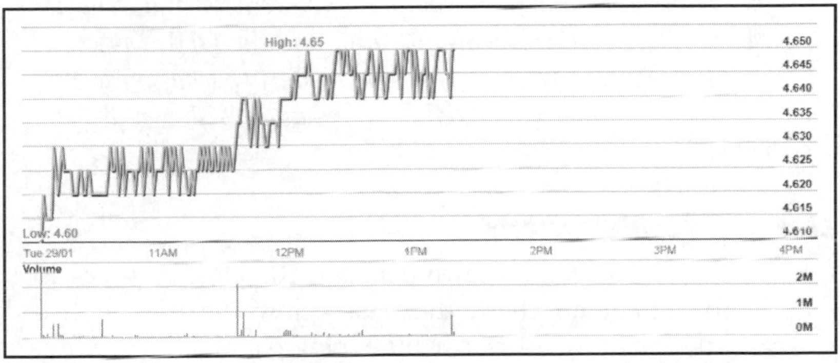

Source: www.CommSec.com.au

Below the price chart, trade volume is shown as a bar chart.

You can see that the shares opened at $4.60 and rose in a series of steps to a high of $4.65. The volume chart is interesting: you can see two high-volume spikes, both of which coincided with an upward price jump.

Types of price chart

There are four different types of price charts commonly available and that you can choose from. They are:

⇨ line and mountain charts

⇨ bar charts

⇨ OHLC charts

⇨ candle (or candlestick) charts.

I'll now discuss these various charts assuming that you're using a daily time scale. If you're using a weekly scale substitute 'week' for 'day'.

> *Tip*
>
> *The CommSec site defaults to the mountain chart but you can call up one of the other types by clicking on 'Chart style' and choosing your option.*

> *Tip*
>
> *On CommSec charts, when you place your cursor in the chart a box will come up showing the date and the OHLC prices. This is also a feature of the Incredible Charts package, except that instead of a box the OHLC information is shown at the bottom of the chart.*

Line and mountain charts

On these charts a line is drawn through the closing prices each day. In the mountain chart, the area below the line is shaded to make the chart stand out a little better and it's known as a mountain chart because the profile resembles a mountain.

Line and mountain charts are the simplest and most easily interpreted types of chart and are usually the default choice on most charting packages. However, they omit significant data of importance because you can't see the range of prices each day and you can't pick out gaps or spikes.

> *Tip*
>
> *Because line and mountain charts omit significant information, I tend not to use them for a single price chart.*

Bar charts

On a bar chart, a vertical bar is drawn each day where the length of the bar indicates the range of daily prices (from lowest to highest). This chart produces a series of vertical lines for each day and allows you to see the range of prices and also to detect any gaps and spikes.

Tip

Bar charts aren't an available option with the CommSec charting software.

OHLC charts

OHLC stands for open, high, low and close (please refer to chapter 7 where I've already discussed these prices). An OHLC chart is essentially a bar chart with the added refinement that two small horizontal lines are superimposed on the vertical bar. The horizontal line to the left indicates the opening price and the line to the right the closing price.

Tip

There's no point accessing a bar chart when you can access an OHLC as it's in essentially the same format but provides additional information.

Candle (or candlestick) charts

This chart provides the same information as an OHLC chart but in a pictorially different way. The vertical bar showing the range between low and high values for the day is a thin line. A wider bar is superimposed on this line showing the range between opening and closing prices. If the closing price is higher than the opening price (price rise), the wide bar is shown in white, and if the closing price is lower than the opening price (price fall) the wide bar is drawn black. On some charting packages other colours, such as green and red, are also common on candle charts to indicate price rises or falls.

Tip

The interpretation of candle charts is a study in itself and devotees use a special vocabulary with commonly identified markers or patterns that includes terms such as 'hammer', 'doji', 'dark cloud cover', 'evening star' and 'morning star'. If you want to delve further, there are many sites that provide further details, including the Incredible Charts site. Also there are dedicated books such as Louise Bedford's The Secret of Candlestick Charting.

These four types of price chart are shown in figure 9.2.

Figure 9.2: various types of price charts

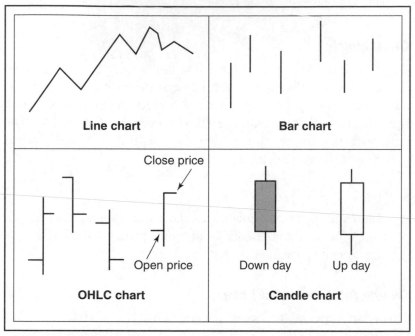

Which of these charts should I use?

At this point you're probably wondering which of the four types of price charts you should use. This depends a great deal on the time period of the chart. A line chart is a simplified plot that's easy to read but omits significant data as you can't see the range of prices each day. Most technical analysts prefer to use price range charts (OHLC or candle charts) that show price ranges rather than just closing prices. In my opinion, a candle chart is the best pictorial representation, but it's not a good chart for long time periods because the candles tend to merge and become difficult to separate visually. Then an OHLC chart is a better option.

Tip

A wonderful advantage of the internet is that you can experiment to your heart's content before making decisions and this certainly applies to charting, so it's a good idea to try all the chart variations available. I favour candle charts for time periods of less than one year and OHLC charts for longer time periods.

Typical mountain and candle charts

In figure 9.3, I've shown a mountain chart from the CommSec site for ASX shares (code ASX) over a six-month period, and in figure 9.4 as a candle chart. Note that the trade volume is shown following the price chart (I'll discuss this a little later).

Figure 9.3: mountain chart

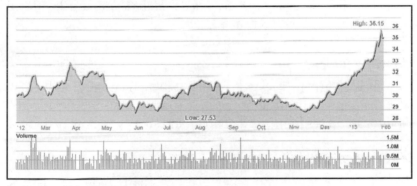

Source: www.CommSec.com.au

Figure 9.4: candle chart

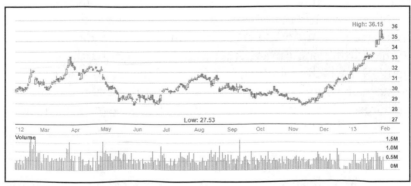

Source: www.CommSec.com.au

Tip

If you look closely at figure 9.4, you will see an amazing downward price spike that doesn't show up at all on the mountain chart and it's a good reason why it's better to use candle charts (as long as the time period isn't too long). On 7 August the shares opened at $31.56, reached a high of $31.71, and then inexplicably fell to a low of $27.53 before recovering to close at $31.64. Despite the price plunge, the share price actually rose on the day. This highlights a downside of stop-loss orders because when the shares were trading at about $31.56 a reasonable stop-loss trigger would have been about $28.40 (10% down). If you had used this trigger, the order would most likely have triggered and the shares would have sold at about this price. You'd have been most annoyed to find that the end of the day you'd sold the shares at $28.40 when they ended the day at $31.64.

Charting indices

As well as charting shares you're able to obtain charts of indices by simply inserting the code of the index rather than the stock code. I'll discuss indices in the next chapter and show you how to do this.

Percentage charts

As well as the four main types of price charts, you can usually obtain another type of chart known as a percentage chart. Rather than showing prices, this chart shows the percentage change in price over the time period of the chart. The chart starts at a zero point on the left hand side of the charting space and then shows the percentage up or down change in price each day compared to the starting point price. A typical percentage chart is shown in figure 9.5 which is a chart of ASX from the CommSec site over a one-year period. You can see that over this period of time the price rose and fell several times but finished up over 11% higher.

Tip

On the CommSec site when the percentage change is positive the line is drawn in green and when negative it is drawn in red.

Figure 9.5: percentage chart

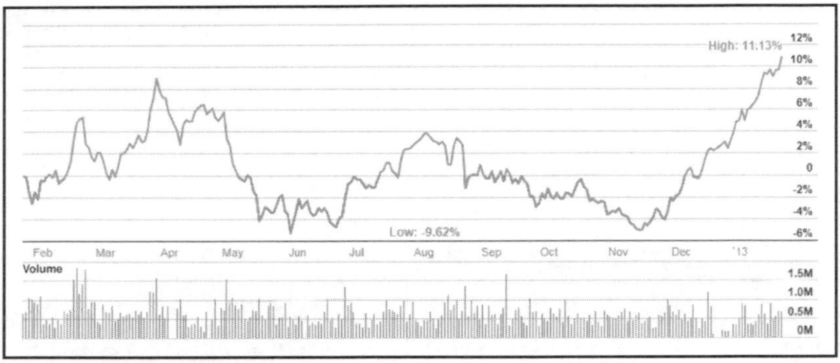

Source: www.CommSec.com.au

Multiple plots

You may want to compare share price changes of different shares over a time period or you may want to compare a share price with an index to see whether the shares have outperformed or underperformed one another or the index. Most charting packages allow you to do this. On the CommSec site you can do this by clicking on the 'Compare' button on the charting web page. When you do this you'll get a percentage chart, because you can't get a good comparison unless all changes in price commence at the same initial point.

As an example of a multiple plot chart, figure 9.6 (overleaf) is a chart of the Commonwealth Bank (CBA) compared with the other three major banks: ANZ Bank (ANZ), NAB and Westpac (WBC). On the CommSec site different colours are used so you can distinguish each one better, but on this chart CBA is the thicker line, and ANZ and WBC closely follow the CBA line. You can see that these three banks all finished around 22% higher. The performance of NAB (lower line) initially kept up with the others but then dropped before picking up again but the shares still lagged the others and finished only about 12% up.

Tip

With multiple plots it's best to use a line chart. Note that the volume bar chart at the bottom applies only to the primary plot — in this case CBA — since that was the primary plot.

239

Figure 9.6: multiple plots

Source: www.CommSec.com.au

Other types of price-based charts

There are two other types of price-based charts available with some charting packages such as the Incredible Charts site—but not CommSec—and they are point and figure charts, and equi-volume charts. For more information on these types of charts please consult my book *Charting Made Simple*.

Volume charts

As I've mentioned before, it's important to consider trade volume in conjunction with price movements. Trade volume each day is conventionally drawn as a bar chart, and on many charting packages (including CommSec) it appears by default as a smaller chart below the price chart as you can see in figures 9.3 and 9.4 (see p. 237).

Volume is important because the larger the volume the more significant the price move. That's to say, price moves on small trade volumes aren't usually of great significance as they're usually indicative of a few investors or traders who just want to purchase or sell small packages of shares where price isn't a significant issue. For example, a price move of 5 cents on a parcel of 10 000 shares represents $500, whereas for a parcel of 1000 shares, it's $50. A trader might well be prepared to accept a loss of $50 but not one of $500.

You can see what I mean if you look at figure 9.4 (see p. 237); the dramatic downward price spike in August 2012 occurred on small volume and significantly didn't herald any major change in sentiment because the share price quickly recovered.

Tip

Uptrending volume indicates increasing interest in trading the shares whereas downtrending volume indicates falling interest.

Volume spikes

Volume spikes are significant increases in volume above the average number of trades, and if you examine figure 9.3 or 9.4 you can see several volume spikes. In some cases volume spikes are significant and accompany major trend changes, as might occur when a mining company makes a significant find or an industrial company announces a major change to its operations. In other cases, spikes appear for no apparent reason and may be difficult to explain.

Tip

Like price spikes, volume spikes are worth investigating.

Effect of a dividend

Not all shares have a dividend associated with them—indeed the majority of listed companies don't pay dividends. These are generally small cap and speculative companies such as medical research and mining companies that run at a loss or make only a small profit and therefore can't distribute any to the shareholders.

For dividend-paying shares the price will invariably fall when the shares go ex-dividend. Remember that if you buy (or hold) the shares prior to this date, you'll receive the current dividend but thereafter you won't. Therefore the opening price of the shares on the ex-dividend day will almost always drop compared with the closing price on the day before. The reason for this is simple — you can't get something for nothing, which would be the situation if the price didn't drop. In that case you could simply buy the shares a day or so before the ex-dividend date, collect the dividend and sell them the day after at the same price, thereby making a fast profit.

The amount of the drop at opening on the ex-dividend day will usually be the same as the dividend per share or somewhat greater to reflect the benefit of franking credits (if any). However, if there's negative sentiment about the shares the drop could be more, or if there's positive it could be less. The price drop due to the dividend should appear as a noticeable downward gap in the price chart. You can see this effect if you look at figure 9.4, and I've shown the same share as figure 9.7 with the ex-dividend date marked.

Figure 9.7: effect of a dividend

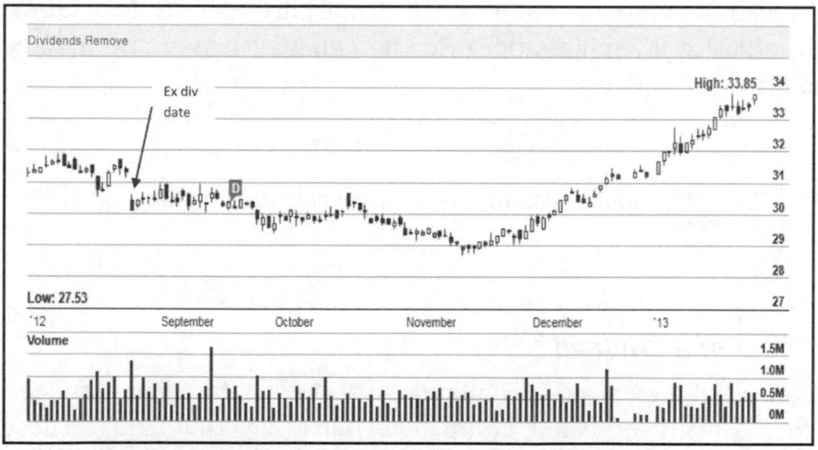

Source: www.CommSec.com.au

Tip

On the CommSec charting package if you click on the 'upper indicators' tab and then scroll down and click 'dividends', a 'D' will appear on the chart as shown in figure 9.7. This is the date the dividend is actually paid to shareholders but it's not an important date that affects the share price.

On 27 August 2012 ASX shares went ex-dividend and I've marked this in figure 9.7. On this day the shares opened at $30.41 and on the previous trading day (24 August) they closed at $31.31. The dividend was 85.1 cents per share. The price drop of 90 cents ($31.31 − $30.41) was greater than the dividend, most likely to take some account of the benefit of the franking credit associated with the dividend.

Tip

When you look at a price chart and detect a downward gap between one day and the next, check the ex-dividend date and the amount of the dividend as the gap could be due to the dividend.

Trends

The primary purpose of charting is to identify trends; that is, the general direction in which prices (or volumes) are changing. I use the word 'general' because the market doesn't move in a smooth fashion but rather as a series of up and down leaps. Short-term traders trade those short-term fluctuations for small but fast profits, but longer term investors look for the general movement over the longer term.

The value of identifying trends is expressed in the well-known saying:

The trend is your friend.

That's to say, it's usually better to go with a trend rather than to go against it. 'Contrarians' are those who trade against a trend and refuse to 'follow the herd'. In some cases this can result in great returns and beating the market but it's a risky strategy and one you should adopt only if you have good reasons to do so.

Tip

Trends seldom continue indefinitely and generally falter at some stage, and may even reverse and form a new trend. If you can identify trends and pick up changes in trends promptly you can trade with minimum delay and maximise profits.

Basic trends

The basic trends are as follows:

⇨ sideways drift

⇨ uptrend

⇨ downtrend.

Sideways drift

This is a directionless trend where the up and down moves balance each other over the longer term. You can think of it as one step forward, one back, or perhaps two forward followed by one back and then another one back. On a chart, this trend is a horizontal line.

Uptrend

This is a generally rising trend where the up moves are greater than the down moves. You can think of it as two steps forward, one back. On a chart, this trend is an upward-sloping line.

Downtrend

This is a generally falling trend where the down moves are generally greater than the up moves. You can think of it as one step forward, two back. On a chart, this trend is a downward sloping line.

The three basic trends are illustrated in figure 9.8.

Tip

For the purpose of technical analysis trends are usually drawn as straight lines, but this is more a matter of convenience than reality, because there's no reason why trendlines can't be curved.

Trend changes

As I said, trends seldom continue indefinitely, and even the strongest trend generally falters at some point. Detecting changes in trends is just as important as identifying the trend in the first place. For example, if you buy some shares that are in a rising price trend and you're showing a good paper profit, all this profit can be eroded or even turn into a loss if you don't act promptly should the uptrend change to a downtrend.

Figure 9.8: basic trends

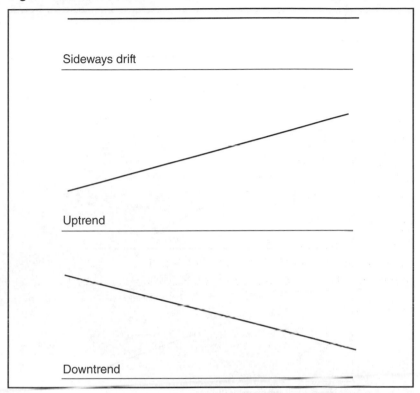

Sideways drift

Uptrend

Downtrend

There are many ways a basic trend can change. The trend change can be a smooth transition or a sudden change and there may be a gap at the trend change point. Three common trend changes are illustrated in figure 9.9 (overleaf).

Detecting trends and trend changes—line chart

The simplest way of detecting trends and trend changes is by visual inspection (eyeball method) using a line (or mountain) chart. The trend and change in trend can be fairly self-evident, but most charting software allows you to insert trendlines on the chart. On some sites (such as the Incredible Charts site), the trendlines will be saved so next time you log in to the site and call up the chart you'll see it with the trendlines you previously inserted.

Figure 9.9: some basic trend changes

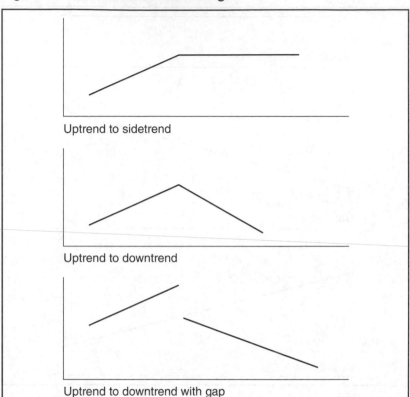

Uptrend to sidetrend

Uptrend to downtrend

Uptrend to downtrend with gap

In figure 9.10 I've shown a line chart from the CommSec site for Suncorp (SUN). The long-term uptrend from August 2012 until the end of January 2013 is clear but I've inserted a trendline of best fit by visual inspection. The break in trend is also clear and this was due to investor concern about the impact of the Queensland floods on the company's profits.

Tip

On the CommSec site you can insert a trendline by clicking on the 'Draw trend lines' box at the upper right hand side of the chart. Then it's just a matter of clicking on the point in the chart where you wish to start the line and dragging along to the end point. If you're not satisfied you can change the position of the line by clicking on an end point and re-positioning the line.

Figure 9.10: trendline on a line chart

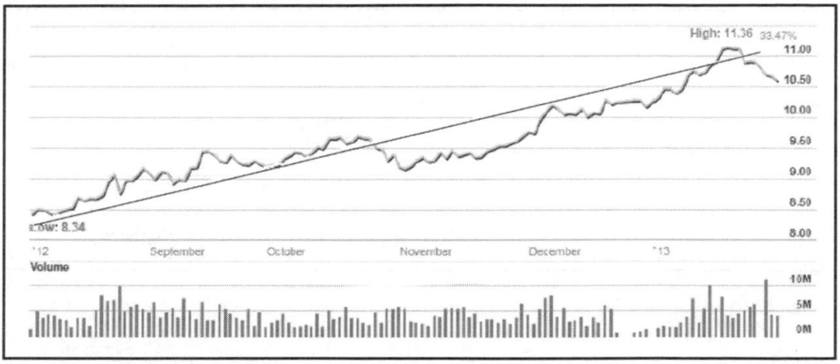

Source: www.CommSec.com.au

Detecting trends and trend changes—price range chart

As I said previously, a price range chart such as an OHLC or candle chart is generally preferred for technical analysis, but with such a chart trends are defined and identified somewhat differently, as follows:

⇨ *Uptrend:* the lows are higher and are identified by joining the lower ends of the price bars. This line slopes upward.

⇨ *Downtrend:* the highs are lower and are identified by joining the upper ends of the price bars. This line slopes downward.

⇨ *Sidetrend:* these criteria aren't as clear for a sidetrend but in most cases both the highs and lows will be approximately level and parallel.

The minimum number of bars you can use to identify a trendline on a price range chart is two, because you need two points to be able to draw a line. However, two points aren't really enough and you need at least three to get reasonable confirmation of the trend.

Tip

The more bars you can draw your trendline through on a range chart, the more confidence you can have in the trend you've identified.

The three basic trends on a price range chart are shown in figure 9.11 (overleaf).

Figure 9.11: basic trends on a range chart

| Uptrend | Downtrend | Sidetrend |

Tip

One or two price bars may overlap the trendline, but this doesn't detract from the validity of the line provided sufficient bars touch the line.

Support and resistance levels

If a share price bounces upward above a certain price and falls back to it a number of times this price becomes a support level. A support level is a consensus level where buyers support a price because they believe it to be a fair price and the buying pressure stops the price from falling below the support level price. If prices bounce below a certain price and rise back to it a number of times, this price becomes a resistance level. A resistance level is a consensus level at which sellers exit the shares at this price because they believe it to be a maximum fair price or they're taking profits in the expectation of a downturn from this price. The selling pressure prevents the price from rising above the resistance level.

A support or resistance level can't be identified unless it is 'tested' several times—at least two and preferably three or more times.

Support and resistance levels are illustrated in figure 9.12.

Tip

Support and resistance levels are horizontal lines. On a price range chart an uptrend is equivalent to an upward sloping support level and a downward trend is equivalent to a downward sloping resistance level.

Figure 9.12: support and resistance levels

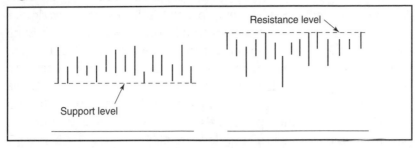

Channels

Parallel support and resistance levels are known as channels and indicate a sideways drift. They seldom last indefinitely, and eventually prices may break upward through the resistance level or downward past the support level, heralding a change in investor sentiment. A favourable change causes an upward break, whereas an unfavourable one causes a downward break. After these breaks, a new channel is often established. If the break has been upward then the new support level is often the old resistance level. Conversely, if the break has been downward then the new resistance level is often the old support level.

An upward channel breakout is illustrated in figure 9.13.

Figure 9.13: upward channel breakout

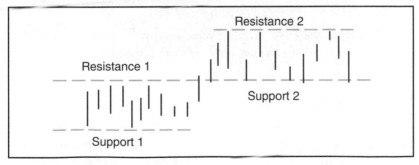

Tip

It is not necessarily the case that in an upward break a new support level is the old resistance level or in a downward break that the old support level is the new resistance level, but it occurs frequently enough for it to be worth taking into account when analysing charts.

Wedges

A channel where the sides aren't parallel is known as a wedge or triangle and it can be converging (getting closer together) or diverging (moving further apart). The converging wedge is interpreted as a sign that traders are reaching agreement on a fair price and a breakout from the wedge is considered to be significant as it heralds a change in sentiment. If the breakout is upward it suggests optimism and a likelihood of further price rises, but if downward it indicates pessimism and that further price falls are likely.

Tip

Wedges are usually short lived, and a breakout will follow.

Patterns

In addition to the basic chart features I've mentioned, many charts have recognisable patterns that technical analysts identify and describe. These include double tops and bottoms, head and shoulders, inverted head and shoulders and wave patterns. Clearly, I can't discuss all these in a single chapter—for further information please refer to *Charting Made Simple*.

Tip

Identifying the basic trends I've defined will serve you well; the more sophisticated patterns aren't really essential.

Simple moving averages

The inspection (or eyeball) method is one way you can identify trends but it's a subjective method. An objective method (that doesn't depend on your judgement) is to identify trends using a moving average. The most basic one is the simple moving average (SMA), which is the average of the closing prices over a certain number of trading periods. You can choose the number of past trading periods, and it can be as short as 5 days or as long as 250 days. If you're using a weekly chart then the closing price each week would be used to calculate the moving average but then you certainly wouldn't use an average of 250 weeks.

The method of calculating a moving average is best illustrated by example. To simplify the maths I've used a very short moving average of only three days.

Consider table 9.1.

Table 9.1: 3-day simple moving average

Day	1	2	3	4	5	6	7
Closing price	1.00	1.20	1.10	1.05	1.12	1.15	1.10
3-day SMA			1.10	1.12	1.09		

The moving average figure in the third column is 1.10 (average of 1.00, 1.20 and 1.10); the figure in the fourth column is 1.12 (average of 1.20, 1.10 and 1.05) and the figure in the fifth column is 1.09 (average of 1.10, 1.05 and 1.12).

Now fill in the last two columns yourself to see if you get the idea.

You should have calculated 1.11 for day six and 1.12 for day seven.

When you're using a charting website you don't need to perform this calculation as the charting software will do it for you and superimpose the moving average on the price chart.

As an example, figure 9.14 is an OHLC chart of Telstra (TLS) for a one-year period from the CommSec site, and on it I've superimposed a 13-day SMA (the default value on the CommSec site). To get the moving average, click on the 'Upper indicators' tab and select from the drop-down menu.

Figure 9.14: SMA

Source: www.CommSec.com.au

You can see how the 13-day SMA closely follows the price action and clearly shows the initial downtrend that's then followed by an almost unbroken uptrend that faltered only briefly in August—some of which was due to the dividend.

Tip

Moving average lines are usually curved lines on a price chart and differ from support, resistance, uptrend and downtrend lines, as these are usually drawn as straight lines.

Exponential moving average and weighted moving average

When calculating an SMA, all data in the series is given equal weight. For example, in a 31-day moving average, the price 31 days ago influences the average as much as yesterday's price. Many analysts believe that this gives an average that responds too slowly to price changes and argue that what happened 31 days ago isn't as significant as yesterday's price move. Also, a single price affects the SMA twice (initially, and then again when it's taken out of the calculation).

The exponential moving average (EMA) and weighted moving average (WMA) are designed to overcome these difficulties as they're calculated using formulas where the weighting of prices varies with time. That's to say, the most recent prices are given greater weighting than older ones so the average is more sensitive to recent price movements than older ones. As time goes on, prices decay and their effect on the average fades away. This overcomes the discontinuity that occurs with an SMA, when the oldest price is deleted from the average and is replaced by the most recent price.

Tip

While very different formulas are used to calculate SMAs, EMAs and WMAs, I've found that it really doesn't make a significant difference to chart analysis which of these you use. I suggest you experiment for yourself and form your own conclusions regarding the one you prefer.

Moving average time periods

The advantage of a moving average is that it smooths the price action and allows you to more clearly see a trend. The disadvantage is that the moving average lags the price action which means that a price trend change won't reflect in the moving average until sometime after the change occurs. The time period of the moving average affects both the smoothing and the time lag as follows:

⇨ *longer time period:* greater smoothing and greater reliability but the average is slower to respond to changes in price action (increases the time lag)

⇨ *shorter time period:* less smoothing and faster time response but less reliability.

So when choosing the moving average time period, it's a matter of compromise, as summarised in table 9.2.

Table 9.2: comparison of short-term and long-term moving averages

	Short term	Long term
Smoothing	Little smoothing	Much smoothing
Sensitivity	Trend changes can be detected more rapidly	It takes longer to detect trend changes
Advantage	There's potential to enter or exit trends at better prices	Greater reliability in the trend and less chance of an unprofitable trade
Disadvantage	Less reliability in the trend and greater chance of an unprofitable trade	Prices can move significantly before a trend change is detected and this can reduce the potential trading profit

Tip

For short-term trend identification use a moving average in the range 5 to 11 days. For intermediate trend identification use a moving average in the range 13 to 31 days. For longer term trend identification and longer term investing, use a moving average in the 50- to 250-day range.

Example 1

You can see the difference between shorter term and longer term moving averages if you study figure 9.15, which is a candle chart for ANZ Bank (ANZ) showing 11-day and 50-day EMAs taken from the Incredible Charts site.

You can see how the 11-day EMA closely follows the price action, although there's a delay of some days before a change in price trend reflects in the EMA trend. You can also see how the 50-day EMA shows the longer term trend.

You can see a strange price spike that occurred on 18 October 2012, where the shares jumped up from their close on 17 October of $25.92 to open at $27.63 and then fell all day to close at $25.95, which was only 3 cents higher. As I mentioned before, spikes like this merit further investigation.

Tip

Charting packages use different colours to distinguish the various moving average lines, and this makes them easier to identify.

Multiple moving averages

It is often useful to chart more than one moving average simultaneously. On most websites you can draw two moving averages simultaneously (as shown in figure 9.15) but some sites (including CommSec and Incredible Charts) allow three or more. If you're using two, you might choose an 11-day and a 31-day, whereas with three you might use 9, 21 and 50 days.

Tip

In order to access multiple moving averages on the CommSec site, hover your cursor over the moving average and a pop-up box will appear with a blue + sign. If you click on this sign you can add more moving averages (and also change the time period of the moving average).

Figure 9.15: candle chart with 11-day and 50-day EMAs

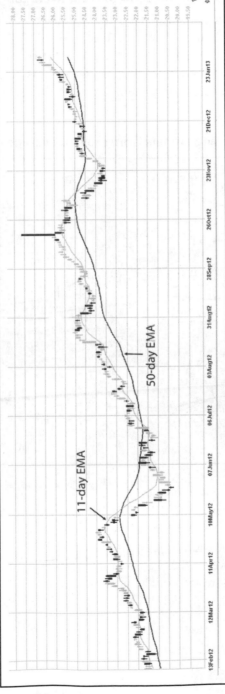

Source: www.incrediblecharts.com

Trading signals from multiple moving averages

Suppose you are using two moving averages—a short one (9 to 13 days) and a longer one (31 to 50 days). Trading signals you can obtain from these are described in the following pages and illustrated in figure 9.16. In this figure the lighter line is the shorter moving average and the heavier line is the longer one.

Figure 9.16: trading signals from moving averages

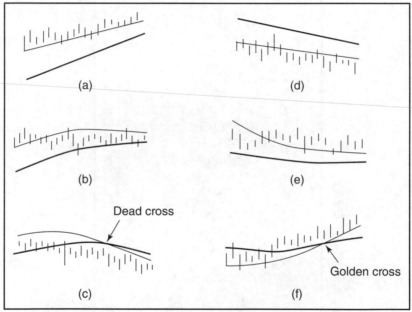

(a) Strong uptrend—buy

In a strong uptrend, the price bars are consistently above the short moving average, which in turn is consistently above the long moving average, and all three are moving upward. The greater the separation between the short- and long-term moving averages, the greater the strength of the uptrend.

(b) Uptrend faltering—caution

Strong uptrends seldom last forever and eventually most uptrends falter and lose momentum. Sometimes this faltering may be only temporary and the price takes off again, but in other cases a sideways drift or a trend reversal may follow. This is a time for caution and close monitoring of price action.

This signal appears on the chart when price bars start to drop below the short moving average, which starts to turn down and the long moving average line starts to flatten out.

(c) Uptrend reversal—sell (or stay out)

Should the faltering uptrend develop into a trend reversal, this is the time to sell (or stay out of the trade).

This signal (known as a dead cross) appears on the chart when the short moving average crosses and drops below the long moving average. The price trends down and the long moving average will generally start to move down as well.

(d) Strong downtrend—sell (or stay out)

In a strong downtrend, the price is consistently below the short moving average, which is consistently below the long moving average, and all three are moving downward. The greater the separation between the short- and long-term moving averages, the greater the strength of the downtrend.

(e) Downtrend faltering—monitor closely

Strong downtrends seldom last forever (unless a stock liquidates) and eventually most downtrends falter and lose momentum. Sometimes this is a period of consolidation before the price heads down again but it may also be the end of the downtrend or a precursor to a trend reversal. This is a time to monitor closely.

This signal appears on the chart in a downtrend when the price starts to rise above the short moving average and soon after the short moving average starts to rise upwards. The long moving average line flattens out as downward momentum loses pace.

(f) Downtrend reversal—buy

Should the faltering downtrend develop into a trend reversal, this is the best time to buy because when downtrends reverse it can be an excellent buying opportunity. At around the reversal point you can buy at a low price and make maximum profit in a re-established uptrend.

The signal is known as a golden cross (for obvious reasons). It appears on the chart when the short moving average crosses and rises above the long moving average. The price is trending up and the long moving average may start to move up as well.

Tip

If you want to check out trading signals from three moving averages please refer to my book Charting Made Simple.

Example 2

Study figure 9.15 (see p. 255) and see if you can identify these trading signals (answer later).

Whipsaws

Moving averages (like all trading tools) aren't infallible and can produce some unproductive trading signals known as 'whipsaws'. These occur when you get a trading signal but soon after you receive a contrary signal indicating the opposite trade. For example, you receive a buy signal, but soon after you receive a sell signal. If you act on the initial buy signal and the later sell signal you are most likely to make a loss on the combined buy/sell trades.

Example 3

Study figure 9.15 (see p. 255) and see if you can identify any whipsaws (answer later).

Acting on a trading signal

The quandary you are faced with when you detect a signal on a chart is this:

⇨ If you act immediately and trade you can be whipsawed unprofitably.

⇨ If you delay acting and wait for confirmation of the signal, much of your profit may be lost because prices can move significantly in short periods of time.

Tip

If you're a longer term investor I believe it is best to forgo some profit and be surer of your trade before you act. Your delay in acting could be based on time or price, as follows:

- Time confirmation: *delay acting for several trading days until you're more confident.*

- Price confirmation: *delay acting until the price moves by a certain amount in the right direction. For example, a 3% rule is common—using this rule you wait for the price to move by 3% from the current price before you act.*

In figure 9.17 (overleaf), I've marked the chart in figure 9.15 with the trading signals (marked *a* to *g*) and a whipsaw (marked *w*).

These are as follows:

(a) strong uptrend
(b) uptrend faltering and reversing
(c) dead cross—sell signal
(d) downtrend established
(e) downtrend faltering and reversing
(f) golden cross—buy signal
(g) strong uptrend
(w) whipsaw—dead cross sell signal followed soon after by a golden cross buy signal.

Figure 9.17: trading signals

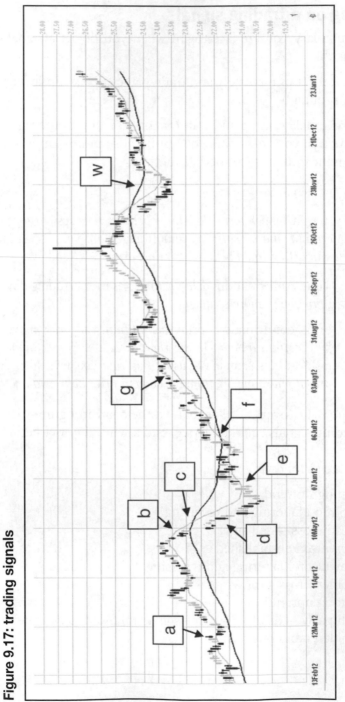

Source: www.incrediblecharts.com

Bollinger Bands®

Share prices generally range between limits that can be mathematically calculated. A method of doing this and charting the limits was invented by John Bollinger and is known as Bollinger Bands®. Many charting websites allow you to call up Bollinger Bands® and on the CommSec site they're accessible via the 'Upper indicators' tab.

Figure 9.18 shows an example of Bollinger Bands® superimposed on a candle chart for Flight Centre (FLT).

Figure 9.18: Bollinger Bands®

Source: www.CommSec.com.au

The mid band is essentially a 20-day SMA of closing prices and the upper and lower bands are the calculated likely price ranges on either side of the mid band. These bands are calculated so that, in the long run, 95% of closing prices should fall between the upper and lower band limits.

You can use Bollinger Bands® in two ways:

⇨ *The width of the bands is a measure of volatility.* That's to say, the closer the bands are together the lower the volatility, and the further apart the higher the volatility. In strong uptrends or downtrends the bands are wider apart than will be the case in sideways drifts where the prices are varying between fairly narrow price limits.

⇨ *Movement of the price bars away from the upper or lower bands and crossing toward the other band is an indicator of a trend change.* For example, if the bars move away from the lower band and head toward the upper band, this heralds an impending uptrend. You can see this clearly in figure 9.17 (see p. 260) in mid December when the bars dived down from the upper to the lower band, then headed back up again and remained around the top of the upper band as the uptrend gathered momentum.

Tip

Bollinger Bands® are a worthwhile charting tool because they're drawn on the primary share price chart (and not as an additional chart below it) and provide a lot of useful information.

Additional indicators

Moving averages used in conjunction with basic trend identification and Bollinger Bands® will serve you well for basic chart analysis and help you to recognise trends and identify when trends falter and change. If you use these tools you'll increase the likelihood of making profitable share trades. However, none of these tools are infallible and you can be unprofitably whipsawed into or out of trades on some occasions. As I've already outlined, one way of being more confident in a trading signal is to use a time or price delay for confirmation or denial but this can erode some of your profit due to the price moves that can occur.

A tactic that helps avoid this difficulty is to use one or more additional indicators (known also as filters). There are many additional indicators you can use—there are at least 50 that have been devised and are accessible on some sites. The CommSec site alone gives you a choice of the following additional indicators available on the 'Lower charts' tab that can be charted below the main chart (in addition to volume):

⇨   on balance volume (OBV)

⇨   money flow index

⇨   fast stochastic

⇨   slow stochastic

⇨ relative strength index (RSI)

⇨ momentum

⇨ Chaikin's volatility

⇨ moving average convergence divergence (MACD).

Tip

Some traders use a system with five or more indicators. I suggest you keep it simple by using only a few that you thoroughly understand. If you want more information about additional indicators please refer to my book Charting Made Simple.

Using additional indicators

If you use an additional indicator there are two possible results:

⇨ The indicator confirms the signal received from the primary indications and this gives you more confidence to act.

⇨ The indicator contradicts the primary signal and this saps your confidence to act. This situation is known as a divergence. In some cases a divergence can present a trading opportunity; that is, a chance to get a jump ahead of the crowd and to trade at a good price while others ignore the potential that's available.

Tip

Divergence trading is more suitable for contrarians and a more risky strategy, so I suggest you use a divergence as a warning or caution and refrain from trading.

The most important trading rule

In this book I've conscientiously tried to avoid using the words 'always' or 'never' because with shares there are very few occasions when these words apply. Shares have a habit of confounding the best of analysts at times and behave in unforeseen ways. However, I'm now going to give you the best tip I possibly can and I will use the word 'never'.

Tip

Never buy shares when the price is in a falling trend mode. If you are going to buy them wait until the price bottoms and the trend reverses. You may lose some potential profit, but in the long run you'll avoid disasters.

Key points

⇨ Charting (or technical analysis) is a useful technique that you can use in conjunction with fundamental analysis to help you make profitable trading decisions.

⇨ For short-term trading fundamental analysis has little relevance; technical analysis is far more valuable.

⇨ Most online broking sites provide a charting facility as well as a variety of technical analysis tools. There are also some public-access sites that provide charting and technical analysis and I have found the Incredible Charts site particularly valuable for this purpose.

⇨ There are no right or wrong answers to chart interpretation—personal skill and experience affect the conclusions drawn.

⇨ The most essential chart is a price chart, and this can be presented in various formats, of which the line or mountain chart and the candle or OHLC chart are the most commonly used.

⇨ Candle charts provide most information but aren't good for longer term charting as the candles tend to merge and become difficult to distinguish.

⇨ The primary purpose of charting is to identify trends, which can be short term or long term. Traders trade on short-term trends but investors look for longer term trends.

⇨ The three basic trends are uptrends, downtrends and sidetrends.

⇨ Over a time period trend combinations may form recognisable patterns.

⇨ The timeframe over which the chart is drawn can vary from very short (one day) to very long (10 years or all data) and you need to consider an appropriate timeframe when you call up a chart.

⇨ Gaps and price spikes sometimes occur in charts and these merit investigation.

⇨ A downward gap inevitably occurs when shares go ex-dividend. This gap doesn't signify a trend change.

⇨ Trends can be identified using inspection or the 'eyeball' method.

⇨ With a price range chart (OHLC or candle chart) trends should be identified by drawing lines through the extremities of the price bars.

⇨ When identifying an uptrend or support, the trendline should be drawn through the base of the bars, and to identify a downtrend or resistance the trendline should be drawn through the tops of the bars. Two bars are the minimum required for this purpose but three or more give better confirmation.

⇨ Trends in volume are important when considered in conjunction with trends in price, and strong price trends are usually accompanied by large trade volumes.

⇨ Moving averages can be used for a more objective analysis of trends than the 'eyeball' method. The time period of the moving average should be appropriate to the timeframe of the proposed trade.

⇨ Multiple moving averages using both short-term and longer term periods can be used to identify trading signals. Of these, the 'golden cross' is regarded as a relatively reliable buy signal and the 'dead cross' as a relatively reliable sell signal.

⇨ Bollinger Bands® are a useful charting tool that can identify changing volatility and help you to recognise trend changes.

⇨ When you're confident that a trend is in place, it's usually the best strategy to trade with the trend rather than against it; that is, to buy in an uptrend and sell in a downtrend. Contrarians trade against the trend, but this is a risky strategy unless you have strong reasons for doing so.

⇨ If you act too quickly on a trading signal you can be 'whipsawed' and this is an unprofitable exercise. You can minimise the likelihood of whipsaws by using a time delay or a price delay.

⇨ Another option to avoid the likelihood of a whipsaw is to use one or more additional indicators (or filters) in conjunction with the primary signal. There are many filters available, of which some commonly used ones are MACD, RSI, M and OBV. I suggest you learn more about them and experiment by studying charts where they're included before you decide which of them (if any) you might use.

⇨ Keep it simple. When analysing charts don't use too many additional indicators until you gain confidence and expertise.

⇨ Never buy shares in a falling trend.

chapter 10

Online indices

In this chapter I'll describe the various indices you can access online and how to use them. I'll outline the makeup of the indices and how they're derived and, most importantly, how you can use this knowledge to your advantage.

Bottom-up and top-down approaches

So far I've discussed analysing shares by two main methods; that is, by fundamental analysis and also by technical analysis (charting). These are known as 'bottom-up' approaches because you're starting at the bottom by selecting a stock and then looking at the unique factors that affect its performance. You can then decide if the shares are worth buying or whether, if you're holding them, you should consider selling.

An alternative approach is known as the top-down approach where you start out by looking at the factors affecting an economy as a whole and then work down through sectors in the economy and finally shares within the sector. In order to apply a top-down approach you need to use indices as these allow you to form an impression of the price performance of the shares in a group of stocks rather than just a single one.

To give you a better idea of the top-down approach and the value of indices let's look at investment property. Suppose you wanted to buy an Australian investment property so you can make capital gains in a rising property market. One approach you could use would be to conduct an internet search of properties, find one that looked promising, then investigate this property further and finally decide whether to purchase. This approach would be a bottom-up one.

An alternative approach would be to examine the statistics relating to the various states and territories in Australia to determine which ones had the fastest growing property markets. Having selected a state or territory, you could then search for the best suburbs within that state or territory and finally hone in on properties within that suburb that look the most promising. This approach would be a top-down approach.

The same principles apply to shares rather property as an investment. A true top-down approach is a global one, where you start your search by looking at the countries offering investment prospects and deciding which ones looked the best. Because this book is about investing in shares on the Australian market, I'm not going to look at the global approach and will confine my discussion to Australia.

Tip

Bottom-up and top-down approaches are two fundamentally different ways of evaluating share investments, but you don't need to adopt only one or the other approach. Indeed, I recommend you use both approaches for evaluating shares.

Indices

Indices are the sharemarket equivalent of grouping properties according to their geographical location, as indices allow you to gauge the performance of a number of stocks rather than the performance of a single one. An index viewed in isolation has no significant meaning and bears no direct relationship to any dollar values. However, changes in an index have significant meaning, particularly the percentage change in the index and whether it's a rise or fall. Using the change in an appropriate index you're able to:

⇨ gauge how the sharemarket as a whole is performing

⇨ gauge how specific sectors of the sharemarket are performing

⇨ compare the performance of one sector of the sharemarket with another and determine the best sectors to invest in.

Index codes

ASX market and sector indices are assigned a three-letter code which distinguishes the index in the same way that each listed stock is assigned a three-letter code. Each code starts with the letter 'X'. For example, the most widely used Australian index—the All Ordinaries—has the code XAO.

Tip

The index code is particularly useful when you want to chart the index. All you need to do is type in the index code rather than a shares code when you want to chart an index.

Types of index

There are two main types of index:

⇨ price index

⇨ accumulation (total return) index.

I'll now explain these.

Price index

A price index is calculated by dividing the dollar value of a hypothetical basket of shares by a benchmark value. The result is a number that's a ratio and doesn't have a dollar value. The benchmark value doesn't change but the value of the index changes as the value of the shares in the index changes. The reason why the dollar value of the shares is divided by a benchmark value is simply to produce a more easily understood number that's in the thousands rather than in the millions or billions, which would be the case if the raw dollar value of a large share portfolio was used.

Tip

Most indices are price indices. The qualifier 'price' isn't usually stated so when you see an index quoted you can assume it's purely a price index.

Accumulation (total return) index

The return from longer term share investing consists of both capital gains and dividends and a price index reflects capital gains (or losses) only, so it reflects only one aspect of financial performance. An accumulation index (also called a total return index) overcomes this disadvantage as the index is calculated by including dividends for the shares in the basket. Therefore an accumulation index provides a better measure of total longer term investor return.

As you'd expect, an accumulation index will show a higher growth rate than the corresponding price index because many shares in the index may have a dividend. While an accumulation index gives a better measure of investor return, it still understates the true return because it doesn't take into account the value of imputation credits that are often associated with the dividend.

Tip

Unfortunately (for some reason that's a mystery to me), accumulation indices aren't as widely quoted or available as price indices. However, you can convert a price index into a total return index by including the average dividend return. For example, if the price index showed a gain of 10% in a year and the average dividend paid was 6%, the total return index would show a gain of 16%. In addition you could add another 1% to 2% to take into account the value of the imputation credits, but it's difficult to be accurate because the franking level associated with dividends can vary from 0 to 100%.

Weighted and unweighted indices

The share mix chosen for the calculation of a price or accumulation index can be weighted or unweighted. An unweighted index is a basket of shares where there's equal number of shares in each stock. For example, there might be 100 CBA shares, 100 BHP shares, 100 WPL shares and so on. On the other hand, in a weighted index the number of shares is weighted according to the market capitalisation of the stocks that are included in the index. Market capitalisation is explained in chapter 8 and it's the amount of dollars invested in a stock; that is, the market price multiplied by the number of shares on issue.

This means that in a weighted index stocks with higher market capitalisation make up a greater proportion of the index than stocks with lower market capitalisation. The reasoning is that the higher the market capitalisation, the more dollars are invested in the stock and the greater the effect a price movement in this stock will have on the majority of share portfolios. Therefore a weighted index provides a more accurate measure of performance for most investors than an unweighted one.

The only disadvantage of a weighted index is that because market capitalisation of a stock changes when its share price changes, the mix of stocks included in the index isn't constant and can change as share prices fluctuate. This particularly affects stocks at the fringes of the index. For example, a stock just outside the index may move into the index when its share price rises, while another stock just inside the index moves out because its share price drops.

Tip

All Australian indices are weighted but not all indices outside Australia are weighted. For example, the Dow Jones index, based on a hypothetical portfolio of 30 stocks on the New York Stock Exchange, is an unweighted index. Therefore the composition of the stocks in this index always remains the same regardless of any changes in their share price. This index is still used and quoted because it's been around for a long time, is well known and—despite its simplicity—is a good barometer for the US market. However, the S&P 500 index (based on 500 stocks) is really a better measure of US market performance.

Example 1

At the time of writing, Commonwealth Bank (CBA) had a market capitalisation of about $104 billion and constituted 31% of the banking sector whereas Bank of Queensland (BOQ) had a market capitalisation of about $2.7 billion and made up about 0.8% of the banking sector. Therefore, a certain price movement in CBA shares would have about 38 times the effect on the banking index compared with the same price movement in BOQ shares.

Market and sector indices

As we've seen, there are several different ways an index can be calculated. In addition, there are different types of indices depending on the types of shares included for the hypothetical basket. There are two main variations, namely market and sector indices.

Sector index

In a sector index, the stocks included in the index are all companies from the same sector; that is, they are all companies that are in the same type of industry. For example, a financial index is made up entirely of companies in the finance industry (banks and so on), whereas a telecommunication index consists entirely telco companies (of which Telstra is the main one).

Market index

In a market index, the basket of shares used in the index calculation isn't sector-dependent and is chosen from the market at large. In a weighted index (as all Australian indices are), the stocks included in the index depend on their market capitalisation only and not on the nature of the business. This means that the index can be heavily weighted with stocks in the same sector if they are large companies with a big market cap. For example, in Australia the big four banks all have high market capitalisations and so are most likely to be included in any Australian market index.

Tip

A market index gives you a good idea of how the market as a whole is performing, but use a sector index when you're interested in a specific sector's performance.

Liquidity

Another variation is possible in an index calculation and that's liquidity. Most Australian indices apply liquidity criteria and this means that to be included in the index the stock needs to meet liquidity criteria based on the average number of shares traded per day. The idea of this is to exclude illiquid companies from the index and include only those where traders and investors are able to freely trade the shares.

Tip

Liquidity criteria apply to all Australian indices other than the All Ordinaries index (XAO).

Example 2

To show you how an index is calculated and used let's compile an index of your share portfolio. Suppose your portfolio had a value at the end of last financial year of $53 520. You could divide this by a benchmark value of $535.20, so at the end of the last financial year your portfolio had an index value of 100 ($53 520 ÷ $535.20).

Suppose that at the present time the value of your portfolio is $58 937. Then your portfolio index would now be 110.1 (58 937 ÷ 535.20). So if a friend asked you how your portfolio was performing, you could answer, 'My portfolio index has increased by a little over 10% since last financial year.'

In a similar way you could compile a sector index of your portfolio by dividing your portfolio up according to sectors and performing the same calculation for each sector.

Tip

When looking at an index, you don't need to know the initial benchmark value in order to use the index to gauge performance changes. If your friends know your portfolio index has increased from 100 to 110.1 they know exactly how your shares have performed without the need to ask what your benchmark value is.

Averaging share prices

You might wonder why indices are used rather than average share prices—wouldn't you get the same picture by averaging share prices? The answer is no. To understand why consider the following example.

Example 3

To simplify the maths, suppose your share portfolio consisted of only two stocks—10 000 shares in A and 500 shares in B. At the end of the last financial year, the shares in each were worth $10 000 because A was trading at $1 and B was trading at $20.

Since last financial year the price of each had risen by $1 so Stock A was trading at $2 and Stock B was trading at $21.

If you measured the change in value of your portfolio by the average price, you would conclude that the average price was initially $10.50, which is (1 + 20) ÷ 2. Later it was $11.50, which is (2 + 21) ÷ 2, and the change in average price was 9.5%, calculated 1 ÷ 10.5 × 100.

However, consider the change to your portfolio value. Your portfolio is now worth $30 500 (10 000 × $2 + 500 × $21) and the change in the value of your portfolio is 52.5% (10 500 ÷ 20 000 × 100).

These are clearly very different results, so which is the correct interpretation? Have your shares gone up in value by 9.5% or by 52.5%?

The correct interpretation is that your shares have gone up in value by 52.5%. Averaging the share price gives a false impression because of differences in the share prices of the stocks in the portfolio.

The same logic applies to the broad market, and because prices differ so much between the various shares in an index, averaging prices would give a false impression of how the index has changed. For example, at the time of writing Commonwealth Bank shares were trading at around $70 whereas Telstra shares were around $5, yet both of these companies are major Australian ones.

Australian market indices

The major ASX market indices with their makeup (at the time of writing) are shown in table 10.1. Australian indices are compiled by a global company that specialises in the compilation of indices—Standard & Poor's—and that is why the index is prefaced with the letters 'S&P', but when referring to an index the 'S&P' is often not included.

Table 10.1: market indices

Index	Code	Makeup	Market cap (%)
All Ords	XAO	500 largest market cap stocks	99
S&P/ASX 300	XKO	300 largest market cap stocks	81
S&P/ASX 200	XJO	200 largest market cap stocks	80
S&P/ASX 200 Total Return	XNT	Same as XJO with dividends reinvested	80
S&P/ASX 100	XTO	100 largest market cap stocks	74
S&P/ASX 50	XFL	50 largest market cap stocks	63
S&P/ASX 20	XTL	20 largest market cap stocks	46
S&P/ASX Midcap. 50	XMD	Stocks in the ASX 100 but not included in the ASX 50	11
Small Ords	XSO	Stocks included in the ASX 300 but not the ASX 100	7

The last column in this table shows the approximate percentage of the entire market capital investment (at the time of writing) represented by the stocks in the index. The figures given in this column are approximate because they change from time to time.

Note that table 10.1 isn't a complete list as there are other specific market indices that I haven't included, such as the All Australian 50 and 200 index and the Emerging Companies index.

Tip

The name 'All Ordinaries' implies that the index measures the movement of all ordinary Australian stocks. At the time of writing there are about 2000 ASX-listed stocks, so even though the All Ords measures 99% of the Australian market, it's made up of only about 25% of all listed entities. This is another example of Pareto's principle (the 80–20 rule) because a small number of stocks have a high market capitalisation and there are a large number of stocks with a low market capitalisation. In other words, most investor dollars are concentrated in the shares of a relatively small number of large companies. You'll probably find this also applies to your own portfolio—most of its value is likely to be in the shares you hold in a relatively small number of stocks.

Using market indices

You can use Australian market indices to aid your share investing decisions in the following ways:

⇨ To gauge the overall performance of the Australian market. For this purpose the All Ords is often quoted. Market change helps you to decide whether to increase or decrease the amount you've invested in Australian shares.

⇨ To measure the performance of sections of the market such as the 20 or 50 largest market capitalisation stocks. This helps you decide whether to weight your portfolio toward the larger, more blue-chip types of shares.

⇨ To provide a benchmark against which the performance of your share portfolio can be evaluated. This is a subjective judgement and you can choose whichever index you think is most appropriate for your share portfolio.

⇨ If you have money invested in a managed fund or superannuation fund (including your own SMSF) you can use an appropriate index as a benchmark to measure the fund's performance. When choosing the most appropriate index you should take into account the nature of the fund. Most funds invest most of their capital in large blue-chip type companies so the S&P/ASX 100 or S&P/ASX 200 indices are often used as the yardstick. However, I believe that the S&P/ASX 200 Total Return index is the most appropriate because dividends are included.

⇨ To provide a benchmark against which the performance of a particular share can be measured. For example, you can compare how a share is performing relative to the market as a whole and this helps you make trading decisions.

Tip

When monitoring the capital gains in my share portfolio and SMSF, I use the All Ords. As my portfolio is strongly weighted toward large-market-capitalisation stocks (blue-chip and green-chip stocks), I believe that the All Ords provides a realistic benchmark for capital gains. Another advantage is that because it's widely quoted it's a convenient one to use.

Online market indices

Most broking websites and many other websites provide a list of market indices and allow you to see how they're performing. On the CommSec site if you click on the 'Quotes and research' tab at the top of the home page and then the 'Indices' link on the left hand side, you'll access a list such as the one shown in figure 10.1 (overleaf).

Figure 10.1: CommSec market indices

Market Indices Download CSV				Tue 12 Feb 2013 12:09 PM (Sydney time)		
Code	Name	Last	Change	Change (%)		
▲ XAO	ALL ORDINARIES [XAO]	4,990.900	10.600	0.200	☑	▤
▲ XJO	S&P/ASX 200 [XJO]	4,969.100	9.800	0.200	☑	▤
▲ XFL	S&P/ASX 50 [XFL]	5,062.300	8.200	0.200	☑	▤

Download CSV

More Indices						
Code	Name	Last	Change	Change (%)		
▲ XTO	S&P/ASX 100 [XTO]	4,088.600	7.300	0.200	☑	▤
▲ XTL	S&P/ASX 20 [XTL]	3,068.600	3.500	0.100	☑	▤
▲ XDJ	S&P/ASX 200 Cons Disc [XDJ]	1,512.500	0.100	0.000	☑	▤
▲ XSJ	S&P/ASX 200 Cons Staples [XSJ]	9,570.400	34.900	0.400	☑	▤
▼ XEJ	S&P/ASX 200 Energy [XEJ]	13,114.400	-4.800	0.000	☑	▤
▲ XFJ	S&P/ASX 200 Financials [XFJ]	5,163.900	7.200	0.100	☑	▤
▲ XXJ	S&P/ASX 200 Fin-x-Prop [XXJ]	5,964.300	7.600	0.100	☑	▤
▲ XHJ	S&P/ASX 200 Health Care [XHJ]	12,269.500	12.800	0.100	☑	▤
▲ XNJ	S&P/ASX 200 Industrials [XNJ]	3,821.700	49.700	1.300	☑	▤
▲ XIJ	S&P/ASX 200 Info Tech [XIJ]	679.800	12.300	1.900	☑	▤
▼ XMJ	S&P/ASX 200 Materials [XMJ]	10,913.400	-26.400	-0.200	☑	▤
▲ XPJ	S&P/ASX 200 A-REIT [XPJ]	1,019.800	2.000	0.200	☑	▤
▲ XTJ	S&P/ASX 200 Telecomms [XTJ]	1,594.000	13.600	0.900	☑	▤
▲ XUJ	S&P/ASX 200 Utilities [XUJ]	5,378.400	27.100	0.500	☑	▤
▲ XKO	S&P/ASX 300 [XKO]	4,944.800	9.800	0.200	☑	▤
▲ XMD	S&P/ASX MIDCAP50 [XMD]	4,149.000	13.500	0.300	☑	▤
▲ XSO	S&P/ASX SMALL ORDINARIES [XSO]	2,403.900	10.500	0.400	☑	▤

Source: www.CommSec.com.au

On the top section of this table are the three most commonly used market indices, namely XAO, XJO and XFL, with their last value and the change in value compared with yesterday's close.

Below these three indices is another table with the same information for other market indices and sector indices (I'll examine sector indices shortly).

Tip

In the CommSec table the indices are shown in green when the change in index value is positive and in red if it's negative.

Charting market indices

You can chart a market index in exactly the same way as you do shares, using the same available chart formats, by inserting the three-letter index code instead of the share code. You can also chart a number of indices on the same chart to compare their relative performance.

Example 4

Figure 10.2 is a chart (taken from the CommSec site) that compares the All Ords (XAO) and the S&P/ASX 20 (XTL) indices over a one-year period to February 2013.

Figure 10.2: XAO and XTL

Source: www.CommSec.com.au

You can see that both indices stayed in phase for a few months, and turned down to lose about 5% in June–July 2012 due to global jitters and unrest about the European Union. Then they both picked up and started rising as optimism returned to world markets, with XAO finishing about 14% higher and XTL outperforming it by finishing about 19% higher.

Conclusion

The 20 largest companies in the Australian market outperformed the general market by about 5% in this one-year period, clearly showing the preference by investors to defensive type shares; that is, the large market cap, high-dividend-paying blue-chip ones. Also, as interest rates fell, investors were transferring cash from low interest bank accounts to higher dividend-paying shares. So if your portfolio (or any managed fund) had comprised the

20 shares in the XTL index, the portfolio or fund would have outperformed the general market in terms of capital gains. If you add the dividends, you would have been well in front.

Tip

It isn't always the case that the largest blue-chips will outperform the general market, but in times of uncertainty and volatility, investors get the jitters and flee to safer and more stable defensive shares.

Investment timing using market indices

You can use market indices to time your investment in shares using the following strategy:

Increase your investment in shares when the market is rising and reduce your exposure when the market is falling.

While this strategy is logical and seemingly obvious, in practice it has a few prickles:

⇨ There are capital gains tax implications that may be unfavourable for you. For example, suppose you decide to sell most of your shares because you foresee that the market is likely to turn down. If you've made good capital gain on these shares, all this gain will have to be included as income in your taxation return for the one year. This could push you up into a higher tax bracket or have other unfavourable financial implications on a higher education loan program (HELP) debt and or the Medicare levy. Another problem is that you may not have held some (or all) of your shares for one year and so may not get the benefit of the 50% reduction in capital gains tax. If you decide to repurchase later on when the market picks up, the capital gains clock starts from zero and you have to hold the shares for another year in order to get the 50% taxation reduction benefit.

⇨ You incur additional brokerage if you sell and repurchase later on. There are also additional paperwork and record-keeping hassles.

⇨ With hindsight it is easy to calculate the additional profit you would have made by trading your shares rather than hanging on, but in practice these gains may not be nearly as good as this calculation indicates. This is because it is impossible to get the timing just right in real time. If you think a bull market is ending and you sell, the downturn could prove to be only a temporary breather and the market may subsequently track higher. Conversely, if you think that after a fall the market has bottomed and you buy in again, this might prove to be only a temporary bounce and the market could drop lower again.

⇨ Pareto's principle crops up again with share price rises because the majority of the price growth in the market occurs over a relatively small number of trading days (typically about 30). As most of us don't have crystal balls, it is extremely difficult to predict on what days the big gains will occur. If you've sold, the big gains could well take place while you're out of the market. Realistically, unless you're a very active day trader, your best way of participating in high market gains is to remain in the market as a long-term investor.

Tip

You need to consider all the factors involved before you trade most of the shares in your portfolio in an attempt to benefit from market rises and minimise losses in times of market falls. Sometimes it can be a good strategy but at other times it can be counterproductive.

Sector indices

Sector indices are calculated by breaking the market up into groups of stocks according to the primary nature of their businesses. The simplest sector grouping is to simply classify them into one of two sectors:

⇨ industrials

⇨ resources (mining and oil stocks).

While such a simplistic division of stocks is often used in newspaper listings and in news commentaries, it's really not adequate for investment research. The ASX (through Standard & Poor's) uses a more sophisticated system to identify sectors of the Australian market. The system conforms to the Global Industry Classification Standard (GICS), so that Australian sectors align with global sector groupings.

The GICS sectors are listed in table 10.2. The three-letter code for the index applicable to each sector is shown along with the types of industries included in that sector.

Table 10.2: sector indices

Sector	Code	Industries included
Energy	XEJ	Energy equipment and services. Oil and gas exploration, production, refining and marketing.
Materials	XMJ	Chemicals, construction materials, containers and packaging, metals and mining, steel producers, paper and forest products.
Industrials	XNJ	Aerospace and defence, building products, machinery and equipment, commercial services and supplies, transportation (air, sea, road and rail) and transportation infrastructure.
Consumer discretionary	XDJ	Cars and car components, household durables, leisure equipment, textiles and apparel, hotels, restaurants, casinos, gambling and leisure facilities. Media production and services, and consumer retailing and services.
Consumer staples	XSJ	Manufacturers, distributors and retailers of non-durable household goods and personal products including food, beverages and tobacco products. Also drug retailers.
Health care	XHJ	Health care equipment manufacturers and service providers. Research, development, production and marketing of pharmaceuticals and biotechnology products.

Sector	Code	Industries included
Financials	XFJ	Banks and financial services, insurance, property trusts and real estate investment and management.
Financials excluding real estate investment trusts	XXJ	Same as XFJ but excluding stocks in the XPJ sector.
Real estate investment trusts	XPJ	Real estate ownership and rental.
Listed investment companies	XIC	Companies whose income is derived from investment in Australian and international equities.
Domestic listed investment	XID	Same as XIC but includes only companies that invest in Australian equities.
International listed investment	XII	Same as XIC but companies that focus on investment in international equities.
Information technology	XIJ	Manufacturers and providers of electronic, computer and internet software and communications equipment and services.
Telecommunication services	XTJ	Telecommunication services.
Utilities	XUJ	Electricity, gas and water utilities and power producers and distributors.
Metals and mining	XMM	Companies from the S&P/ASX 300 index that are classified as being in the metals and mining industries.
Resources	XJR	Companies from the S&P/ASX 200 index that are classified as being in the energy or metals and mining industries.
Gold	XGD	Companies from the All Ordinaries index that are engaged in the mining and production of gold.

Tip

Index groups don't always conform to what might appear logical. For example, household durables, textiles and apparel are included in the Consumer Discretionary sector index, whereas alcohol, tobacco and personal products are included in the Consumer Staples sector index!

Applying sector analysis

The overall market performance is the aggregate performance of all sectors, and during different periods some sectors outperform or underperform others. When applying a top-down approach with sectors, you try to identify the sectors that are the best performers and concentrate on shares in those sectors. In theory, if your portfolio is concentrated with shares in the best performing sectors, your portfolio should outperform the general market. However, there's no guarantee of this because, while a certain sector may be outperforming the general market, it's not necessarily the case that all shares within that sector are also outperforming the market. Indeed, it's often the case that a sector can be trending up while some shares within that sector are neutral or trending down.

Tip

While not all shares making up a sector follow the overall sector trend, there's a higher probability that most will be. So by biasing your portfolio with shares in the best performing sectors you increase the probability of your portfolio outperforming the general market.

Identifying the best sectors

The question then is: how do you identify the best performing sectors?

One way you can do so is to look at some key financial statistics relevant to the various sectors and compare them. A sector analysis (taken from the CommSec site) is shown in table 10.3. To access this table on the website, click on the 'Quotes and research' tab on the top of the home page and then the 'Sectors' link on the left hand side.

This table shows the average annualised growth in earnings per share (EPS), the price/earnings ratio (PE) and dividend yield for the current financial year up to the present time as well as the forecast projections of these statistics for the next two years. Unfortunately, the sector table from the CommSec site doesn't include all sectors and contains only 10 of the total 16 sectors currently published for Australian shares and therefore doesn't give the complete picture.

Table 10.3: sector analysis

| | Sector Analysis | | | | | | | | |
| | EPS Growth (%) | | | Price/Earnings (x) | | | Dividend Yield (%) | | |
Sector	Current	Forecast Y1	Forecast Y2	Current	Forecast Y1	Forecast Y2	Current	Forecast Y1	Forecast Y2
Total Market	6.98	10.46	13.23	3.93	16.76	19.08	5.12	4.42	4.78
Energy	12.59	63.49	–7.52	–92.60	16.09	20.35	2.61	3.04	3.03
Materials	2.58	–7.04	30.13	14.51	10.50	33.13	2.87	2.85	3.32
Industrials	53.44	23.05	26.38	–13.32	47.71	26.79	3.76	3.67	4.00
Consumer Discretionary	5.33	4.53	10.45	14.19	17.53	15.99	4.20	3.42	3.36
Consumer Staples	7.42	3.43	9.94	14.18	17.86	16.23	4.94	4.34	4.76
Health Care	7.89	17.10	10.08	14.48	17.04	17.22	3.19	4.04	4.79
Financials	–1.77	9.50	7.54	11.81	13.45	12.51	6.75	5.55	5.92
Information Technology	–2.65	12.63	13.61	16.45	19.43	17.13	4.15	3.50	3.77
Telecommunication Services	9.79	5.76	10.65	11.81	15.44	13.93	8.41	5.99	6.58
Utilities	10.02	4.15	11.00	15.59	17.77	16.20	6.43	5.32	5.47

Source: www.CommSec.com.au

You can see from this table that at the time of writing (February 2013) the highest EPS growth was in the industrial sector, with the lowest growth in the information technology sector. While there was a large divergence in EPS growth for the various sectors, the dividend yield growth showed far less variation. Somewhat surprisingly, this table shows negative growth for the financial sector, but this was no doubt due to the fact that REITs (real estate investment trusts) are included in this sector and they didn't enjoy the positive growth experienced by the banking sector.

Tip

Remember the saying 'what goes around comes around', or a similar sentiment expressed in the saying 'every dog has its day'. There's no guarantee that the best performing sectors currently (or in the past) are necessarily the ones that will perform best in the future. So you need to monitor the sectors in the same way as with shares to detect trend changes.

Charting sector performance

Another way of identifying the best performing sectors is to chart sector performance relative to one another or to an appropriate market index using the percentage chart, as this gives you a comparison that is easy to interpret. Once you have set up the parameters for the charts, you can quickly run through the sectors and identify the best performing ones.

When you do this, you need to decide on an appropriate timeframe for the chart. A suitable timeframe for longer term investing would be one to three years, and for shorter term investing three to six months.

Tip

For the purpose of long-term sector performance comparison, I suggest you use a weekly (rather than a daily) chart, as this will provide a clearer picture of the long-term trends.

Example 5

A typical weekly sector performance chart over a one-year period to February 2013 is shown in figure 10.3. In this chart, the performance of the Financials sector (XFJ) and the Industrial sector (XNJ) is charted relative to the All Ordinaries index.

Figure 10.3: sector performance chart

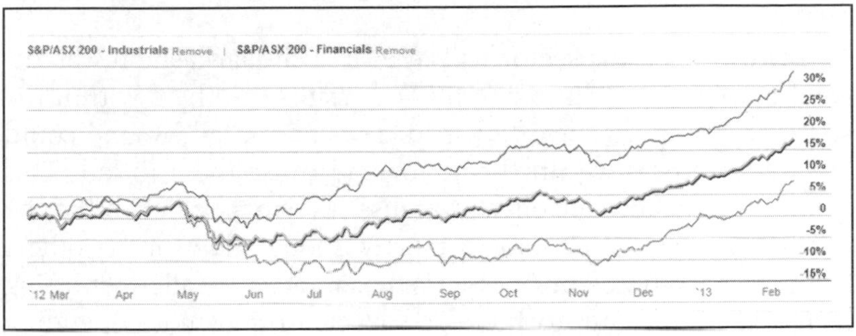

Source: www.CommSec.com.au

On this chart the top line is XFJ, the centre line XAO and the lower line XNJ. You can see that the financial sector grew over 30% in the year and outperformed the general market, which grew by about 17%, whereas the industrial sector (XNJ) underperformed the general market with a growth rate of about 8%. Also, you can see that while each sector performed differently, the lines all had the same general shape, confirming the saying that 'all boats rise or fall with the tide', meaning that when the market rises or falls most shares tend to follow suit and usually very few sectors buck the market trend.

Tip

You can chart many sectors together to compare performance, but if you chart too many the lines may merge and cross and make interpretation difficult. Therefore I suggest you limit the chart to no more than four (or preferably no more than three) sectors simultaneously.

Sector conformity or divergence

An important question for share investors is how changes in the fortunes (and share price) of one stock within a sector may impact on others within the same sector. Three scenarios are possible:

⇨ similar effect

⇨ neutral effect

⇨ opposite effect.

Similar effect

All shares within the sector will react in a similar fashion; that is, good news resulting in a rise by one results in others within the sector also rising. Conversely, bad news and a fall by one could flow on to others within the sector and cause them to fall. This is known as a 'flow-on' effect, because investors perceive that the good news that affects one company should flow on to others in the same type of business. For example, a retailer reporting increased profits due to increased levels of consumer spending will most likely tend to lift all other similar retailers in the sector

Neutral effect

A change in the fortunes of one company within a sector is seen to be unique and of no relevance to others in the same sector. For example, a change in governance in one company affecting their share price really has no relevance to others within the sector.

Opposite effect

In this case a change in the fortunes of one company within the sector may have the opposite effect on others. For example, bad news and a fall in the share price of one may result in a share price rise for others within the sector (or vice versa); for example, if a large company within a sector experiences major quality control problems that results in product withdrawals and a steep drop in its share price. However, shares in other companies within the sector rise because investors perceive that these companies will be able to increase their market share to take up the slack.

Tip

When evaluating the effect of a change in fortunes (and share price) of one company on others in the same sector there's no general guideline and each case needs to be considered as a unique situation.

Sector and industry groups and subgroups

The sector indices listed in table 10.2 are based on the main types of business companies can be involved in. However, the business type can be quite broad with a range of diverse types of activity included. For example, the Materials sector includes a wide range of business activities including chemicals, paper/packaging, glass, construction materials and metals and mining. Similarly, the Energy sector encompasses oil, gas and coal exploration, and production and energy equipment and services. I think you'd agree that from an investor's point of view there's a huge difference between an energy explorer and an established provider of energy or a provider of energy services such as storage and transportation.

This problem is addressed by dividing each of the main sectors further into more specific industry types. Australia has adopted the Global Industry Classification System, where a numerical code (not an alphabetical one) is used for the sectors and industries. Each main sector is given a two-digit code, which is then subdivided into an industry group by adding two digits to obtain a four-digit industry group. A further two digits are added to give a six-digit industry classification. Finally, a further two digits are added to give an eight-digit sub-industry classification.

The most recent listing of the numerical sector, industry groups and industry classifications as compiled by Standard & Poor's (30 June 2010) is shown in table 10.4 (overleaf). In this table I've gone as far as the six-digit industry code only, as the complete table up to the eight-digit sub-industry code is a large document.

Table 10.4: sector and industry numerical codes

Sector		Industry Group		Industry	
10	Energy	1010	Energy	101010	Energy Equipment & Services
				101020	Oil, Gas & Consumable Fuels
15	Materials	1510	Materials	151010	Chemicals
				151020	Construction Materials
				151030	Containers & Packaging
				151040	Metals & Mining
				151050	Paper & Forest Products
20	Industrials	2010	Capital Goods	201010	Aerospace & Defense
				201020	Building Products
				201030	Construction & Engineering
				201040	Electrical Equipment
				201050	Industrial Conglomerates
				201060	Machinery
				201070	Trading Companies & Distributors
		2020	Commercial & Professional Services	202010	Commercial Services & Supplies
20		2020	Commercial & Professional Services	202020	Professional Services
		2030	Transportation	203010	Air Freight & Logistics
				203020	Airlines
				203030	Marine
				203040	Road & Rail
				203050	Transportation Infrastructure

Sector		Industry Group		Industry	
25	Consumer Discretionary	2510	Automobiles & Components	251010	Auto Components
				251020	Automobiles
		2520	Consumer Durables & Apparel	252010	Household Durables
				252020	Leisure Equipment & Products
				252030	Textiles, Apparel & Luxury Goods
25		2530	Consumer Services	253010	Hotels, Restaurants & Leisure
				253020	Diversified Consumer Services
		2540	Media	254010	Media
		2550	Retailing	255010	Distributors
				255020	Internet & Catalog Retail
				255030	Multiline Retail
				255040	Specialty Retail
30	Consumer Staples	3010	Food & Staples Retailing	301010	Food & Staples Retailing
		3020	Food, Beverage & Tobacco	302010	Beverages
				302020	Food Products
				302030	Tobacco
		3030	Household & Personal Products	303010	Household Products
				303020	Personal Products
35	Health Care	3510	Health Care Equipment & Services	351010	Health Care Equipment & Supplies
				351020	Health Care Providers & Services
				351030	Health Care Technology
		3520	Pharmaceuticals, Biotechnology & Life Sciences	352010	Biotechnology
				352020	Pharmaceuticals
				352030	Life Sciences Tools & Services

(continued)

Table 10.4: sector and industry numerical codes *(cont'd)*

Sector		Industry Group		Industry	
40	Financials	4010	Banks	401010	Commercial Banks
				401020	Thrifts & Mortgage Finance
		4020	Diversified Financials	402010	Diversified Financial Services
				402020	Consumer Finance
				402030	Capital Markets
40	Financials	4030	Insurance	403010	Insurance
		4040	Real Estate	404010	Real Estate — Discontinued effective 04/28/2006
				404020	Real Estate Investment Trusts (REITs)
				404030	Real Estate Management & Development
45	Information Technology	4510	Software & Services	451010	Internet Software & Services
				451020	IT Services
				451030	Software
45	Information Technology	4520	Technology Hardware & Equipment	452010	Communications Equipment
				452020	Computers & Peripherals
				452030	Electronic Equipment, Instruments & Components
				452040	Office Electronics
		4530	Semiconductors & Equipment	453010	Semiconductors & Semiconductor Equipment
50	Telco Services	5010	Telecommuni-cation Services	501010	Diversified Telecommunication Services
				501020	Wireless Telecommunication Services

Sector		Industry Group		Industry	
55	Utilities	5510	Utilities	551010	Electric Utilities
				551020	Gas Utilities
				551030	Multi-Utilities
				551040	Water Utilities
				551050	Independent Power Producers & Energy Traders

Source: GICS table, June 30, 2010. See disclaimer on p. viii.

Tip

You can access the full table up to the eight-digit sub-industry code on the Standard & Poor's website or via the ASX site. These web addresses are given in chapter 3. You will find the table (as an Excel spreadsheet) if you search for 'GICS map'.

Using sector and industry numerical codes

The numerical coding system provides a high level of refinement that enables you to focus very closely on the differences between all the various types of business a company can be engaged in. Information and statistics using the alphabetical coding system are readily available on websites, but unfortunately those based on the numerical codes aren't so readily available. For example, using the alphabetic codes you can readily chart the sector groups and also compare one group to the other (as I've demonstrated), but very few free websites (including broking sites) provide the same facility for the numerical codes. However, there are some charting packages that you can purchase (such as Stock Doctor) that allow to you view sector and industry charts using the numerical codes. Some even break down to the sub-group and sub-industry-group level.

Tip

Even if you can't use the numerical codes to obtain sector and industry charts, the GICS map (as shown in table 10.4) allows you to be more discerning when looking at sectors and to make more refined decisions based on the type of industry a company is engaged in.

Trading an index

Using alphabetic codes it's possible to trade a market or sector index as you would trade shares using their three-letter code. In other words, you can 'buy' or 'sell' an index, depending on whether you think the index will rise or fall. Clearly you can't do so with an ordinary share trading facility, but you can if you trade CFDs (contracts for difference). While the principles of share trading and technical analysis are the same for CFD trading as for shares, detailed discussion of the ins and outs of CFD trading is outside the scope of this book. If you want to trade CFDs you need to set up an account with a CFD provider. Many online brokers offer a CFD trading facility (please refer to chapter 4 where I give the web addresses of several sites that compare brokers and include the facilities offered by each).

Index tracking funds

If you'd like your share portfolio to match the performance of a market index, you could do so by setting up a portfolio of the same shares included in the index and in the same proportion. However, this isn't really a practical proposition for the average share investor unless the index contains a small number of different shares only. Another way of doing so is instead of buying shares in all the companies included in that index you can buy units in an index tracking fund. Many online brokers (including CommSec) provide online investing in managed funds in a similar way as to online share investing. As the name suggests, index tracking funds are set up with the specific purpose of tracking an index. They do so by setting up a portfolio of shares in all the companies included in an index and in the same proportion as they're weighted in the index. Clearly for the All Ords index this requires a portfolio of 500 stocks, which wouldn't really be feasible. However, it's certainly a feasible proposition for a market index based on only 20 or 50 stocks.

The idea of an index tracking fund is that the fund's performance should exactly match the index performance, so by buying into the fund you can effectively buy into the index in only one transaction.

Tip

An index tracking fund won't usually perform as well as the index being tracked—can you see why? The answer is because the fund charges management fees that can be around 2% or so. Consequently, if the index being tracked rises by, say, 10% in a year then the fund would rise by only 8%.

Sector funds

If you'd like your share portfolio to match the performance of a sector index, you could do so by setting up a portfolio of the same shares included in the sector index and in the same proportion. Another way of doing so is instead of buying shares in all the companies included in that index, you can buy units in a sector fund. The sector fund will invest in shares included in that sector only and so will give you exposure to a number of different companies in the sector with only one transaction involved.

Tip

There are many different sector funds on offer—you can check the ones available with your online broker if you're interested in this type of investing.

Key points

⇨ Market and sector analysis is a useful 'top-down' approach that attempts to identify markets and sectors outperforming (or underperforming) others. It differs from the 'bottom-up' approach that uses fundamental analysis based on the analysis of individual shares from the grass roots. The bottom-up approach using fundamental analysis was outlined in chapter 8.

⇨ There's no reason why top-down and bottom-up approaches can't both be used together when you're evaluating shares; indeed, it's a good idea to do so.

⇨ You use the top-down approach to maximise the probability of your portfolio outperforming the market by weighting your shares in the best performing markets and sectors.

⇨ Market indices in Australia comply with the Global Industry Classification System (GICS).

⇨ Australian indices are weighted according to the market capitalisation of the shares included in the index.

⇨ Market indices provide a method of evaluating market performance and provide a useful benchmark for comparing the performance of a fund or portfolio relative to the most relevant market index.

⇨ Industry sectors are based on the main type of business companies are involved with. Some sectors (such as the Energy sector) have many companies in them while some sectors have relatively few (for example, the Telecommunication sector).

⇨ Sector analysis allows you to identify the best performing (or worst performing) sectors within the general market.

⇨ You can analyse market and sector performance in the same way as you would analyse share performance because market and sector indices are identified with unique alphabetic codes that can be used to chart their performance and allow you to apply technical analysis to identify trends.

⇨ Sector groups can be very broad, and so are refined further into industries and sub-industries using a numerical code (rather than an alphabetic one). Depending on the degree of refinement, the numerical code can be 2, 4, 6 or 8 digits.

⇨ You can invest in an index tracking fund if you wish to track index performance. However, fund performance won't match index performance because of the fees involved.

⇨ In a similar way you can invest in a sector fund if you particularly like one market sector.

chapter 11

Managing online investing risks

Online share investing involves some risks. In this chapter I'll look at the various types of risk associated with online share investing and suggest strategies for managing those risks. Because this book is about online share investing, I'll concentrate on the online risks and strategies you can use for managing them. However, many of the risks and management strategies apply equally well to offline share investing.

Tip

If you want more information about share investing risks and the management of them please refer to chapter 13 of my book Teach Yourself About Shares.

Risk management and risk minimisation

In many people's minds, risk management is synonymous with risk minimisation because in most activities in life we manage risks by trying to minimise them. For example, when we're in a motor vehicle we should fasten our seat belts because this minimises the risk of personal injury should the vehicle be involved in an accident.

With share investing, you need to adopt a different mindset—risk management isn't the same as risk minimisation. The reason for this hinges on the connection between investing risk and investing return. Simply stated, if you want a higher profit (return on your investment), you need to take more risk. If you're not happy with a higher level of risk, you need to be satisfied with a lower return.

Let's suppose you want to minimise investing risk to the lowest possible level. One way of doing so is to deposit your funds in an interest-bearing account with one of the major banks. This is about as low an investing risk as is possible as it's extremely unlikely that the bank will default on interest payments or that you won't be able to withdraw funds without loss when you want to do so. However, the return isn't going to be very spectacular; based on today's interest rates, you'll get a return of only about 3%. The interest is taxable income, so if you're liable to pay income tax, the after-tax return will be around 2% (or even less). Australia's inflation rate usually runs at about 3%, meaning that the purchasing power of money reduces by this amount each year. If you deposit your investing capital in an interest-bearing bank account, your after-tax return of 2% is less than the inflation rate of 3%, so you're going backwards. Your real wealth (in terms of purchasing power) is reducing and not increasing.

Naturally, we'd all love to find a really safe haven for our investing capital that produced high, reliable returns year after year with no risk of ever incurring a loss or reduction in the expected profit. Unfortunately this type of investment exists in cloud-cuckoo land only, and in the real word the higher the expected return from an investment, the greater the risk involved. You will note that I used the qualifier 'expected' when referring to the return. This qualifier is needed because it's another fact of life that when you invest your capital in some type of investment you're leaping into the future because you can't receive a return on this capital retrospectively. Your profits will be made in the future, and any leap into the future contains an inherent degree of uncertainty. So with all investing, profits can be 'expected' or 'anticipated' only; it's not a certainty that the actual return will match expectations. Even a comparatively safe interest-bearing bank account isn't a certainty as interest rates can (and do) change and can reduce as well as increase. It's certainly not without precedent that banks in some countries have run into financial difficulties and have suspended or limited withdrawals, although this hasn't happened with Australia's major banks and is extremely unlikely.

The very fact that you're reading this book implies that you recognise these facts and are interested in share investing because you want a higher return from your investment than you can expect from a bank deposit. You most likely realise that share investing carries an inherently higher risk but you're prepared to accept that higher level of risk so you can participate in the higher gains possible. With shares the name of the game isn't to minimise risks, but rather to manage risks so you don't take unnecessary risks. To do this you need to adopt sound strategies to ensure that the risk doesn't exceed the level you're comfortable with.

Tip

With any investing (and certainly share investing), you need to shift focus from risk minimisation to risk management.

Risk profile

Because risk and return are inextricably linked, the first step in managing investment risk is to decide what level of risk you're comfortable with. This is an individual issue as everyone's different in this regard. It depends on your personality and a whole host of factors, including your age, gender and life experiences. For example, risk tolerance usually decreases with age and younger people are prepared to take higher risks than older people. As a general rule, men are prepared to take more risks than women of comparable age. Also your risk tolerance level is influenced by your financial and family situation; for example, a married person with children and a sizeable mortgage will be more focused on minimising the possibility of losses than on taking more risk with the possibility of higher profits.

Before you can match your investments to your risk tolerance level, you really need to determine what that level is. You'll no doubt have an inherent idea of how much investing risk you're comfortable with but you can get a more definitive and less subjective idea of this by completing a risk profile quiz.

There are several risk profile quizzes available online; one I've personally tried and recommend is available for free on the following website: www.riskprofiling.com. This site will link you to the FinaMetrica site where there's a 25-question quiz. After you complete the quiz you'll be asked to estimate your risk score, which can lie in the range 0 to 100, with the average person having a score of 50. The higher your score, the more risk you're comfortable with. After you've submitted your score estimate, the program calculates your score based on your responses to the quiz. It's very interesting to see how your estimate compares with the program score. In my case I estimated a higher score than was indicated by my quiz responses, indicating that I perceived myself to be a higher investing risk taker than I actually am.

Tip

I strongly suggest you complete a risk management quiz like the one I've indicated, in order to get a more definitive and more objective idea of your risk profile. Your shares planning (as discussed in chapter 6) should take into account your risk profile as you should match the types of shares you trade and your trading duration and frequency with your risk tolerance level.

Volatility

As the name suggests, volatility is 'jumpiness', the extent to which there's a variation up or down from an average or general trend. Volatility applies to all facets of share investing but most importantly to price, earnings and income. Volatility is the opposite to stability; that is, the greater the stability, the lower the volatility and vice versa. For example, consider figure 11.1 where I've shown the performance of two shares: A (solid line) and B (dashed line).

Figure 11.1: volatility

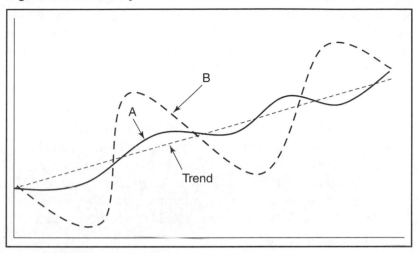

You can see that both A and B follow the same trendline and start and finish at the same points, but A is far more stable (less volatile) than B.

Tip

Volatility is closely related to risk, and the higher the volatility the greater the risk. This is because the greater the amount of historical variation, the greater the uncertainty of the future. Speculative shares are the most volatile and carry the greatest risk but have the potential for fast capital gains profits.

Share investing risk

There are three main risks associated with share investing, and these are:

⇨ earnings risk

⇨ dividend risk

⇨ price risk.

Earnings risk

This is the risk that there'll be an earnings downgrade; that is, the earnings per share (EPS) will reduce below that of previous periods or below that which has been forecast (or anticipated) by the market. Investors love to see a stable and growing EPS and shares that have a track record of stability and growth in EPS are rated highly. Earnings downgrades are regarded as bad news, and should they occur, the share price is usually punished — often to a greater degree than the downgrade warrants.

Tip

With shares there's always a risk of unexpected bad news causing an earnings downgrade. This can come out of left field at any time and can be very difficult to foresee. The best way of managing this risk is to invest in companies that have a stable earnings record over several years. Better still, stick to companies that have been able to steadily increase their EPS, despite market downturns.

Managing the earnings risk

As I've said, the best way of managing the earnings risk is to invest in companies that have a stable earnings record. One way you can check the earnings stability is with published fundamental data (as explained in chapter 8). On the CommSec site, the earnings stability is shown in the 'Key measures' data and is expressed as a percentage per annum. It's shown for the company in question, the market as a whole and the relevant sector. The closer the figure is to 100%, the greater the stability (the lower the volatility). If you refer to figure 8.1, you can see that in my example for Flight Centre (FLT), the earnings stability for this company is given as 77.5%. For the market as a whole it's 55.4% and for the sector it's 51.9%. Therefore we can conclude that FLT has a relatively stable earnings record.

Tip

If the shares haven't been listed for very long or don't have a history of earnings (not making a profit), earnings stability can't be calculated.

Several other ways of assessing earnings stability are given on the CommSec site in the 'Company research' section and the 'Forecast' tab. There are two bar charts as shown in figure 11.2.

Figure 11.2: earnings surprises for FLT

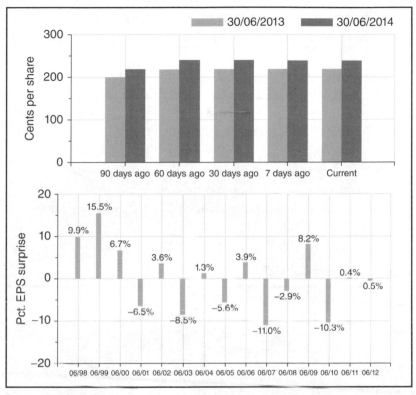

Source: www.CommSec.com.au

The top chart shows analysts' earnings trend estimates for the current financial year (left bar) and next financial year (right darker bar) over the last three months. You can see that analysts are expecting next year's earnings for FLT to be rather higher than this year's, and also that their earnings estimates are relatively stable.

The lower chart shows EPS surprises over a past number of interim and final periods. You can see that for FLT there's been about an equal number of upgrades and downgrades over the last 15 reporting periods, with the best surprise being 15.5% better than expected and the worst being 11% lower than expected.

Yet another way you can gauge earnings stability and growth (or reduction) is from the historical EPS data. This data for the CommSec site was shown in chapter 8 as figure 8.2. From this data you can see that EPS for FLT for the last 10 financial years was as follows in table 11.1 (overleaf).

Table 11.1: historical EPS for FLT

Year	2003	2004	2005	2006	2007	2008	2009	2010	2011	2012
EPS	76.4	89.4	71.9	84.5	96.6	146.5	98.0	138.8	170.8	198.6

By examining this table it's clear that the EPS has generally risen over the last 10 years and this is an excellent indication. However, there were hiccups in 2005 and 2009 when the earnings were lower in these years than in the previous years.

Tip
You can get a better visual impression of the EPS trend by charting EPS using a program such as Excel, as I've done in figure 11.3.

Figure 11.3: EPS for FLT

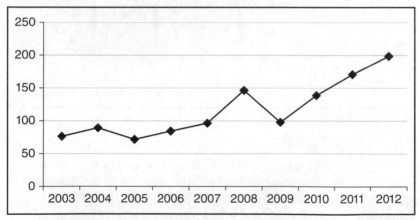

Dividend risk

If there's no dividend payable clearly there's no dividend risk, but if there's a dividend that's of importance to you, there are several risks involved, namely:

⇨ reduced dividend

⇨ reduced level of franking

⇨ suspension of the dividend reinvestment plan (DRP).

Reduced dividend risk

If the shares have produced significant dividends in the past, there's a risk that the dividend could be reduced (or even suspended entirely) in the future or that future dividends will be less than the market anticipates based on company announcements and performance metrics. This is an important risk if you're relying on dividends for income or you're reinvesting the dividend so as to build up your share investment capital. A reduction or suspension of the dividend is double-barrelled bad news as it reduces future payouts to shareholders and, in addition, the market will almost always react unfavourably and the share price will fall.

Tip

Dividends paid to shareholders are a share of the profits, so it follows that in order to pay consistent or rising dividends the company needs to make consistent or rising profits. In some cases, after an earnings downgrade company directors may decide to maintain the dividend at the previous level. This isn't really good news for shareholders as it's not a sustainable practice in the long run because the company needs to dip into its assets in order to do so.

Managing the reduced dividend risk

You can manage this risk in a similar way to the earnings risk. Firstly, you can check the dividend stability. If you refer to figure 8.1, you can see that for Flight Centre (FLT) the dividend stability is 90.4%, which is a high value, although a little below the market value of 90.9% and the sector value of 94.2%. You can also check the historical dividend data as given in figure 8.2 (see p. 218). For FLT it was as shown in table 11.2.

Table 11.2: historical DPS for FLT

Year	2003	2004	2005	2006	2007	2008	2009	2010	2011	2012
DPS	43.5	61.0	50.5	52.0	66.0	86.0	9.0	70.0	84.0	112.0

Tip

You can get a better visual impression of the DPS trend by charting the EPS using a program such as Excel, as I've done in figure 11.4.

Figure 11.4: DPS for FLT

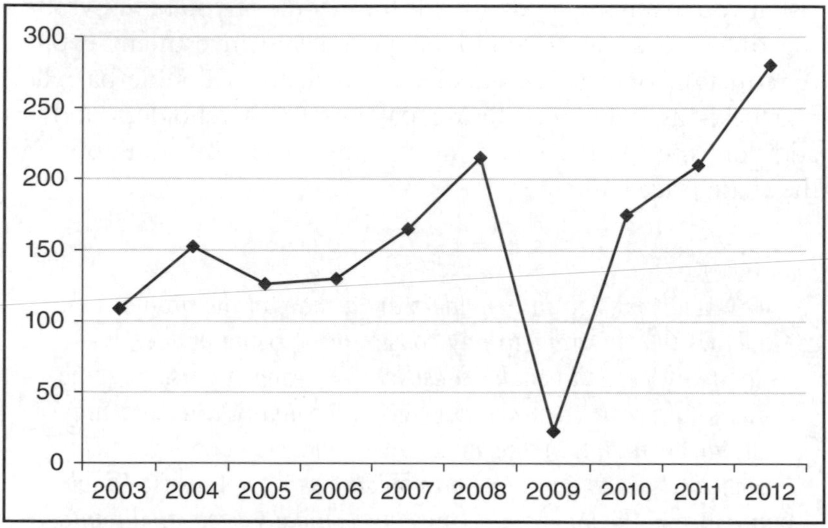

Reduced level of franking risk

Many dividend-paying shares have franking credits (imputation credits) associated with the dividend. There's a risk that there could be a reduction in the level of franking for future dividends and this will reduce the value of the dividend.

The imputation credit associated with the dividend varies according to the franking level and can vary between 0 and 100%. If the dividend is fully franked (100% franking), shareholders receive full credit for Australian income tax paid by the company and can claim this credit as a rebate (offset) from the ATO (or as a cash payment if the shareholder doesn't have a taxable income).

Tip

As outlined in chapter 1, the Australian company tax rate is 30%, which gives a grossing-up factor of 1.429, which means that a fully franked yield is almost 43% better than an unfranked one.

Managing the franking risk

Ways of managing the franking credit risk include:

⇨ Invest in companies that earn all (or most) of their profits in Australia and therefore pay Australian tax on their profits that automatically carries franking credits.

⇨ Check franking credit history and ensure that the level of franking has been stable over a number of years. This data appears in the historical data under DPS, and you can see that for FLT the level of franking has been 100% consistently over the last 10 years.

Tip

If the franking level has been consistently maintained over the last 10 years, there's very little risk of it being reduced in the future.

Suspension of the DRP risk

As I've said in previous chapters, if you're more interested in building up your nest egg than in obtaining income from your shares, a dividend reinvestment plan is a great way of doing so, because your dividends are automatically converted into shares without brokerage and often at a favourable price. The availability of a DRP may indeed be a decisive factor in your initial decision to invest in the shares. Companies offering a DRP can suspend it at any time at the discretion of the directors — usually because the directors don't want an increase in the number of issued shares. This is a small (but possibly significant) risk if you value the DRP.

Managing the DRP risk

You can check if there's a DRP on offer at the time you purchase shares in the published financial data. For example, on the CommSec site this is given in the 'Company info' section screen on the right hand side in the 'Company details' box.

Unfortunately there's no clear-cut way of managing this risk as there's no easily accessible historical data showing how long the DRP has been in operation. The best you can do is to keep alerted to company announcements to see if there's any talk of suspending the DRP at any time in the future.

Tip

If the availability of a DRP is important to you, ensure that one is in operation before you invest in particular shares.

Price risk

Price risk is the risk that the price could fall after you've purchased shares, so that if you want to sell later on you'll make a capital loss. The possibility of a price fall is a definite and ongoing risk with share investing, and is the main reason why many potential investors shy away from shares.

As I've said, price risk is closely related to earnings risk because an earnings downgrade will almost always cause a share price fall. Of course, that applies only to companies making profits, but there are many listed companies that don't make a profit or pay dividends, so for these companies price risk is more dependent on future earnings possibilities or 'blue sky potential' rather than a definite earnings downgrade.

Managing the price risk

Like all share investing risks, the price risk can be managed if you use good strategies and stay in the game for a reasonable time period. In the longer term you'll end up in front compared with 'safe' investments such as bank deposits.

So far in this book I've outlined many strategies you can use to manage the price risk. I'll briefly summarise the most important ones:

⇨ Have a written trading/investing plan and stick to it — please refer to chapter 6.

⇨ Regularly monitor your share investments and use indices to keep tabs on market and sector performance. Take action if necessary — please refer to chapter 6, and consider using conditional orders to limit losses as outlined in chapter 7.

⇨ Invest in shares whose fundamentals match your risk profile—please refer to chapter 8, and be prepared to re-jig your portfolio when there's a change in the fundamentals—in particular earnings or dividend changes.

⇨ Use technical analysis to maximise the likelihood that you'll trade at a good price and at a good time—please refer to chapter 9. At all times keep in mind the golden rule that you should never buy shares if the price is falling.

Tip

Using the strategies I've suggested above is the most reliable long-run way you can manage the price risk with shares.

Downside potential

In the planning stage when you're evaluating the risk of a share price fall, it's a good idea to consider the downside potential, which is essentially the worst-case scenario. One way of doing this is to try to identify a realistic price support level. With speculative shares you might decide that a realistic downside level is zero (the shares could become valueless), but could you see this happening with one of the major banks or retailers? Can you see Commonwealth Bank or Woolworths becoming bankrupt and their shares falling to zero value?

As well as downside potential you should consider the upside potential; that is, a realistic resistance level or price which the shares could conceivably rise to in the foreseeable future. With any proposed trade you can then calculate the up/down ratio (reward/risk ratio) by dividing the upside potential by the downside potential. The higher the ratio, the greater the profit potential and the lower the price risk.

For example, consider two shares, A and B, with support and resistance levels as shown in table 11.3 (overleaf).

By this method of evaluation, it's clear that shares in A represent a better and less risky investment than B because there is a much higher upside to downside ratio. Indeed, this calculation indicates you should avoid B altogether unless you were very confident that the price was in a strong uptrend mode.

Table 11.3: downside/upside potential

	A	B
Price	$1.86	$5.34
Support	$1.75	$5.00
Resistance	$2.11	$5.60
Downside potential	$0.11	$0.34
Upside potential	$0.25	$0.26
Ratio up/down	2.27	0.76

Tip

It's always a good idea to have realistic downside and upside potential price estimates before you initiate a share trade.

Price risk and volatility

Price risk is closely related to price volatility; that is, the degree to which the price fluctuates up and down. If price volatility is low, the price is relatively stable and moves up or down by relatively small amounts and therefore there's less risk of a sudden and significant price fall. If volatility is high, the price fluctuates up or down significantly in a relatively short time and therefore there's more price risk.

Tip

Shares in companies that don't make profits are generally more volatile and therefore more risky.

Managing the price risk

Three common ways of evaluating price volatility (and risk) are as follows:

⇨ beta

⇨ volatility formula

⇨ chart inspection.

These methods will now be outlined.

Beta

As discussed in chapter 8, beta is a statistic that provides an estimate of the volatility of shares (or a sector), and the higher the beta value the higher the volatility. A beta value of around one indicates volatility that's about the same as the general market, below one there's less volatility and above one there's greater volatility.

As an example, in figure 8.1 (see p. 208) the beta values for Flight Centre (FLT) were as follows:

Company 0.87, market 1.07, sector 0.93

You can see that the beta value for FLT is relatively low and better than both market and sector, indicating that the price is relatively stable and that there's a relatively low price risk associated with these shares.

Tip

The beta of the All Ords isn't exactly one due to the statistical calculation method used with the selection of shares that comprise the index.

Volatility formula

A simple way of assessing price volatility is from the range in prices—the difference between the highest and lowest prices in a period of time.

The volatility formula as given below gives a volatility percentage score, and the higher the score the greater the volatility:

$$\text{Volatility (\%)} = \frac{(\text{Period high} - \text{Period low})}{\text{Period low}} \times 100$$

Conventionally, the time period is the most recent 52 weeks, so the formula will calculate the annual volatility.

Tip

You may wish to set a limit on the volatility you consider acceptable as part of your 'health test'—please refer to chapter 8. For volatile shares the annual volatility can be above 100%.

Example 1

I'll use the formula to calculate the price volatility for FLT. If you refer to figure 8.1, in the top right-hand corner the 52-week high for FLT is given as $29.10 and the 52-week low is given as $16.82. Applying the formula:

$$\text{Volatility \%} = \frac{(29.10 - 16.82)}{16.82} \times 100 = 73\%$$

This is a relatively low value and confirms the conclusion from the beta value.

Now consider a mining stock that I chose at random: Alkane (ALK). At the time of writing, the 52-week high was $1.615 and the 52-week low was $0.565. Applying the formula:

$$\text{Volatility \%} = \frac{(1.615 - 0.565)}{0.565} \times 100 = 186\%$$

This is well above 100%, confirming the volatility of the price of these shares.

Chart inspection

A third way that you can form an impression of price volatility is by examining a price chart and looking at the amount of price variation. A good way of doing this is by using a candle chart as this chart shows daily variations rather than just end-of-day prices. In figure 11.5 I've shown candle charts of FLT and ALK together.

You can see the greater variations in price (bounciness) that occur with ALK, confirming the greater price volatility.

Tip

You can also form an impression of shorter term price volatility from Bollinger Bands®. The further apart the bands are the greater the volatility, and the closer together the lesser the volatility. Please refer to chapter 9 where I briefly discuss these bands.

Figure 11.5: FLT and ALK compared

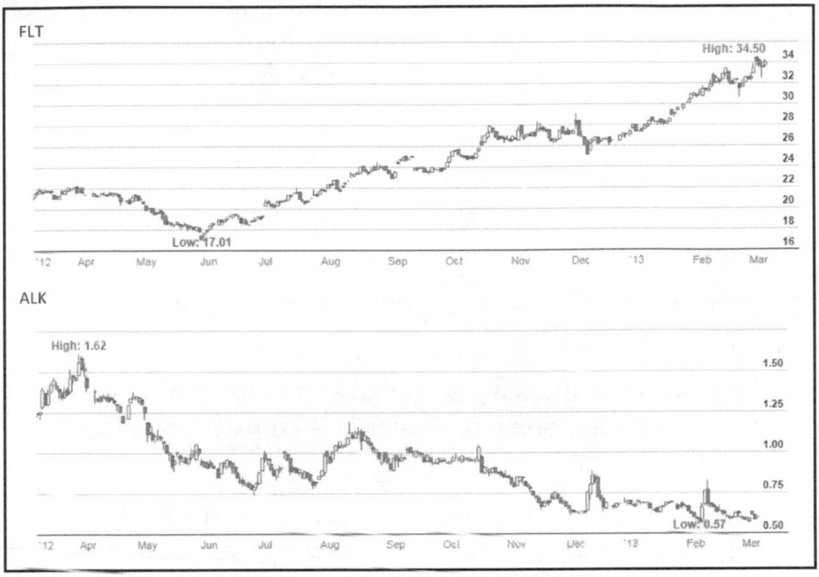

Source: www.CommSec.com.au

Risk management—a top-down approach

One approach to risk management is a top-down approach, which is based on progressively climbing down the risk ladder in the following sequence:

⇨ global market risk

⇨ Australian market risk

⇨ sector risk

⇨ specific risk.

Global market risk

This is the risk associated with major world economies, particularly the US, Europe (including Britain) and the so-called developing 'BRIC' economies—Brazil, Russia, India and China. There's usually a flow-on effect from one major economy to another—in particular, the Australian market is strongly influenced by the US, China and European markets. Our market is only a very small one in the world scene and usually follows global trends. It used to be said that 'when the US market sneezes the rest of the world catches a cold', but nowadays our market is usually affected as much by other major global economies, including China and the European Union.

Managing global risk

Obviously you can't influence the course of global markets but you can manage the global risk as it could affect your share portfolio in the following ways:

⇨ keep your ear close to the ground; that is, monitor global markets regularly

⇨ be aware of changes in the global scene that can have financial implications for Australia — in particular global commodity prices

⇨ access and assess analysts' predictions as to the likely impact of world events on the Australian sharemarket or Australian companies

⇨ plan your share investing strategies according to how the above factors are varying.

Tip

Another way of managing global risk is by investing globally, either in international shares or in currencies (forex). There are higher risks involved with global investing so I suggest you stick to the Australian market unless you have particular global investing expertise.

Australian market risk

This is the risk associated with the Australian market. There are many unique factors that can cause our sharemarket to rise and fall. These include changes in the following factors:

⇨ federal government political party in power

⇨ Australian financial legislation

⇨ government policies

⇨ government spending and where the funds are being directed

⇨ economic data such as employment, retail sales and balance of trades

⇨ interest rates.

Managing Australian market risk

You can manage the Australian market risk in the following ways:

⇨ assess the level of risk by keeping yourself up to date with Australian economic data as it's released

⇨ study analysts' forecasts and comments regarding the Australian sharemarket or particular companies or sectors

⇨ analyse charts of market indices and use technical analysis tools (as outlined in chapter 9) to identify market trends and to assess the likelihood of trend changes.

If your analysis leads you to the conclusion that the Australian sharemarket is upbeat you can increase your exposure to Australian shares, and when you think the market is due for a correction or downturn you can decrease your exposure to these shares.

An alternative strategy for managing market risk is to be a long-term participant; that is, simply hold tight and ride the up and down fluctuations. The Australian market has proven to be among the best in the world for growth and stability and in the last 100 years there's never been more than two consecutive years of negative performance. Therefore, Australian market risk is virtually eliminated if you hold a portfolio of quality Australian shares and continue holding them over the long term.

Tip

Long-term participation is a simple and effective strategy for managing Australian market risk, but for it to be effective your portfolio needs to consist of quality shares; that is, shares with sound fundamentals. It's usually not productive to hold speculative shares over the long term.

Sector risk

This is the risk associated with specific sectors of the Australian market rather than the market as a whole. For example, changes in export demand or the price of resources, such as gold, coal or oil, affect the relevant resource sectors but may have little impact on other sectors of the Australian market.

Managing sector risk

You can assess sector risk in the same ways as previously outlined—by keeping up to date with sector performance, studying analysts' forecasts and comments regarding sectors of the Australian sharemarket, and analysing charts of sector indices and using technical analysis tools to identify sector trends and to assess the likelihood of trend changes.

You can then manage the sector risk by balancing your portfolio with shares in sectors that align with your risk profile. For example, if like me you're a relatively low-risk investor you can bias your portfolio so that the majority of your shares are in stable (defensive) sectors. These sectors are those where fluctuating economic conditions don't affect the sector greatly, generally because demand in the sector is relatively inelastic. That's to say, the products or services marketed by companies included in that sector have a relatively stable demand despite changing economic conditions. These safer and less volatile sectors include the following:

⇨ banking

⇨ alcohol and tobacco

⇨ gambling and gaming

⇨ infrastructure and utilities

⇨ property trusts

⇨ consumer staples.

The riskier and more volatile sectors include the following:

⇨ mining

⇨ tourism and leisure

⇨ biotechnology

⇨ telecommunications

⇨ internet and new technology.

Tip

Be aware of the differing risk levels associated with differing sectors and choose shares in sectors whose riskiness aligns with your risk profile.

Specific risk

Specific risk is the risk associated with a particular share that doesn't necessarily apply to others (even in the same sector). For example, if the XYZ oil exploration company were to announce that a promising well proved to be uneconomic and was to be capped, the share price would usually fall. However, this will probably have no impact on any other shares in the Australian market—even those in the same sector. In a similar way, even in the relatively stable and defensive financial sector there are considerable differences in risk associated with the various companies in the sector according to the source of their income and investments.

Managing specific risk

You can assess and manage specific risk in the same ways that apply to sector risk, including: close monitoring of share prices and announcements, analysts' forecasts, fundamental analysis to check the historical financial statistics (particularly earnings risk and debt) or by using charting and technical analysis to detect changes in market sentiment about the shares. Also you should match your risk profile with the riskiness of the shares in your portfolio. If you're a low risk taker your portfolio should consist of mainly relatively safe and defensive shares. If you're more of a high risk taker, your portfolio could contain a higher proportion of the more speculative shares.

Tip

If you want a low specific risk, invest in shares with good fundamentals; that is, blue- or green-chip shares in established companies with good fundamentals that have a proven track record of good returns for shareholders with consistently growing profits and good dividends.

General risk management strategies

I'll now outline some general risk management strategies you can use with shares. I don't claim this to be a comprehensive discussion; I'll just outline some easily applied strategies that I've found useful and that you may wish to adopt.

Tip

An essential part of any risk management strategy is to minimise the likelihood of trading mistakes. You may wish to revisit chapter 7, where I outline possible online trading mistakes and suggest strategies for avoiding them.

Concentrated portfolio risk

This is the risk of having a concentrated portfolio of shares; that is, one where a substantial amount of your investing capital is invested in shares of a similar type in the same sector. The risk is that if there's a downturn in this particular group of shares, your portfolio performance will suffer greatly.

Managing concentrated portfolio risk

The most commonly recommended method of managing concentrated portfolio risk is to have a diversified portfolio that's balanced with shares in diverse sectors. In a diversified portfolio there's a sharing of risk as summarised by the well-known saying, 'Don't put all your eggs in one basket'. Diversification is based on the idea that poor performance in a particular group of shares can be offset by good performance in others (unless of course the whole market trends down).

On the other hand, there's the potential for a concentrated portfolio to outperform a balanced one and this will occur if the portfolio is concentrated with shares in the best performing sectors. As an example, my portfolio is heavily weighted with banking shares because I'm a self-funded retiree and relatively low risk taker. My priority is to obtain steady and reliable dividend income from my shares and for there to be a low downside risk with most of them. My strategy has been vindicated in recent years as my banking shares have returned good, steady income in the form of substantial fully franked dividends and they've also experienced high capital growth. In this way I'm getting the best of both worlds, and in recent years I've been able to consistently beat the overall market. However, I realise that by adopting this approach I'm accepting the risk that a downturn in the banking sector will have a more negative effect on my portfolio than in one that's balanced with a variety of shares in many diverse sectors. In a sense my portfolio strategy doesn't align with my low-risk profile because it's not a well diversified one. However, while my portfolio isn't balanced, it's concentrated in low-risk shares so I don't really think I'm taking a high risk by adopting this strategy.

Tip

There are both advantages and disadvantages to a concentrated portfolio compared to a balanced one, and there's no right or wrong approach so you really have to decide which of these options you prefer.

Tracking error

The stability of your portfolio compared to the overall market (represented by the All Ords) can be measured by what's known as tracking error. The higher your diversification, the lower the tracking error and vice versa. This effect is shown in figure 11.6.

Figure 11.6: tracking error

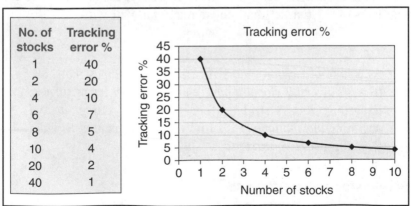

No. of stocks	Tracking error %
1	40
2	20
4	10
6	7
8	5
10	4
20	2
40	1

The law of diminishing returns kicks in as the number of stocks in your portfolio increases. That is, you significantly reduce tracking error by holding five or six stocks rather than one or two, but there's only a further 2% reduction in tracking error by holding 20 stocks rather than 10. A large number of Australian shareholders have portfolios consisting of only a few stocks, with more than 50% of shareholders holding three or fewer stocks. This indicates that most Australian shareholders don't diversify sufficiently to bring their tracking error down to a low level (say, less than 5%).

Tip

If you want a well-diversified portfolio you should hold at least five and preferably ten stocks in different industries or sectors. However, bear in mind my previous discussion about the advantages and disadvantages of a concentrated portfolio compared to a diversified one.

Company diversification

Many companies practise diversification with the range of products they market and the markets they service. History shows that product or market diversification of Australian companies increases their overall profitability only when the business doesn't diversify into products or markets that don't align with their established core competencies. As a general rule, Australian conglomerates don't usually achieve better financial performance than Australian companies that concentrate on specific types of products or segments of the market that they're really familiar with.

Tip

As a note of caution, many Australian companies that have tried to diversify globally have ended up with burnt fingers. Exporting from Australia is one thing, but setting up and operating internationally is entirely another kettle of fish and it often proves to be an unsuccessful venture.

Single-stock diversification

As well as diversifying the shares in your portfolio, you can diversify by investing in a single entity such as a diversified managed fund or investment company. Many diversified funds are available that offer a mix of different asset classes such as cash, fixed-interest, property, Australian shares and global shares, and many of these are accessible online. There are a number of Australian listed investment companies (LICs) that invest in a wide variety of different shares in the Australian market. You can trade shares in a listed investment company using your online broker just as you would for ordinary shares.

Tip

If you have a relatively small share portfolio I suggest you consider holding at least one listed investment company. By doing so you obtain some diversification with just one stock and, in general, Australian LICs have a good track record.

Irrational optimism or pessimism risk

In previous chapters I've outlined the strategy that it's generally safest to follow a trend rather than to go against it; that is, to be a contrarian. While this is usually the safest and best strategy, you need to be aware of the risk of irrational optimism or pessimism. This occurs when traders get 'carried away' and drive share prices to unreasonably high or low levels that prove to be unsustainable. Irrational optimism or pessimism can occur with specific shares, sectors or the market as a whole.

To see why it can occur consider the likely result if a share price rises for some time. Traders and investors look at the share price chart and sense the mood of optimism driving the share price higher. Before long, others want to jump on board and get a slice of the action. This drives prices higher and puts more fuel on the fire in a self-driven rush that can spiral out of control. Prices can rise beyond a sustainable level because it's a level that can't be justified by any rational analysis of realistic earnings prospects. The opposite effect can occur when prices drive down in a mood of pessimism that can end up being almost a panic.

When irrational optimism or pessimism take hold in the market, the inevitable consequence is that eventually some traders 'pull the plug' and this results in a sudden reaction in the opposite direction. I've illustrated this in figures 11.7 and 11.8 (overleaf) which are pictorial representations of irrational optimism and the subsequent correction to the long-term trendline.

Figure 11.7: irrational optimism

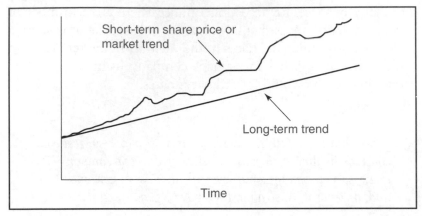

Figure 11.8: irrational optimism correction

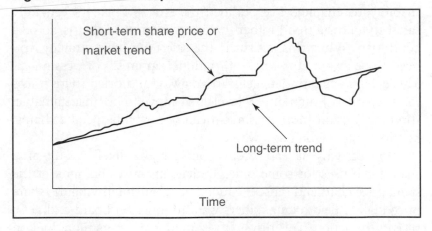

Managing irrational optimism or pessimism risk

There are two signal markers that help you identify irrational optimism (and the opposite effects for irrational pessimism). These are:

⇨ the price rises upward well above the longer term trendline

⇨ the P/E ratio (price/earnings ratio) rises to well above the historical sector level to a level that's unsustainable. That's to say, the share price can't be justified by realistic earnings analysis.

Tip

When a share price climbs high above the long-term trendline or when its P/E rises to a level than can't be justified by earnings (and is much higher than the sector average), beware, as sooner or later a downward correction is inevitable. On the other hand, price corrections after falls to irrationally low levels can present good buying opportunities, provided the bounce is a sustained one and not a 'dead cat' bounce.

Personal bias risk

We're all human and have our own personal likes and dislikes, and this applies to our share trades and our share portfolios as much as it does to everything else in our lives. Personal bias on the sharemarket causes us to take a 'blinkered' view that disrupts our rational decision making. For example, it's a well-known communication bias that we tend to take on board new information that reinforces our own belief system and ignore (or play down) information that contradicts it. With share investing this bias causes us to look at shares we like through 'rose coloured spectacles' and ignore the negative signs. At the same time we tend to ignore the positive signs affecting shares we don't like (often because we've had our fingers burnt with them in the past).

As much as you might think you're making rational share investing decisions you can't avoid a certain amount of personal bias, so you need to consider this at all times. In particular try to avoid 'falling in love' with certain shares. These are shares that in the past have been good performers and that you feel a particular attachment to. The world is constantly changing and good past investments won't necessarily be the best ones going forward so you need to constantly re-evaluate your shares in the light of changing circumstances.

Managing personal bias risk

The best way of managing personal bias risk is to avoid making share trading and investing decisions based on 'gut feeling' and instead use rational decision-making procedures based on sound fundamental and technical analysis.

Another aid to the management of personal bias risk is to seek the ideas of others and put them through the 'grist of the mill of your own mind' before making decisions. Many online sites provide forecasts and opinions of one or more financial analysts about specific shares, sectors or the market as a whole. In addition, the internet has opened the door to communication with others and there are many internet sites devoted specifically to share investing forums and chat rooms. However, you need to take into account that others also have their own personal biases or 'axes to grind' and their suggestions could reflect these biases.

Tip

Be aware of the risk of personal bias affecting your share investing and trading decisions, and try to make rational and objective decisions rather than subjective ones. It can also be helpful to seek the ideas of others (but don't necessarily act on them).

Share partnership

Another way of managing share investing risk is by setting up a share club or partnership. Share investing clubs (usually set up as partnerships) are now quite common.

Advantages

⇨ more investing capital available, as 10 investors with $5000 each now have a combined investment capital pool of $50 000

⇨ sharing of the risk among the investors

⇨ you can obtain several viewpoints and discuss ideas with others and this helps you to overcome your personal bias.

Disadvantages

⇨ it takes time (and some cost) to set up the bank accounts, partnership agreements and to obtain a tax file number

⇨ the partnership needs to file a separate tax return

⇨ if you decide to have personal meetings you need a mutually convenient time (and place). However, it's possible to set up conferencing using the internet or to keep in touch using Facebook or other internet conferencing methods that allow members to make joint decisions without the need for personal meetings.

Tip

If you're in touch with other like-minded share investors, consider the possibility of a share partnership. Apart from the fact that it may be a profitable venture you're sure to pick up some ideas that will broaden your perspectives.

Profit erosion risk

Profit erosion risk is the risk that occurs when you're holding shares that show a good 'paper' profit. The risk is that the price could fall and your 'paper' profit could evaporate or even turn into a loss.

Managing profit erosion risk

An obvious strategy to manage this risk is to set a profit stop (or profit target) with your online broker. This is a conditional selling order that crystallises your profit. If your profit stop is activated, the risk of a price fall is eliminated. After your order transacts, it makes no difference to you if the price falls because you have the cash value of the sale in your account.

Profit stops were outlined in chapter 7 and you may wish to review this discussion now. The chief disadvantage of profit stops is that they limit your profits when prices are rising. Because of this I tend not to use them because they violate my fundamental principle of not selling in a rising market. However, this is a personal preference and many authors and trading systems advocate the use of profit stops. They justify this strategy by quoting the stock market saying:

You can't go broke by taking profits.

To which I counter:

You can't become rich by selling too soon when the price is rising.

Tip

I feel it's better to let profits run until there's a trend change rather than selling when a pre-set profit stop price is reached. However, you need to make up your own mind about this as many analysts advocate the use of profit stops.

Sequential trading risk

Sequential trading occurs when you sell shares in one stock and reinvest all your capital from that sale into the purchase of shares in another stock. This risk occurs because of a mathematical quirk that has nothing to do with the specific shares involved.

For example, consider the following scenario:

⇨ You buy a parcel of shares for $1.00 each.

⇨ The price rises by 50% and then falls by 50%.

Are you better off, worse off, or do you break even?

The answer is that you're worse off. If the price rises by 50%, the share price will be $1.50. If the price now falls by 50%, the price will be $0.75 and you've made a 25% loss! Strangely, the same effect occurs when the price falls by 50% and then rises by 50%. You still make a loss of 25%!

The risk applies to your share trades when you trade sequentially; that is, you reinvest all proceeds from one sale into another. For example, you buy a $2000 parcel of speculative shares. Subsequently the price rises by 50% and you sell the shares for $3000. You use the proceeds to buy a $3000 parcel of shares—this is trading sequentially. Now if the price falls by 50% you'll make a loss of 25% because your capital has dwindled to $1500, so you've lost $500!

Tip

In my example I've assumed you've suffered a 50% price fall in shares you purchased. If you adopt the suggestions I've repeatedly made throughout this book you shouldn't suffer this type of loss and you should stop any losses before they reach such a high level.

Managing sequential trading risk

One way of managing sequential trading risk is to not reinvest all your capital from one trade into another. In the previous example you invest only $2000 on the next trade and keep $1000 in cash. If, on the next trade, the price falls by 50% and you sell the shares for $1000 the net result on the combined trades is a break even and not a loss, because you still have $2000 of capital.

Another strategy is to split your trades. For example, if you buy two different shares and invest half your capital on each trade, if the share price of one goes up 50% and the other goes down 50% you break even and don't make a loss on the combined trades.

Tip

If you can pick a string of winners, sequential trading can produce large profits. But it's a very risky strategy and one I suggest you avoid unless the market is in a prolonged bull phase (or you're very good at picking a string of winners).

'Getting it wrong' risk

I'll now discuss a risk that's involved with all share trades; that is, the risk of getting it wrong. This is the risk that the price will move in the opposite direction to what you expected when you placed the trade. For example, you buy shares when you're expecting the price will rise, or at least not fall. If you think the price will fall, you're better off delaying the trade until the price bottoms and then starts to rise. On the other hand, if you're selling shares you're expecting the price will fall, otherwise if you think the price will rise you're better off delaying the trade until the price reaches a peak and then starts falling.

When you trade in the expectation of future price action, you naturally think you're right. But it's a sobering thought to remember that you can't buy unless someone else sells and you can't sell unless someone else buys. Clearly, another trader is taking the opposite view to yours. I hope by now you've taken on board my suggestions and are planning your trades using sound fundamental and technical analysis to give yourself the best chance of getting it right. Perhaps you're inclined to think you have an edge on other traders who aren't quite as clever or disciplined as you are. There's no doubt that some people have a natural flair for predicting price movements and getting it right more often than they get it wrong, but in my experience there aren't many fools trading shares and it's not easy to consistently make winning trades. I suggest that a good bottom line for you is to adopt the mindset that despite all your good planning it may turn out that you're right only 50% of the time.

This might seem like a rather depressing thought, but all is not lost—even if you're right only half the time, there are three strategies I'll now outline that enable you to make a profit even under these conditions. The only time these strategies won't work is when the entire market is in a strong bear phase, in which case 'all boats fall when the tide goes out'.

The three strategies are:

⇨   multi-parcel trading (cost or price averaging)

⇨   the 1% rule

⇨   let profits run but limit losses.

I'll now describe these strategies.

Strategy 1—Multi-parcel trading

This strategy applied to purchases is also known as 'cost averaging' and when applied to selling as 'price averaging'. The multi-parcel strategy is based on the well-known principle of 'not putting all your eggs in one basket'. As an example of the strategy, suppose you have $20 000 trading capital and you want to buy particular shares because you're expecting their price will rise. Rather than buying a single $20 000 parcel, you buy an initial parcel of $10 000. You then wait to see what happens. If you're right and the share price rises, you buy another $10 000 parcel. If you're wrong and the price falls you don't buy more shares and, indeed, if the price falls to your stop-loss limit you sell.

This strategy has sometimes been compared to having an 'each way' bet, but in fact it isn't the same type of strategy at all.

When you place a wager, you can't change your bet after you've placed it, regardless as to how the race progresses. Multi-parcel trading is more like placing an initial bet and then being able to watch how the race progresses before you decide whether to wager more or to cut your losses and get out.

You might wonder about the value of the multi-parcel strategy if you assume you're correct in your judgement 50% of the time. It seems that half the time you'll make more profit and half the time you'll make less profit. Since there are additional trading costs involved, in the long run it seems you'll make less profit by using a multi-parcel trading strategy. But, in fact, multi-parcel trading when applied with sound strategies can improve long-run trading profitability, as the following example will demonstrate.

Example 2

You have about $20 000 to invest in shares and after careful analysis you've selected XYZ shares, currently trading at $10.00. For the purpose of this exercise, I'll assume you can trade online a parcel value up to $20 000 for a cost of $20.

Single-parcel strategy

Buy 2000 shares at $10.00.

If the price rises, hold the shares but set a trailing stop loss of 10% of the market price.

If the price falls to $9.00 after the original purchase, sell.

Multi-parcel strategy

Buy 1000 shares at $10.00.

If the price rises to $10.50 buy another 1000 shares and use a trailing stop loss of 10% for the total shareholding.

If the price falls to $9.00 after the original purchase, sell.

I'll now look at the right and wrong scenarios and assume that they're equally probable.

Scenario A—you get it right and the share price rises to $12.00.

Scenario B—you get it wrong and the share price falls to $8.00.

Single parcel

Buy cost: 2000 shares @ \$10.00 = 20000 + 20 = \$20020

Scenario A: Price rises to \$12.00

Shares value = 2000 × 12 = \$24000

Profit = 24000 − 20020 = \$3980

Scenario B: Price falls to \$8.00 but you sell at \$9.00

Revenue from sale = 2000 × 9.00 − 20 = \$17980

Loss = 17980 − 20020 = \$2040

Assuming equal probability for each scenario the probable value of both trades is:

3980 − 2040 = \$1940

Multi parcel

Buy cost: Initial parcel: 1000 shares @ \$10.00 = 10000 + 20 = \$10020

Scenario A: Price rises to \$12.00

You buy another 1000 shares when the price is \$10.50

Buy cost: 1000 shares @ \$10.50 = 10500 + 20 = \$10520

Total buy cost for both parcels: 10020 + 10520 = \$20540

Shares value = 2000 × 12 = \$24000

Profit = 24000 − 20540 = \$3460

Scenario B: Price falls to \$8.00 but you sell the parcel of 1000 shares @ \$9.00

Revenue from sale = 1000 × 9.00 − 20 = \$8980

Loss = 8980 − 10020 = \$1040

Assuming equal probability for each scenario the probable value of both trades is:

3460 − 1040 = \$2420

Conclusion

You can see that if you get it right the single parcel trade results in $520 more profit than the multi-parcel trade, but if you get it wrong it results in a $1000 greater loss. This is because if the price rises both single and multi-parcel trades produce profit on 2000 shares but in the multi-parcel trade, if the price falls, the loss is incurred on only 1000 shares and not 2000. So if you assume that it's just as likely that you could get it wrong as get it right, you can still swing the odds in your favour by multi-parcel trading. In other words, you've better managed the trading risk.

Note that in this example, when the share price has risen I've assumed you continue to hold so the profit at this stage is an unrealised one; that is, a paper profit. If you did crystallise profits, the actual profits would be slightly less ($20) due to brokerage.

Tip

Multi-parcel trading is a very good risk management strategy for online trading because the low trading cost doesn't have a significant impact on profits. If the total value of the shares you want to trade is high, you can extend multi-parcel trading to three or even more parcels.

Strategy 2 — The 1% rule

Another strategy you can use to manage the 'getting it wrong' risk is based on the 1% rule. The rule is to limit your loss on any one trade to only a small proportion of your available capital; that is, 1% of it. The rule is:

Limit your downside risk on any one trade to no more than 1% of your investing capital.

As an example of the rule, suppose your total investing capital is $100000. You buy parcels of maximum value $10000, and set a maximum 10% stop loss on any one trade. If you get it wrong your maximum loss on a trade is $1000, which is 1% of your trading capital. With smaller amounts of investing capital you can still use the 1% rule provided you reduce the parcel value of any one trade. For example, with $20000 investing capital you would need to limit the parcel value to $2000 in order to apply the rule with a 10% stop loss. By doing so, if you get it wrong you'll still lose no more than 1% of your investing capital.

I've derived the following formula to allow you to calculate the maximum parcel value for any single trade using the 1% rule:

$$\text{Maximum parcel value} = \frac{\text{Total investing capital} \times 0.01}{\text{\% stop loss (expressed as a decimal)}}$$

For example, if your share investing capital is $70 000, and you apply a 10% stop loss (0.1 decimal), the maximum parcel value would be:

$$\frac{70\,000 \times 0.01}{0.1} = \$7\,000$$

When you set a 10% stop loss on this parcel, your maximum loss if you get it wrong is 10% of $7000, which is $700. This is equal to 1% of your investing capital, because 1% of $70 000 is $700.

Note that for simplicity's sake I don't include trading costs when I use the 1% rule. Therefore, if a stop loss is activated, the actual loss will be a little higher than indicated.

Tip

Some authors and share advisers recommend a 2% rule, but a 1% rule gives a higher margin for safety and is the one that I suggest you use. The beauty of the 1% rule is that even if you get it wrong with five trades in a row you'll lose only 5% of your total investing capital. Assuming there's an equal likelihood of getting it wrong as getting it right, the chances of getting it wrong five times in a row is only 1 in 32 or about 3% — which, I don't need to tell you, is very unlikely.

Strategy 3 — Let profits run but limit losses

As I've said before in this book, the strategy of letting your profits run but limiting your losses is the single most important strategy you can use to manage the risks involved with share investing and trading. If you apply this strategy in combination with the 1% rule you can still make profits if you're right only half the time, even if the market is directionless (sideways trend). I'll demonstrate how this works in the following example:

Example 3

Let's say you have $20000 to invest and you purchase shares in 10 different shares for your portfolio, investing $2000 in each. I'll assume that your choice of shares turns out to be a 50/50 proposition; that is, it turns out that you've chosen as many losers as winners and the up and down movements are equal. The letters A to J have been used to denote these shares.

After one year, the situation is as shown in table 11.4.

Table 11.4: share price movements

A	up 50%
B	up 20%
C	up 10%
D	up 5%
E	no move
F	no move
G	down 5%
H	down 10%
I	down 20%
J	down 50%

If you adopt a buy and hold or 'bottom drawer' strategy you'll finish the year even—with no capital gains profit or loss on your total portfolio.

Let's now see what happens if you use strategy 3 and limit your losses but let your profits run. A simple form of this strategy is as follows: if a share price goes down 10%, sell—otherwise hold.

The profit/loss using this strategy is summarised in table 11.5 (overleaf). Note that for the sake of simplicity in this example I've ignored brokerage.

(continued)

Example 3 *(cont'd)*

Table 11.5: profit/loss using strategy 3

Shares	Invested ($)	Price change over year	Sell (S) or hold (H)	P/L ($)
A	2000	+50%	H	1000
B	2000	+20%	H	400
C	2000	+10%	H	200
D	2000	+5%	H	100
E	2000	0%	H	0
F	2000	0%	H	0
G	2000	−5%	H	−100
H	2000	−10%	S	−200
I	2000	−20%	Sell at −10%	−200
J	2000	−50%	Sell at −10%	−200
Total	20 000		Total	1000

By using this simple strategy you're showing a $1000 capital gain on your portfolio, as compared with breaking even with a 'buy and hold' strategy. Note that, as with the previous example, the profits shown in this table are actually 'paper' profits because you're still holding your winners.

Tip

This example illustrates the tremendous importance of the strategy of cutting losses while letting profits run. Even if you select as many losers as winners in a sideways trending market, you still can make a 5% capital gain with your portfolio. If your selected shares pay a reasonable dividend of about 4% fully franked, giving a grossed-up yield of about 6%, your portfolio actually shows a total profit of about 11%—and this in a directionless market and with only 50% winners! Imagine how well you can do if you improve your selection expertise so you select more winners than losers—particularly if the market is in a bull phase where most share prices trend up!

Key points

⇨ Risk and potential return (profit) are linked, and if you want a high potential return on your investing capital you need to accept the higher risk.

⇨ Share investing is more risky than safer alternatives, such as bank deposits, but in the long run produces higher profits in the form of both dividends and capital growth.

⇨ With share investing, you need to change your mindset from risk minimisation to risk management.

⇨ You can maximise the probability of success (and avoid disasters) by adopting sound risk management strategies.

⇨ The first step with share investing risk management is to establish your risk profile; that is, the amount of risk you're comfortable with. You can do this by completing an online quiz. You can then select shares whose riskiness is compatible with your risk score.

⇨ Risk is closely related to volatility (or jumpiness)—the amount of fluctuation above or below the average. The greater the volatility the higher the risk.

⇨ There are three main risks associated with share investing: earnings risk, dividend risk and price risk. These risks are related and earnings downgrades almost always result in the share price being hammered. As well as this, a company can't maintain high dividends when earnings fall.

⇨ You can manage the earnings risk by checking the earnings stability and from the historical EPS data. Steady growth in EPS over a number of years is the best indication of low earnings risk.

⇨ You can manage the dividend risk in a similar way to managing the earnings risk. If a consistent dividend is important to you (as it is for me), look for shares that have a history of good, reliable dividend payments that are preferably fully franked.

⇨ You can manage price risk with sound planning and research before you buy shares using all the methods I've outlined in this book.

⇨ You can form a good impression of price volatility using beta, a volatility formula or a chart inspection.

⇨ One method of risk management is a top-down approach where you work your way down from global risk, Australian market risk, sector risk and finally share risk.

⇨ Obviously you can't do anything to influence markets or sectors but you can monitor these closely on a regular basis and plan your risk management strategies accordingly.

⇨ The Australian sharemarket rises and falls over the years but overall the rises well outnumber the falls. In addition to the capital gains potential, many shares pay a good fully franked dividend that provides a steady income stream regardless of the price fluctuations. Therefore a simple but effective way of managing market risk is to be a long-term investor.

⇨ Some sectors are more risky than others and you should invest in shares in sectors whose riskiness matches your risk profile.

⇨ Shares within the same sector can have different levels of risk and it's a good idea to formulate your own list of the more risky ones. You can manage the risk by ensuring that the proportion of risky shares in your portfolio is in accordance with your risk profile.

⇨ Diversification is an effective strategy to reduce portfolio risk but it also reduces the likelihood of substantial gains above those achieved by the general market. A concentrated portfolio is more risky but offers the potential for above-market returns.

⇨ The lowest portfolio risk occurs when you have a well-diversified portfolio with at least five and preferably ten stocks in different industries or sectors.

⇨ A good way of diversifying is by investing in a listed investment company. This achieves effective share diversification with only one stock.

⇨ When considering a share trade, consider the downside potential as being the worst-case scenario. Evaluate this in conjunction with the upside potential and try to maximise the ratio of upside to downside potential.

⇨ You can reduce the downside potential risk by using stop-loss orders (particularly on your more speculative trades).

⇨ Profit stops effectively eliminate the risk of a paper profit subsequently turning into a loss. However, profit stops violate the strategy of letting profits run, so you need to take this into account before using profit stops.

⇨ Beware of personal bias in your investment decisions and particularly 'falling in love' with shares that have been good ones for you.

⇨ Sequential trading carries an inbuilt mathematical risk that can be managed by diversifying and keeping the parcel value of each trade approximately the same.

⇨ Beware of irrational optimism and pessimism in the market. Almost always, if these occur a correction will follow.

⇨ Signal markers for irrational optimism are when the price rises upward well above an established trendline and the P/E ratio rises to well above the historical sector level to one that's unsustainable. That's to say, the share price can't be justified by realistic earnings analysis.

⇨ When irrational pessimism corrects irrational optimism, this can be a good buying opportunity.

⇨ With each share trade you make, you run the risk of 'getting it wrong'. Remember that's there's always a trader who is taking the opposite view to yours.

⇨ There are three strategies you can use that enable you to still make a profit even if you get it wrong 50% of the time.

⇨ One of these strategies is multi-parcel trading. This strategy is particularly applicable to online trading because of the low brokerage. This strategy will reduce your profits if you get it right but will more than compensate for this over the long run by reducing your losses if you get it wrong.

⇨ Another strategy is the 1% rule, which limits your losses on any single trade so that even if you get it wrong several times in a row it won't be disastrous.

⇨ Last but not least, the most important strategy of all is to maximise capital gains with your winners and minimise your losses with your losers. You use this strategy when you cut losses but let profits run. This strategy allows you to make capital gains in a directionless market even if you get it right only as often as you get it wrong.

⇨ If you apply the principles I've outlined in this book to the planning of your share trades and the management of your portfolio you should be able to improve your share selection and trading expertise so you select more winners than losers and make excellent profits from share investing in the longer term.

Index

Note: underlined entries indicate websites.

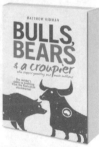

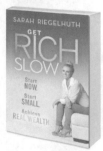
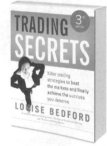